t
6.11.07

ESSENTIAL
reporting

In memory of Joan
A fine reporter

Dedicated to trainers
and trainees everywhere

ESSENTIAL
reporting

THE NCTJ GUIDE FOR
TRAINEE JOURNALISTS

JON SMITH

SAGE Publications
Los Angeles ▪ London ▪ New Delhi ▪ Singapore

nctj

© Jon Smith and the NCTJ 2007

First published 2007

SAGE Publications Ltd
1 Oliver's Yard
55 City Road
London EC1Y 1SP

SAGE Publications Inc.
2455 Teller Road
Thousand Oaks, California 91320

SAGE Publications India Pvt Ltd
B1/I 1 Mohan Cooperative Industrial Area
Mathura Road, New Delhi 110 044
India

SAGE Publications Asia-Pacific Pte Ltd
33 Pekin Street #02-01
Far East Square
Singapore 048763

Library of Congress Control Number:

British Library Cataloguing in Publication data

A catalogue record for this book is available from
the British Library

ISBN 978-1-4129-4750-3
ISBN 978-1-4129-4751-0

Typeset by C&M Digitals (P) Ltd, Chennai, India
Printed in Great Britain by TJ International, Padstow, Cornwall
Printed on paper from sustainable resources

CONTENTS

CONTENTS

PREFACE

THE world of the media is changing fast, but there is a constant that underpins it all. We might call it the spirit of journalism.

The desire to inquire, the will to question, the urge to inform or entertain: these apply no less to the news websites of the 21st Century than to the newspapers of the 19th. Without that spirit you should question whether journalism is really for you. With it, you will find this book an invaluable guide.

You can learn the technical bits – shorthand, intros, writing for the web – as you go on, and there's more than enough practical advice in these pages. But first you should take in those basic principles that are also set out here, the lessons we should carry with us wherever we go: the essence of accurate reporting; the benefits of clear communication; the vital role of a free press in a democratic society.

Adopt those principles and you can work anywhere, because the foundations of journalism are the same in print, broadcast and on the web. There's a lot of laughter in newsrooms, but the men and women who work in them also know that this is a serious business that demands the highest standards.

There are no better guides than people who have done it themselves. Here you will find terrific advice, great wisdom and fascinating insights about the media world as it really is. Better still, you'll find it conveyed with the clarity that's at the heart of great journalism and the passion that's in the hearts of great journalists.

This is a job that repays the effort that you put in, for who knows what is behind that door where no one else has knocked? It is a job where every day can be different, because the nature of news is so varied; a job that gives you a ringside seat at the drama, comedy and tragedy that make human lives. And a job that can be so much fun you sometimes – *sometimes* – can't believe they are actually paying you to do it.

Kim Fletcher
Chairman
National Council for the Training of Journalists

ACKNOWLEDGEMENTS

THIS book could not have been written without the help of many people.

I owe the greatest debt to Steve Nelson of the *York Press*, a fellow member of the NCTJ's journalism board, who cast his sub-editorial eye over the book so many times that he probably knows it off by heart. His suggestions have been invaluable.

I am very grateful to Nigel Burton of *The Northern Echo*, who contributed enormously to the chapter on working with the web; to Olwen Vasey, former municipal reporter for the *Telegraph & Argus* in Bradford, who provided much of the chapter on covering councils; to Malcolm Wright, Arthur Pickering and Andy Kluz of Tyne Tees Television for their great help with the section on broadcasting; to Tom Welsh, co-editor of *Essential Law*, who dusted off unpublished notes for his own book on reporting and told me to help myself, an offer which he will see has been gratefully accepted; to media consultant Andy Bull for his help with online reporting; to Richard Parsons of the *Sportsbeat* training company for helping to knock the sports reporting section into shape; to Lindsay Jennings of *The Northern Echo* for her assistance with the feature writing chapter; and to Bob Satchwell, executive director of the Society of Editors, for his enthusiastic encouragement and useful suggestions after reading through the first draft.

I would like to thank past and present colleagues at Darlington College, especially Sue Campbell, Robin Crowther, Barry Davis, Joyce Hutchinson, Dawn Johnson, Sue Kelly, Mark Parry, Eric Walsh and Guy Williams, for their help and encouragement over the years; my friends at *The Northern Echo*, notably editor Peter Barron and former managing director David Kelly, for their advice and inspiration; my drinking partner Richard Davies, also from the *Echo*, for regularly diverting me from the task of authorship when it threatened to become an obsession; and, of course, Sheila, Jay and the rest of my family for putting up with me when it did.

I am grateful to David Baines of the National Union of Journalists, Neil Benson of Trinity Mirror, David Rowell of Johnston Press, Keith Stafford of Reuters, Margaret Strayton of Newsquest, and many others for passing on the request for working journalists' tips and encouraging their colleagues to contribute.

ACKNOWLEDGEMENTS

Finally, my thanks go to Joanne Butcher of the NCTJ for inviting me to compile the book and to her unfailingly cheerful staff.

No one mentioned above, of course, is responsible for any errors or omissions in the book. The blame for those is entirely mine. Corrections, amendments and suggestions for improvement will be very welcome.

Jon Smith

THE INTRO

THOSE of us lucky enough to work in the media have three main functions: to inform, guide and entertain. The emphasis varies. Serious national newspapers put great weight on their opinion columns; redtop tabloids concentrate on celebrity gossip. It is generally agreed, however, that the media's most important role is to tell the public what is going on in the world and why, whether it be roadworks delaying their journey to work or a declaration of war threatening their lives.

There may be nothing they can do about it, but they need this information to make the choices necessary in a democratic society. It gives newspapers and broadcasters a vital role as the electorate's watchdogs, reporting truths unpalatable to authority, while those elected or appointed to make decisions rely heavily on the media for information and use it to influence local and national government.

None of this would be possible without reporters. It is their job to gather the news, check its accuracy, and present it in a form which interests and can be understood by the public. It is a job to be proud of, and it is vital to those who undertake it, their audience, and society as a whole that they are well-trained. This book, we hope, will help to ensure that they are.

Essential Reporting is a practical guide to what life as a trainee reporter is all about: who does what, why they do it, and how. It was prompted by demands from trainees, trainers and people working in the media for a standard textbook on reporting. As its title suggests, it covers the basics. It cannot possibly deal in depth with everything a trainee reporter needs to know. There is no substitute for practical experience, and it is intended to be used as an introduction and reference book to accompany vocational training on accredited training courses and in the workplace.

It comes in five sections. The first chapters examine what makes a good reporter and what news is all about. The next look at everyday reporting tasks in and out of the office, on and off-diary. Third is a section on writing for print, working online and handling audio and video. Then come specialist areas, including courts, councils, sport, district reporting and features. The final section includes a chapter on training, a round-up of reference sources, guidance on further reading, and a glossary.

Trainee reporters who read it will be entering a fast-changing world. Technology is obliterating the boundaries between newspapers, radio, television and web-based media, and the days of training reporters for one medium alone are over. Editors expect them to be multi-skilled and flexible, producing words, sound and pictures to appear in print, online and on air, capable of switching from one medium to another with

> *When we embarked on this book, we emailed hundreds of people working in the media asking for their tips, memories and warnings about life as a reporter.*
>
> *The response was over-whelming, and we have included as many contributions as possible.*
>
> *You will see them, and quotes from other sources, in this spot on the righthand pages throughout the book. They have been linked where possible to the content of the main text.*
>
> *Our thanks to all who responded. We hope those whose offerings are missing, because they duplicated others or were reluctantly spiked for lack of space, will forgive us and enjoy the ones that made it.*

This spot on the lefthand pages has been given over to practical tips relating to the accompanying text.

ease and assurance. This book attempts to reflect that demand, recognising that its readers are equally likely to work for newspapers, magazines, websites, radio or television – or for any combination of these simultaneously.

Some things, however, remain unchanged. Whatever the medium, there are core values common to all. Every reporter still needs the ability to recognise news, to gather information, to communicate with people, to produce accurate, balanced and attractive stories. These fundamental attributes are what this book is all about.

One
WHAT YOU NEED

YOU want to be a reporter. Of course you do: it's the best job in the world. How else can you get paid for listening to gossip, digging behind the scenes and telling everyone else what you've discovered?

The first question is whether you are likely to be any good at it. Well, picking up this book and reading so far shows that you have at least three of the vital qualities: ambition, curiosity and self-belief. There's a lot more to it than that, of course, and this opening chapter looks at all you need to be, to learn, to do and to have to be the ideal reporter.

Don't let the length of the list dishearten you. There are thousands of reporters out there, every one of them different and none of them perfect. There are hard-nosed door-stoppers hunting celebrity wives, planet-brained intellectuals hunched over government statistics, mothers of five writing up village shows, front-line correspondents ducking bullets. They are old and young, male and female, left-wing and right-wing, happy and angry, introvert and extrovert, open and devious, teetotal and alcoholic, driven by passion and by money. What on earth do they have in common? What are editors looking for when you apply for a job?

Ask Google *'What makes a good reporter?'* and you will discover hundreds of people who have tried answering that question. A few are convinced that the only requirement is a burning desire to overthrow the system (any system), but those who know what they are talking about show a high level of agreement about the essential qualities a reporter needs. Some are innate, some can be nurtured, some you can learn.

- Character
- Attitude
- Knowledge
- Skills
- Equipment

QUALITIES YOU ARE BORN WITH

YOU NEED...

Curiosity

A desire to know what is going on and how things work. You have to be inquisitive about everything, constantly asking questions about the world around you. What has happened? Who did it and why? What happens next?

An interest in people

Fascination about what makes them tick and how they feel, whoever they are and whatever they are doing. You need to know and appreciate what grips your public before you can recognise what is newsworthy and how to handle it. If you are bored by sports players, find politicians

The only qualities essential for real success in journalism are rat-like cunning, a plausible manner, and a little literary ability.

NICHOLAS TOMALIN
(1931-1973)
Journalist
The Sunday Times

a turn-off and couldn't care less what is happening in Coronation Street, reporting may not be the job for you.

Intelligence

Bright enough to grasp what people are talking about most of the time, sharp enough to discern nuances and inferences, quick-witted enough to think on your feet. A good all-round education is useful but you don't have to be academically brilliant.

Health

You need to be fit. Physically fit, because you will be working long and odd hours, not always in the most comfortable environment. Mentally fit, because you will have to cope with pressure from deadlines, stressed-out news editors, angry readers and distressed relatives. It helps if you can survive irregular sleep patterns, possess a good digestion, and can keep a steady head after a couple of drinks... or more.

Courage

The self-assurance to accost strangers and ask them awkward questions, to speak out at a press conference in front of dozens of other journalists, to stand up in court and tell magistrates they are wrong when they try to ban you reporting someone's name. You may need the strength to face jail for refusing to reveal your sources. If you are planning to be a foreign correspondent, you will need a strong nerve the day you find yourself under fire.

Belief

If you believe in yourself, are keen to succeed, listen to what you are told and learn from your mistakes, you will get there.

YOU NEED TO BE:

Out-going

Cheerful, optimistic, confident, able to get on easily with all sorts of people and work in a team. A sense of humour is vital. So is being a good listener, sensitive to people's feelings, appearing sympathetic even when you disagree with what you are being told. It is handy to be able to exude enough charm to talk your way past protective secretaries and petty officials, especially if you can do it over the phone. You need to be flexible, willing to adapt to change whether it means having to cancel a night off to cover an emergency or re-train in the latest technology.

Enthusiastic

You have to believe that you are a force for good, a vital part of society, that what you are doing benefits your fellow man and woman – and to argue forcefully with those who disagree. It helps if you have a well-developed sense of justice, so long as it doesn't override your ability to report objectively. You need enough idealism to make you indignant about injustice but not so much that you can't see both sides of an argument.

Determined

You must want to succeed. You need the strength to persevere in the face of opposition and refuse to accept failure, a sense of urgency to work fast to deadlines, and a desire to get there first.

Accurate

You must be committed to getting the facts right and the quotes correct. Every word you write will be read carefully by those involved; your stories may be cut from the newspaper and kept for years. If a name or a fact is inaccurate, readers dismiss your newspaper as *'the local rag – which always gets things wrong'*. Your commitment to accuracy should be coupled with a strong desire to find out the truth and expose falsehood. This means being open-minded, willing to listen, wary of making assumptions, aware of your own beliefs and prejudices and capable of putting them to one side.

Sceptical

You need a healthy distrust of authority, whether it is a government minister, a petty official at the town hall or a slick-spoken press officer. You have to question what you are being told and why you are being told it (but not with so much scepticism that you are too cynical to recognise good news when you come across it).

Thick-skinned

You need a skin thick enough to take criticism from your seniors and the public, and not mind looking faintly foolish when you don't understand everything first time or have to admit you have got something wrong. Not so thick, though, that you are impervious to the feelings of others.

Innovative

You need to be able to see beyond the immediate, come up with ideas, work on your own, and make decisions.

> The main ingredient I look for in a reporter is hunger. Do they really get excited about breaking news? Do they really want to be a journalist? What have they done to prove it?

PETER BARRON
Editor
The Northern Echo

> The skills I look for are compassion and tenacity.

SIMON REYNOLDS
Editorial director
Lancashire Evening Post

> I look for passion, commitment and a hint of madness. And dreadful clothes on a man: I find those who dress badly often make the best investigative journalists.

DOROTHY BYRNE
Head of News
Channel Four Television

QUALITIES YOU CAN WORK ON

YOU NEED TO BE:

News-conscious

News sense is the ability to put things in context, recognise what is newsworthy and how much it is worth. You will come across journalists who tell you this is something you either have or you haven't, something that can't be taught, but we are all born with it to some degree. Nobody walks past a blazing house without thinking it worth mentioning when they get to the pub. What a good reporter needs is the ability to spot the story that isn't staring them in the face, and that comes with an understanding of the world around them, their audience, their organisation's needs and agenda.

Literate

If your words are going to be read and understood, you need to be able to spell and punctuate them correctly, and put them together in grammatical sentences. Simple errors can radically change the sense of what you are saying, and that can prove very costly. Ignorance of what commas, apostrophes and full stops are for does nothing for your reputation and career prospects. Correcting your errors drives sub-editors up the wall.

Articulate

You will spend a lot of time talking to people (sometimes in front of an audience) and you will need to be able to express yourself clearly and sensibly. The way you speak and sound is important, and vital if you are a broadcaster.

Numerate

Journalists are notoriously bad with figures. Good journalists aren't. Nobody expects you to be a mathematical genius, but you should be able to work out a percentage, understand a timetable, make sense of statistics, differentiate between turnover and gross profit. Knowing how to add up on a calculator is not enough.

QUALITIES YOU CAN ACQUIRE

YOU NEED KNOWLEDGE:

The world around you

You don't have to be an expert in anything (unless you specialise in a subject like health or education, of course) but you do need to be well-informed: to know a bit about a lot, have a good general knowledge and an understanding of the society you live in, and be up-to-date on current affairs. Only then can you judge what is newsworthy.

You need to read a wide range of newspapers and magazines, listen to current affairs programmes on the radio, watch a lot of factual and popular television, regularly delve into the internet for new information. You won't remember it all, but enough will stick in your memory for bells to ring when a name or an event crops up later.

Your industry

You need to understand the role of the media, its powers and responsibilities, how it works, who does what and why, the problems it faces – and your role within it.

Sources of information

If you don't know something, you need to know how to find out. Reporters research a wide range of information sources; you have to know what they are and how to make the most of them. Paramount among these are people. You will spend your working life making and maintaining contacts, sources of information, opinion and advice that you will use time and again.

Law

You have to know what you can and cannot report. Defamation is a danger whatever the story. Contempt is possible whenever you handle courts and crime. You have to be aware of restrictions on naming people, the law of copyright, what you can report about bankruptcy, how to avoid falling foul of election law and scores of other legal issues. A good reporter always has the question *'Is this legally safe?'* at the back of their mind.

Public affairs

A working knowledge of local and central government is invaluable, whatever field you are working in. On a local newspaper, you need real understanding of how the council works and its relationship with Whitehall.

FIRST IMPRESSIONS COUNT

You can't help your looks but you can make sure you are reasonably presentable. It is obviously essential if you are going to be seen in video clips or on television. What you are wearing is part of the overall first impression you give people when you meet, and you won't get far if you look a mess and smell like last night's vindaloo.

Dress smartly but not over the top. You will meet all sorts of people in all sorts of situations and although ideally you would wear designer casuals to interview teenagers in a nightclub and a dark suit when you are covering a civic funeral, you will rarely have the chance to change from one outfit to another.

I look for confidence, detailed knowledge of our papers, a 'hinterland' away from the standard school/college/work route, a driving licence, some tough questions for me at interview – and correct use of apostrophes.

ANDY COOPER
Editor-in-chief
Northcliffe SW Weeklies

I look for intelligence, but not intellectual arrogance; a talent for writing decent plain English; the ability to meet deadlines; a desire to dig under the surface of a story; a real enjoyment of people and all their quirks and foibles; the ability to work as part of a team; a sense of humour.

PAT STANNARD
Editor
Newsquest N London

Courtesy costs nothing; the lack of it will cost you contacts, and lost contacts mean lost stories. Being polite is essential if you are to succeed.

Reporters have very few rights not enjoyed by the rest of the public.

Nobody <u>has</u> to talk to you, and they won't if you are aggressive or give the impression that you think you're someone special.

A working knowledge of a foreign language or two is handy, but GCSE French isn't going to guarantee you a job as a foreign correspondent.

Fluency in Arabic or Chinese might help, though.

Real stories come from real people – and the best way to get them is to be part of the community.

Codes of conduct

You need to know how you are expected to behave as a professional journalist, how to handle moral and ethical dilemmas, what restrictions professional codes of conduct place upon your conduct, and what defences are available to you.

YOU NEED SKILLS:

Reporting skills

You need to know how to deal with people face-to-face, on the phone and online; how to report courts, meetings and public events; how to cover major incidents and human interest stories; how to deal with complaints; and how to handle a host of other everyday demands.

Recording skills

Shorthand is essential if you want to work in local newspapers – few will even consider you for a job without it – and is a great asset whatever you do.

Being able to record accurately what is being said is fundamental to the job. For the journalist without shorthand it is often difficult if not impossible. Taking down every word in longhand takes forever. Interviewees quickly get fed up of waiting for you to catch up with them, and you end up grabbing snatches of their replies that are certainly incomplete and possibly inaccurate. Tape recorders are forbidden in courts and council meetings and there are other times when they are difficult to use effectively – at press conferences, for instance. Interviewees clam up at the sight of them. Transcribing tapes and trying to work out who said what is time-consuming and leads to errors.

100? THAT'S JUST FOR STARTERS

Teeline is the commonest form of shorthand taught in Britain. The minimum speed required by trainees sitting the NCTJ's final examinations is 100 words per minute.

On a typical college course, this takes around 150 hours of lessons plus plenty of homework practice, though some tutors boast of trainees getting there in much less.

This speed is enough to record someone speaking fairly slowly, but many people talk much faster than 100wpm and the higher your shorthand speed, the better. Teeline rates of 120-130wpm are not uncommon and even 150wpm has been achieved.

There are other shorthand systems around such as Pitman's, harder to learn than Teeline but with a much higher potential speed. It is favoured by parliamentary reporters working at up to 250wpm for Hansard.

Other systems include Gregg's, rare in Britain, and Speedwriting, difficult to do beyond about 80wpm.

Background noise drowns out the words. You can't record anything but the sound – nothing about the way people are acting, for example, or their surroundings. Courts are far less happy about accepting tape recordings than shorthand notes, believing they are easily doctored.

There are advantages of using tape. You can concentrate on an interview without worrying about note-taking, it is easier to thrust a recorder in front of someone's face in a crowd than to scribble in a notebook when all around you are pushing forward, and you can transcribe from it perfectly days later without worrying whether your notes are accurate. Feature writers use tape recorders as back-up for lengthy interviews. But for most news reporters most of the time, shorthand is essential.

Its use is curiously confined to parts of the English-speaking world. Reporters from countries without it are often intrigued, even amused, by our insistence on it as a basic tool of the job. They all acknowledge its usefulness, however, and there are times when they are deeply envious of our ability to record precisely what has been said. No matter how tedious you find learning shorthand, stick with it. You will be glad all your working life that you did.

Writing skills

You need the ability to write in clear, straightforward language appropriate to your audience, whether your words end up in print, online, on the air or on an autocue.

Technical skills

You have to be able to find your way round a computer keyboard, have a basic understanding of relevant software, know how to transmit words and images, understand how to search the internet effectively. If you are working with sound, you need to be able to operate a tape recorder and edit tape. If you are expected to take pictures, you need to be able to handle still and moving-image cameras and know how to edit video and put it on a website.

Organisational skills

Journalists tend not to be the most self-disciplined of people when it comes to paperwork, filing and generally keeping track of their lives. In-trays overflow, notebooks pile up haphazardly, pictures vanish under mountains of unused handouts and discarded letters. However, to work effectively you need some degree of organisation. Newsrooms work to tight deadlines, and you have to meet them. Good reporters manage their time effectively and force themselves to put things in order.

What do I look for in a trainee? Someone who's interested in the world, mainly – someone who listens and learns, and has questions to ask back in return. And someone who makes me laugh.

JOHN FRANCIS
Group editor
Bedfordshire Newspapers

I want reporters who will keep and use a good contacts book – and if you think you can get away without good shorthand, think again.

PAUL HORROCKS
Editor
Manchester Evening News

Shorthand is still an essential skill. Converging skills are needed but we must not forget the importance of good accurate writing and traditional journalism skills.

BARRY HUNT
Editor
Saffron Walden Reporter

👍 *Rule margins down the lefthand side of every page in your notebook before you start, to give you somewhere to make notes, mark important bits, and transcribe difficult words when you come to read it through.*

Leave some space at the end of each entry so you have room for extra information later, and start each new story on a new page.

Date and time every entry, with the name of whoever you are interviewing.

When your notebook is full, write the dates it covers (and major stories it includes) on the front cover.

Libel actions can be initiated up to a year after publication, so keep all your notebooks safe for at least that long, preferably longer.

Driving skills

A driving licence is not absolutely essential – there are some excellent reporters who can't or won't drive – but it is very useful. You will have to travel to and from your office (which may be on an industrial estate miles out of town) to cover assignments all over the place. Time is wasted and stories are lost if you rely on public transport. Few newsrooms will pay for taxis. Bicycles may be fine for short trips through heavy town traffic but are not much use for longer journeys and hopeless in bad weather.

Given the choice between two otherwise equally-attractive applicants for a job, an editor will probably pick the one who can drive. Owning your own vehicle is handy, but being able to use the office car is a good start.

EQUIPMENT

As well as qualities you have got, can develop or can learn, you require some basic tools of the trade before you can start working as a reporter.

Notebooks

The traditional A5 spiral-bound reporter's notebook is still the best for most occasions. Small enough to fit in a pocket or handbag, easy to balance on a knee or hold in one hand, but not so small that you are flipping over to a new page every few seconds. Work through it using alternate pages; when it is full, turn it over and start again from the other end. Smaller, bound notebooks are easier to hide but harder to handle, and they fill up quickly. A4 pads can be useful in the office (if there is room on the desk) because you can get a lot down on one page, but they become cumbersome out in the street or in face-to-face interviews.

Pens

Always have at least a couple of ballpoints handy. Having to ask an interviewee if you can borrow one because yours has run out ranks high in the top ten of most embarrassing moments for a reporter.

Carry a sharp soft pencil as well because ballpoints don't work well in the rain and you may want to write on something – the back of a borrowed photo, for instance – and erase it later. Have a yellow highlighter to identify vital facts or the best quotes when transcribing a lengthy chunk of shorthand.

Diary

Make it pocket-sized, preferably loose-leaf so you can sling out old pages (keep them safe for future reference) and add new ones. Have pages for more than a year ahead so you can enter anniversaries of major stories. Use it to record meetings you are going to cover and people you are going to meet, with names, contact numbers, times and venues.

Contacts book

This is one of the most valuable tools of your trade: somewhere to store the names, addresses, email addresses and phone/fax numbers of all your contacts and sources. Guard it with your life, because that's what it is. Never leave it lying around where someone can steal it, bin it, or (less traumatic but irritating) copy its contents and pinch all the contacts you have worked so hard to build up.

Pick a book that is easy to carry, durable (hard-back, with a water-resistant cover), flexible (loose-leaf, expandable, with A-Z indexing), and ideally with space for a spare pen, business cards, phone money and anything else you might want handy. Put your own name and contact details in big letters on the first page, with a promise to reward anyone who finds it handsomely for its return (believe me, you will pay anything to get it back). Fill it with details of everyone you meet and every person or organisation that might be useful to you, because you never know when they are going to be of value. When the faintly potty old lady who demanded you run a story about her lost budgie wins the lottery six months later, you will mutter a prayer of thanks that you kept her name on file.

Stick in all the obvious contacts – emergency services, hospitals, post offices, pubs, the lot. Raid the office contacts book and steal from your colleagues. Note the names of potentially useful people mentioned in newspapers and magazines. Trawl the Yellow Pages.

Enter people and organisations alphabetically, and cross-reference entries. You may forget someone's name but you will find them under the group or interest they represent. Put all the hospitals under H, all the schools under S, and so on. Photocopy all the pages every so often. It's a chore, but it might save your career if you lose the original.

Style book

This is a guide to your organisation's preferences for spellings, abbreviations, lists and a wide range of other matters. Ask your newsdesk for a copy. More on this later in the book.

Dictionary

Arm yourself with one that is more than just a list of definitions. A good dictionary will contain proper names and places, maps, lists of abbreviations, weights and measures, conversion tables and much more. If it comes with a thesaurus, all the better (if not, get one, or a dictionary of synonyms). Don't rely on your computer's spell-checker: it won't do the job properly.

Mobile phone

Get a mobile with a built-in camera. Stick a label with your office number on it and the offer of a reward if the finder returns it.

> *Build your contacts book into a library of numbers for everyone you meet on your journalistic journey. It is more precious than anything else you have.*
>
> **MARK TURNBULL**
> Producer
> BBC Radio Cleveland

> *Be prepared for the idiosyncratic. The poet WH Auden refused to be interviewed by a reporter using a tape recorder, saying: 'If what I say is not worth writing down, then I'm not worth interviewing.' I had my trusty notebook and he gave me two hours of his time. The story made all the nationals.*
>
> **SHARON GRIFFITHS**
> Feature writer
> The Northern Echo

> *Get a thick skin and broad shoulders – you can't be friends with everyone.*
>
> **DANNY BRIERLEY**
> Assistant editor
> Croydon Guardian

👍 *Don't rely solely on contacts lists held on computer (they crash and you can't take them out of the office), or on mobile phones or electronic organisers (they run out of power and are easily lost). By all means use these as back-ups.*

If you are involved in a really sensitive investigation, you might want to keep contacts' details separate. Police can search your office, home and computer files.

CODE YOUR CONTACTS

Being the only person in the office who knows how to contact the celebrity of the moment gives you a lot of cred. Do your best to keep it that way.

It may seem paranoid, but you could devise a code to disguise your most important contacts, people who have given you their private numbers in confidence and will be furious if strangers get hold of them.

Tape recorder

Essential for broadcasters and, as we have already said, useful for people working in print as a back-up for shorthand notes and to record lengthy interviews. If you are not provided with one, buy a machine that fits in your pocket and is powerful enough to pick up speech more than a foot away. Make sure it uses standard tapes (have spares handy) and works off both mains and batteries (have spares of these, too).

Mini voice-recorders are useful for making notes (on the road, for example – but don't get done for careless driving) but no good for interviews. Label all your tapes with dates and subject matter, and keep them safe.

Camera

You should be provided with one if you are required to take pictures, but having a digital camera of your own available 24 hours a day is a good idea. Know how to use it and how to download to the web.

👍 *Journalists are expected to abide by the code issued by the Press Complaints Commission, dealt with at length in McNae's Essential Law for Journalists.*

You should also be aware of the code issued by the National Union of Journalists.

FATHERS, MOTHERS & CHAPELS

Many news organisations recognise one or more unions for bargaining purposes.

The largest in Britain is the National Union of Journalists (NUJ); others include the Chartered Institute of Journalists (IOJ) and the British Association of Journalists (BAJ).

There are many associations for specialist writers, such as the Sports Journalists Association. There is an International Federation of Journalists, based in Brussels, to which the NUJ and other unions are affiliated.

Apart from their bargaining role, where recognised, unions are involved in many matters affecting members' health, safety and general welfare, and some of them offer an extensive range of training programmes for senior journalists.

Workplace union branches are often known as *chapels*, headed by a *father* or *mother of the chapel* (known as the *FOC* or the *MOC*).

Two
WHAT'S NEWS?

POSE that question to many seasoned reporters and there is a fair chance that they will scratch their heads and say: _'Well, you just... sort of... know.'_ Uncharitable ones may add: _'...and if you have to ask, you're probably in the wrong job'_. If you think that is a bit unfair, you are right. Millions of words have been written trying to define news and nobody has yet come up with the perfect answer.

Attempts range from former Sunday Times editor Harry Evans' three-word offering _'News is people'_ to 26 pages of oft-cited intricate analysis by a couple of Scandinavian academics called Galtung and Ruge who concluded there were at least a dozen factors involved. The Concise Oxford Dictionary settles for _'information about important or interesting recent events'_. The average newspaper reader in the street will offer a chicken-and-egg answer: _'It's what goes in newspapers'_.

It gets easier if you split it into two questions: what do news stories have in common? and why are some chosen and not others?

COMMON FACTORS

News is new to its audience

News is what it says on the tin: it's not 'olds'. It must tell its audience something it doesn't already know. Usually this means information about a recent or forthcoming event. It may be hard news about something that has just happened _(Two die in car crash, Midthorpe United win FA Cup, Vicar runs off with barmaid)_ or been said _(Council warns of 20% tax rise, Tories admit Marx was right all along)_. It may be softer news, entertaining as well as informative _(Big Brother star hits out, Nine out of ten teenagers haven't heard of Shakespeare)_.

The more recent the event, the newsier the story tends to be. On TV, radio or the web, that means things that have happened within the past few hours; on a daily newspaper, within the past 24 hours; on a weekly within the past seven days.

Some stories, however, are about events that have taken place in the past but only just come to light. It is the disclosure now that makes them news _(Baby's skeleton found in wood, War-time papers reveal Hitler kidnap plan)_. Again, the more recent the events, the more newsworthy these stories usually are – but not always: _Scientists prove aliens created world 10 trillion years ago_ will definitely make the front pages.

- What do news stories have in common?

- What decides which ones get used?

> _When a dog bites a man, that is not news. When a man bites a dog, that is._
>
> **CHARLES A DANA**
> American journalist

> _News is something someone, somewhere, wants to suppress. All the rest is advertising._
>
> **WILLIAM RANDOLPH HEARST**
> US Newspaper proprietor

'True' should mean more than just getting the facts right. The selection of facts should be fair and the story balanced, giving both sides and a true picture of what that took place: in the language of the Defamation Act, 'a fair and accurate report of the proceedings'.

That's a tall order. Although good reporters on honest newspapers aim to fulfil it all the time, it isn't always the case.

Readers often contact the local media with problems, and not all of them make stories.

Sometimes you find yourself acting as a combination of social worker and citizen's advice bureau volunteer. It's all part of the reader service, and if you solve their problems, it can be quite rewarding.

Not all news stories are about single events, now or in the past. Some are about trends which only make headlines when something acts as a catalyst: a report, for example, gathering together a number of events *(Crime figures up)* or a survey analysing what many people say *(Poll shows Lib Dems in lead)*. Some things go unreported for years until suddenly a case is highlighted and everyone jumps on the bandwagon as the media and public go into a mass (though probably short-lived) panic. What makes it news is the reader or listener knowing about it for the first time.

News is true (or at least believed to be)

Contrary to popular belief, newspapers and broadcasters rarely say anything they know to be an outright lie. There are notorious exceptions (the *Sport* used to revel in spoof stories such as *Elvis alive and driving double-decker bus on moon*), but in general editors strive hard to get things right. Their credibility is on the line. Like the rest of us, they don't like having to admit they are wrong and face the consequences. They hate printing corrections or being sued for defamation.

Mistakes do get made. There isn't a newspaper in the world that hasn't mis-spelt a name or got an age wrong. But they don't do it deliberately and they don't make things up.

That does not mean, of course, that they don't publish claims that they cannot prove, or doubt, or flatly disbelieve. Precious little would appear in print if that were the case: nothing about court cases, for a start. 'True' means the report is an accurate account of what has happened or been said, and anything the reporter does not know to be correct has been attributed to its source. It may not be true that *Abattoir stench killed pets* but it is true that somebody made a statement claiming that it did: *Abattoir stench killed pets, say angry neighbours* or *Abattoir blamed for pet deaths*.

News is about people

Most of us are interested in what the rest of the world gets up to. We want to know what other people do, say, feel and believe – and what happens to them. We are surprised or amused or worried by their behaviour and experience. We like to know there are others who share our view of the world, to be warned about those who don't, to feel relieved when things go wrong for other people, not us.

We prefer people to be doing things rather than just saying them, and we love it when they disagree: conflict is at the heart of many of the best news stories, whether they are about nations at war, litigants in court, residents fighting development plans or just 22 players battling for the ball on a football pitch.

Not everyone is of equal interest, of course. There are celebrities and the rest of us. Celebrities may be people who can affect our lives (politicians), people we welcome (soap stars and rock singers), people

BRINGING COLOUR INTO LIFE

What people think is news hasn't changed over the years.

In 1949 a Royal Commission on the Press compiled a list of topics that newspaper proprietors, managers and journalists thought were of most interest to readers.

Sport came top, followed by 'news about people, news of strange or amusing adventures, tragedies, accidents and crimes – news, that is, whose sentiment or excitement brings some colour into life'.

Public affairs did not rate highly.

---

inflicted upon us (serial killers), or even fictitious (Harry Potter). They come top of the newsworthiness league when they do the unexpected or outrageous *(MP joins nunnery, Oscar-winner weds for ninth time)* and often when they do pretty ordinary things, too *(Corrie star pregnant, President trips over)*.

Groups of people can acquire celebrity status. Some countries and organisations command more attention than others because of the influence they wield (the United States, Nato, the Church of England) or the work they do (Oxfam, Amnesty, the Red Cross) and even routine activities by these elite groups find a place on the news agenda.

The rest of us make the news when we do something out of the ordinary *(Bank clerk climbs Everest, Fishmonger dies of hiccups)*. Otherwise we are largely ignored – *Bank clerk bikes to work* isn't going to set many news editors' hearts racing – unless a lot of us are involved *(Ten million swap cars for bikes, Anti-war protesters storm Downing Street, Two out of three housewives fancy Tom Cruise)*.

News may be not so much about people doing things as having things done to them. This may be as individuals *(Lightning kills two)* or en masse *(Global warming threatens human race)*. How newsworthy this is depends on how many people are involved, how serious the effect is on them, how long it lasts and how urgent it is the rest of the world gets to hear about it. *Tummy bug hits junior school* scores well below *Black Death wipes out Bradford*. Even when many people are affected we find it difficult to cope with vast anonymous numbers, however, and newspapers may well personalise such stories by concentrating on one or two victims *(Sudan: the face of starvation)*.

'People' extends to creatures other than human beings. They become newsworthy for the same reasons: unusual behaviour by individuals *(Python loose in sewers, Dog can count to ten)* or groups *(Butterflies return to Iceland, Rats immune to poison)* or as celebrities *(Three-time Grand National winner dies, Loch Ness Monster seen again)*.

News is a trigger

News provokes reaction from the audience. That may just be surprise because it is unusual, odd, unexpected, quirky or downright weird

---

Trainees have to learn the real nature of a reporter's job and exactly what we need from them. One told me very earnestly that it was vital for sales of our paper (a tabloid where the readership is largely ex-miners) that we should carry more news about the European Parliament. Another couldn't grasp exactly why we would want to interview a woman who had handed her husband over to the police after discovering he had murdered a prostitute.

GRAEME HUSTON
Editor in chief
South Yorkshire Newspapers

News all depends. But you'll know it when you see it. Clear? Right. Now go out and find some.

TERRY PRATCHETT
The Truth (2000)

👍 *News doesn't always have to surprise us. Some of it is very predictable: weddings, court cases, elections, anniversaries of major events – all things we know well in advance are going to take place, but are covered nonetheless because they offer fresh detail.*

Such stories renew emotional responses and reinforce beliefs and prejudices. They trigger the satisfaction of knowing that what we expect to happen does happen, and that events do reach a rounded conclusion.

👍 *Aim to make at least one new contact every day. When you've met all the obvious ones – councillors, police, and so on – start on all the other people who might be a source of information and stories. You'll find suggestions for contacts throughout this book. Make a list and tick them off one by one.*

(Snowstorm halts test match, 92-year-old weds for third time, Giraffe born with two necks), but it may arouse any of the wide range of human emotions: disbelief *(92-year-old expects twins)*, anger *(Council tax to double)*, pleasure *(Council tax halved)*, envy *(Goalkeeper signs million-pound-a-week deal)*, pity *(Soap star has cancer)*, horror *(Berserk axeman slaughters family)*, disgust *(Man dies in sewage blast)*, hope *(Cancer cure breakthrough)*, laughter *(Getaway car runs out of fuel)*. It may simply satisfy curiosity *(Study reveals how spiders end up in the bath)*. If enough people react strongly enough it will provoke debate, controversy and maybe action.

We tend to react more strongly to bad news than good – contrast your reaction to *Pensioner wins lottery* with *Toddler raped six times* – and news selection reflects this, though there is always a place for *Amazing rescue* and *Miracle survival* stories.

Not every news story will trigger a response from every reader or listener. We are not all interested in the same things and what makes one person react with excitement leaves others cold. But a story that nobody finds interesting isn't news.

DECIDING FACTORS

NEWS is new, true, about people and triggers reaction. So far so good. But there are countless stories around each day that fulfil these basic criteria. Only a tiny few make it to newspaper pages and news bulletins. Why are some chosen and not others?

The reasons divide fairly neatly into three: the story itself, its newsroom context and external influences.

THE STORY

Stories may be chosen because of:

Availability

To make the news, events obviously have to be reported in the first place, and there are many that go uncovered. It may simply be because nobody knows about them. It may be they are known but not recognised as news – the publication of statistics, perhaps, in which important facts are buried. It may be because there are better stories around to occupy reporters' time. It may be because they are too difficult or costly or time-consuming to make coverage worthwhile: many news-gathering organisations have abandoned routine coverage of courts, for example.

Stories are more likely to be covered if they can be planned well ahead because they come from regular, reliable sources such as calls and councils.

Relevance

The closer readers feel to a story, the more likely it is to be used. That may simply mean geographical proximity. Something that happens down your street is more likely to arouse your interest than something a long way away. A weekly newspaper will put *Body dragged out of river* on its front page if it has happened in its circulation area, but ignore *Three bodies found in river* 50 miles away. A national daily will mention six people hurt in a rail crash in Britain, but pass over 16 injured in a similar crash in Belgium or 60 dead in China. In the world of news, distance rarely lends enchantment to the view.

Stories from a long way away can be newsworthy if there is a cultural proximity. British newspapers carry more news about the United States and Australia, which are tied to us historically, have a common language and (generally) share our view of the world, than they do about much nearer but culturally distant countries such as Latvia and Uzbekistan.

Proximity may mean shared interest in a story's subject matter. If foot and mouth breaks out in Cumbria, it is news to farmers not only there but all over Britain; if Avian flu breaks out it may well get mentioned all over the world. Relevance clearly varies with the audience. A newspaper that knows its readers are predominantly female or old or leftwing will adjust its contents to suit. Everyone making decisions about what stories are newsworthy is constantly asking: is this relevant to our audience? Is it significant to them, is it important that they know it, and will they find it interesting?

Scale

The more people involved in an event – taking part or responding to it – the greater the impact. One child born without arms is a personal tragedy; a thousand is a national scandal prompting intensive news coverage, multi-million-pound law suits and a radical overhaul of the law. If the price of hamster food soars, few people care and it goes unreported (except perhaps in *Hamster Owners' Monthly*); if petrol goes up five pence, everyone is affected and it makes the front page.

A one-off event has more impact than a series of events spread over time: *20 die in motorway crash* gets more coverage than 20 stories about *One dead in motorway crash*, a tsunami makes headlines while thousands dying in monsoons over a six-month period doesn't.

On the other hand, something that will affect the audience for a long time is usually stronger news than something that is soon over: *Town centre to be pedestrianised* beats *Town centre closed half a day for gas main repairs*.

> *What's a good story? A good test is what will be the stories people in the pub will be telling their mates about once they've read them in your newspaper: stories that spark comments like 'You'll never guess what!' or 'Have you heard what the council wants to do now?'*

DAVID JACKMAN
Editor
Epping Forest Guardian

> *Local news is what local people are talking about – so find a way to report it. Nothing should be too trivial for inclusion in the local newspaper.*

JEAN MAY
Editor
News Shopper, Orpington

George Bastian, an American reporter, tried to define newsworthiness in mathematical terms.

According to his formula,

1 bank manager plus 1 wife = 0

but

1 bank manager minus $100,000 = News

and

1 bank manager minus $100,000 plus 1 chorus girl = BIG news

It's not really quite that simple, but it does make the point that news is something interesting and about people.

'Good news is no news.' To prove this wrong, one or two editors have tried printing nothing but happy stories.

Readers yawned, sales plummeted, and the newspapers returned swiftly to their usual agenda.

Drama

If there is a choice between two stories, one a mere statement of facts and the other packed with eye-witness accounts of dramatic action, the second wins every time. *Store robbed* will race up the news list if it has shoppers screaming in terror, heroic defiance by the owner, attention-grabbing quotes and a high-speed chase at the end.

Simplicity

A news story is more likely to be used if readers can grasp what it is all about straight away and make sense of what is being said. Complex arguments or swathes of statistics, however important, are no use without explanation or analysis. This means, of course, that it has to be clearly understood and explained by the reporter in the first place.

Timing

News from a press conference just before deadline, offering the chance of an exclusive story, is more likely to get in than one held just afterwards, which will be old news by the time it reaches its audience.

Exclusivity

Newspapers and broadcasters love scooping the opposition. Stories they have to themselves have a better chance of being used prominently than those shared with rival publications or stations.

That said, some stories get used because they *have* been elsewhere. One news medium can set the agenda for others. If a story figures on the early-morning radio bulletins, newspapers may well feel they should cover it too; conversely, radio stations follow up stories that have already been in the newspapers, stories they would not otherwise have known about or covered. A story in one part of the country may prompt reporters elsewhere to look for similar ones nearer home. You can bet that a report of a panther running wild on Exmoor will spawn news of similar beasts being spotted elsewhere.

Trendiness

Times change. What is news in one decade may not be in the next. No one gets excited now about heart transplants, gay weddings or the appointment of female priests. Some topics rise up the news agenda. Privatisation in the eighties, for example, thrust the stock market onto the pages of even the brashest tabloids as more and more readers bought shares. The soaring number of people holidaying and retiring abroad has led to an upsurge in stories about countries hitherto ignored.

Acceptability

Stories have to be legally safe, ethically sound, and conform to what the newspaper is prepared to print and its readers to read. What is deemed acceptable varies with the medium and its audience. Lurid details of a councillor's three-in-a-bed romps with traffic wardens will be splashed across a national tabloid but never see the light of day in the local weekly. British media report full details of inquests and name those involved; in some other countries, the dead are rarely identified.

Pictures

Stories with illustration stand a better chance of being used, whether they are for television, websites or newspapers. Events in obscure countries suddenly make the TV because a camera crew are there, and vanish into obscurity as soon as they leave. A story about 70 people dying in a ferry disaster in Indonesia will be lucky to make a paragraph in a British national – unless there are dramatic pictures of survivors clinging desperately to the upturned boat.

Local newspapers give mundane events more prominence if there are photos to go with them – how many would cover nativity plays without all those little faces? (Very few, we discovered, when schools started banning such photographs to placate parents panicking about paedophiles).

> *Listen and learn. Read the papers. Know what's going on. Stay abreast with the changes.*
>
> *Follow the advice of the old hands.*
>
> *And don't ever think that you will know all there is to know.*
>
> **DAVID ARMSTRONG**
> Editor
> Portadown Times

NEWS IS... EVERYBODY'S

There is no copyright in news. The moment your hard-won exclusive story is published, the rest of the media are free to lift the facts for their own use, repeat them as often as they like, and even claim that they found them in the first place.

They do so, of course, at the risk of looking as foolish as you if the facts are wrong.

They could also find themselves in the dangerous position of repeating libellous allegations, which you can prove but they are unable to defend.

There *is* copyright in the *form* in which stories are published, which is why newspapers stealing rivals' stories usually re-write them and try to add a little new material of their own.

You can and should complain if your copy is reproduced word-for-word without being credited to your newspaper.

There is a defence in copyright law called fair dealing, which permits the reproduction of extracts of original material (apart from photos) for the purpose of review or reporting current affairs, so long as the source is acknowledged.

You won't see this done very often, because newspapers hate having to admit that their rivals have beaten them to a story.

National newspapers sometimes delay the publication of exclusives until later editions to reduce the opportunity for rivals to follow them up.

Papers run crusades – to crack down on litter louts, to improve safety at accident blackspots, to raise money for local hospices – and publish stories that help the cause, even though they may not be intrinsically very newsworthy and are sometimes little more than stunts dreamed up by the newspaper itself.

For broadcasters, sound content is critical. Stories that include recorded interviews fare better than flat reports read by a presenter.

THE NEWSROOM CONTEXT

Stories may be selected because of:

Space

When there is plenty of big news around, lesser stories are jettisoned. Political spin-masters know this and make the most of it. It takes a very strong story indeed to find space, let alone prominence, the day after a princess is killed or terrorists blow up a tube train.

On slow news days, stories that would not normally see the light of day get in. There is less competition for space at certain times of the year – Christmas, for example, and the summer Silly Season, when Parliament, courts and councils are quiet. Sundays are thin news days for daily newspapers, and newsrooms may be grateful for anything they can lay their hands on. It is often a case of 'the best we've got'. On any day of the week, if a newspaper is awash with advertising there will be a greater demand for editorial to fill up the extra pages than if space is tight.

Balance

Readers and listeners want variety, and the daily news menu has to ring the changes. Item after item of serious news about gloomy subjects makes the audience wonder whether it might not be better off swapping its news source for one less depressing.

So those who decide what goes in sprinkle cheerful off-beat stories among the gloom. TV news programmes end with light-hearted items to balance things up a bit. Newspapers decide *Daft duck thinks it's a dog* may not be the most significant news of the day, but should go across the bottom of the front page rather than *Yet another court case.* The Sun slaps topless teenagers on Page 3.

Balance is not just about the tone of stories. Geography matters, too. The media try to make their choice of news stories reflect the spread of their audience across their area or the country as a whole.

Newspapers may produce more than one edition, each aimed at a specific part of their circulation area. First editions of the nationals will focus on the furthest-flung corners of the country because it takes longer to deliver the printed newspapers there, though this is much less of a problem in these days of multi-centre printing than when all were produced in London. Stories are chosen appropriately. The result can be an unhappy mix of stories from widely separated parts of the country – Northern Ireland, Scotland and Cornwall, for example. It leaves readers baffled.

Decision-makers

A tale that excites one news editor may not have quite the same impact on another. When editors change jobs, their replacements bring fresh agendas with new priorities. Everybody in a newsroom has his or her own view about what are the best stories of the day.

In the end, decisions about what tops the news list are made by a handful of people who are all subjective human beings, and, as you can see from the variation in stories chosen by the nationals each morning, they don't always agree.

EXTERNAL INFLUENCES

Story selection may be influenced by:

Ownership

Few proprietors spend their days hovering behind the news desk dictating what goes in. They don't need to. There may be the occasional phone call to make sure the newspaper follows the right editorial line on a major political issue, but they have appointed managers and editors who understand broadly what is acceptable and will make sure the newspaper's image, content and political spin conform with the owner's wishes.

Advertisers

It would be naive to claim that advertising considerations have never influenced a commercial news operation's choice of stories. It isn't easy for the editor of a cash-strapped weekly to run a story exposing price-fixing among local house agents who spend hundreds of thousands a year on much-needed advertising.

Happily, giving in to pressure to keep stories out of the newspapers is pretty rare. Editors fight hard for their independence, and are usually robust in defending their right to publish stories putting companies in a bad light whatever the financial consequences. They argue that nobody advertises out of the goodness of their hearts, and advertisers need newspapers as much as newspapers need them. Bowing once to pressure from advertisers would open the floodgates to many more.

Never ignore the strangest thing. Leaving a village pub one night I heard the sound of bagpipes from a nearby field.

It turned out to be a member of a local bagpipe band, banned from practising at home because it upset his wife and neighbours so much.

ALAN KIRBY
Editor
Coventry Telegraph

The need for light relief can occasionally mean a story gets in the newspaper for no better reason than it offers subs an opportunity to demonstrate their headline-writing skills.

It is hard to believe, for example, that news of a parish council putting Christmas decorations on its public toilet would have made the national press without the headline 'Lav is a many-splendoured thing'.

That said, while virtually no stories are left out in case they upset advertisers, many get in as a result of advertisers' influence. Every newsroom's postbag brings press releases purporting to be news stories, advertising stunts created by publicity agents who know their claims may well go unchallenged by newsdesks under pressure to fill space as quickly as possible. A survey claiming to prove that *TV star has Britain's sexiest legs* made many a national news page (with a photo, naturally). Who did the survey? The agency handling the launch of a new range of stockings, that's who.

Publicity material is the backbone of many an advertising feature with editorial content (known as advertorial) – *Spring Brides, Bank Holiday Days Out, Christmas Shopping*. Some newspapers make sure these are prominently identified as advertising; on others the distinction between what is written because it is news and what appears because it keeps the ads flowing is less than clear.

Three

FINDING OUT

TELL people you are a reporter and it won't be long before they ask 'Where *do* you get all that news?'

Many members of the public seem to think there is some magical gravity-like force that draws news and news-gatherers together. Others assume newspapers and radio stations have scores of reporters wandering happily round town all day, so there is always one on the spot when anything newsworthy happens. They chase every fire engine and ambulance that goes by. If a court is running they are there to cover every case. Police tell them about the latest crimes, councillors keep them posted on town hall secrets, and their office is besieged by people anxious to boast of their exploits, confess their misdemeanours and expose the corruption of others.

If only it were true. In fact, finding the news takes hard work, organisation, persistence and a fair bit of luck.

NEWS SOURCES

AMONG the main sources of news are:

TV, RADIO & THE WEB

The media are cannibals, feeding voraciously on each other's output. TV and radio follow up stories in the newspapers, newspapers follow up TV and radio news. The nationals pursue stories first found in the weeklies, the weeklies find local angles on stories broken by the big operators. In thc middle are freelances and agencies grabbing ideas from each end and selling them to the other. Everyone is constantly watching what the rest are up to.

Daily newspaper and radio newsdesks monitor TV, radio and web-based news sites throughout the day, watching for fresh news. Reporters should keep an eye and/or ear on them, too: you look and feel foolish if you are unaware of a big breaking story. If you have the option, make your computer's home screen one that carries the news headlines and regularly updates them.

Weekly newspapers do not need such a constant check on the rest of the world but still regularly check what is on the local TV and radio news.

- Sources of news
- Sources of information

> *The bcst advice I received as a trainee was: Get out of the office! My editor insisted that we meet people face-to-face and build up useful contacts.*
>
> *I went on a round of calls twice or three times a week, popping in to see head teachers, shop assistants, police officers, firemen, bar staff, waiters and even a lollipop lady.*
>
> *Every week I would pick up a human interest story or a snippet of information which would lead to something.*
>
> **DENNIS SISSONS**
> Editor

👍 *Check which minority publications are on sale in your local newsagents.*

If there is a demand for copies of the Phnom Penh Post you might wonder what some of its readers are doing in town.

Newsdesks monitor websites where there may be information not otherwise available. This applies at local as well as national level: a weekly newspaper may not have the time or staff to cover all the parish councils in its area, for example, but will find details of meetings and activities on their websites.

Other kinds of websites can prove a source of news. There are regular stories to be found, for example, about unusual items for sale on eBay and people finding romance via Friends Reunited.

WIRE SERVICES

Most daily newspapers and radio stations are connected to news agencies which send them a regularly-updated stream of national and international news stories, data, images and video. Content used to arrive by telegraph (hence the name 'wire services' and the many newspapers with *Telegraph* in their titles). Nowadays it comes straight to the computer screen via satellite, cable or internet.

Wire agencies have their own reporting staffs and sub-editing teams. The ones you are most likely to come across include the Press Association (PA), covering the UK, and international agencies such as Reuters, Associated Press (AP), United Press International (UPI) and Agence France Presse (AFP). As well as news, these agencies offer sport, finance, features and pictures, and will provide newspapers with custom-built items ranging from weather maps and football league tables to ready-to-print pages of TV listings and city prices. The subscription fee paid by newspapers to agencies is based on circulation and the services required.

BBC radio stations are also served by a centralised BBC newsroom, and independent stations by Independent Radio News (IRN).

Weekly newspapers concentrating on local news have little need for wire services and few have full access to them.

👍 *Treat leaked information, however reliable the source may seem to be, with caution.*

Ask yourself what your informant's motives might be, how likely it is that they have had access to the information they are offering, what proof there is of documents' authenticity.

Verify the facts from another source and get the other side of the story if you possibly can.

PUBLICATIONS

Your own newspaper

As well as stories that could be developed further, there may be news buried in the advertisements. Small ads are fruitful, particularly those advertising items lost, found, wanted and for sale, and those announcing births, deaths and marriages (often referred to as BDMs or HMDs – hatches, matches and dispatches). Don't skip the Sits Vac. An ad for a new company executive may tip you off about the current post-holder's resignation; an ad for bus-drivers may suggest the firm has problems running its services or is planning expansion. Others worth looking through include notices of planning applications, bankruptcy hearings, footpath closures and traffic diversions.

Other newspapers

Newsdesks scour the nationals and other newspapers, looking for stories that are new or have been missed and that can be followed up with a local angle. Going through the newspapers and reporting what you find to the newsdesk may be one of your first duties when arriving in the office as the early-duty reporter.

Most newsrooms will have a selection of the nationals, but there are many other newspapers available that are worth monitoring for potential stories. Take a look, for example, at the religious press *(The Church Times, Catholic Herald, Methodist Recorder)*, ethnic publications *(New Nation, Asian Times, Muslim News)*, and left-wing newspapers *(Morning Star, Socialist Worker)*. Most are available online. All have readers in your area; all carry information which might lead to stories – visits by newsworthy people, plans for demonstrations, fund-raising activities.

Magazines and journals

At one end of the scale are academic journals and professional publications, of particular interest to specialist reporters. Health correspondents will study *The Lancet* and the *British Medical Journal*; education specialists *The Times Education Supplement*. At the other end are community, society and church newsletters carrying information about local affairs. Some may be very parochial and look amateurish, but all can be rich sources of news items. In between are a host of other publications catering for particular interests – trades, pastimes, sports and entertainment.

DIARY JOBS

Every newsroom has a diary, traditionally an A4-size day-per-page book kept on the news editor's desk but these days replaced in some offices by an electronic version available to everyone with a computer.

Into it go details of everything newsworthy known to be coming up in the future: courts and inquests, councils, public meetings, press conferences, public inquiries and tribunals, sports fixtures, shop openings, village shows, anniversaries, weddings and funerals. Each will be listed with time, venue and contact information. Many will have letters, emails or press releases to go with them, and these will be kept either in the diary itself or in a nearby filing system. Into the diary, too, go reminders for follow-up stories: the date the council promised roadworks would finish, for example, or the birthday of someone you hear about who will be 100 in six months' time.

The newsdesk writes reporters' names or initials in the diary beside the stories they have been allocated. One of the first things you do when you arrive at work is check what you are scheduled to cover, note where you are supposed to be and when, and collect any relevant material. You should check the diary again before you leave at night so you know what

I'm a huge believer in getting out of the office and just talking to folk. I can't understand why loitering with intent – just being one of the lads in the pub – is so frowned upon.

The trick is patience and never switching off.

MIKE AMOS
Columnist
The Northern Echo

What editors look for at interview: Personality, personality, personality – and clean fingernails.

ANITA SYVRET
Editor
Gloucestershire Echo

Get away from the telephone, get out of the office and get to know the patch inside out. Always be curious.

NICOLE GARNON
Assistant editor
South Wales Argus

is facing you next day and can prepare for it if, for example, you have an assignment out of the office first thing in the morning.

The diary forms the basis of news lists compiled by the newsdesk for discussion at daily news conferences. It is updated regularly, as new items are added by the newsdesk and by individual reporters. It also shows reporters' days off, who is on early and late duties, who is on holiday and so on. Each year's diary is stored away for checking anniversaries and other future reference.

A large part of every newspaper and news bulletin consists of stories that have been in the diary, known about and planned for well in advance, and you will spend much of your early reporting life working 'on-diary'.

THE CALLS

One job allocated to a reporter each day is doing the calls – regular checks, by phone or face-to-face, with emergency services and other contacts. These produce information that is followed up at the time or later.

HANDOUTS AND PRESS RELEASES

Scores of these arrive every day, by post, fax and email. Some are useful, some go straight in the bin. Useful ones include notices of meetings, minutes and agendas, government announcements, invitations to meet visiting ministers or celebrities, company reports, the latest job or crime figures, decisions of planning inspectors, and details of forthcoming activities by charities, community organisations and pressure groups.

Many handouts are from company press offices announcing new products and services or claiming improvements on old ones. They are often little more than blatant attempts to win free advertising, but some have news value.

SUBMITTED ARTICLES

These may come from stringers, the name given to local correspondents not on the full-time staff. They may be paid a regular retainer or a fee only when items are used. Other items arrive from freelances, who range from individuals working part-time to full-time agencies employing a dozen or more reporters. They may submit stories on spec or be commissioned by the newsdesk to cover them. Many newspapers use news agencies to cover courts.

From time to time your newsdesk may be offered copy from newspapers elsewhere in the country if their reporters have covered stories involving people from your area. Large newspaper groups with publications dotted all over the country may have a system for sharing stories of mutual interest.

READERS' LETTERS

There are two kinds of these. The first are from people hoping the contents are newsworthy enough to earn space on the news pages. They can succeed. Notices of forthcoming charity events, for example, may merit a paragraph or two in a weekly newspaper; pleas for help in tracing long-lost schoolfriends may find space, especially if there is a faded photo to go with them. Many, though, are simply pleas for free publicity, and usually end up being redirected to the advertising department.

The second kind are letters intended for publication in the correspondence columns. Some are too boring, too badly-written or too libellous to get in; others are luckier, though they may be trimmed to a manageable length. A few will include information, comments, allegations or appeals that are worth following up and turning into news stories. If your newsdesk asks you to do this, they will insist that you contact the writer to explain what you are doing, get approval, and probably obtain additional material.

TIP-OFFS

Readers phone or call in at the office to tell you about things they think are newsworthy. Sometimes they are right, and you are alerted to potentially good stories: a crash on the by-pass, a town centre pub raided by the drugs squad, a neighbour from hell holding three-in-the-morning karaoke sessions.

You get tip-offs, too, from non-editorial people working for your organisation. Advertising reps spend their lives meeting people who run businesses in the area. Van drivers get all over the place. Everyone who works for a newspaper or radio station knows people who are potential news sources. Good newsrooms maintain contact with them all and encourage them to pass on anything they hear.

LEAKS

Not every document marked *Confidential* stays secret. Some find their way into the hands of reporters. Disaffected councillors slip them details

I remember a new journalist who contacted every animal group that existed and by simply calling them every week always had a colourful story.

He could turn out copy on animal rescues, cruelty claims, remarkable animal adventures at the drop of a hat – and of course animals always make excellent pictures.

It was a good example of someone doing that basic job of a journalist, finding out where the stories were and just milking them endlessly.

BILL BROWNE
Editor
Salisbury Journal

DON'T ASK HOW THEY KNOW THAT

Public relations offices produce surveys and try to persuade the media to use them.

Some are newsworthy. Others have only entertainment value, but still make the news when little else is around. Take the survey claiming *42% of Britons make phone calls in the nude*.

It got plenty of exposure one late December, when the annual Christmas/New Year news oasis had editors prepared to use just about anything.

If in doubt, leave out – but better, find out!

LIZ GRIFFIN
Editor
Hereford Times

of town hall plans, union whistleblowers reveal company moves to cut jobs. Politicians have been known to leak proposals in order to gauge public reaction before announcing or (if the reaction is hostile) abandoning them.

PUBLIC OPINION

Newsrooms create news stories by conducting surveys and polls, face to face, on the phone, by email and by text, to find out what people think about the issues of the day. Their views and comments make stories. Some are serious journalism: a survey of every dentist in town, for example, that reveals that not one is prepared to take on new patients. Others are mere snapshots of opinion: the views of half-dozen people selected at random. Some of these are informative, others simply desperate attempts to fill space on a grimly-thin news day *(Is Christmas too commercial? You have your say)*.

The softer kind of surveys are often carried out by reporters; more serious ones claiming to give a genuine picture of opinion, such as polls of pre-election voting intentions, are usually contracted out to professional market survey companies.

IN-HOUSE ACTIVITIES

Newspapers run campaigns, organise events and hold competitions. The motives may be pure *(Save our hospital)* or self-promotional *(Is your dog our Pet of the Year?)*. Whatever the driving force, stories are found – or manufactured – as a result of these activities: *Hundreds sign our petition, Mary scoops our win-a-teapot prize*.

ANNIVERSARIES

These may be national *(60 years of the NHS)* or local *(The day the bombers hit town)*, serious *(Our 12 months of hell)* or light-hearted *(Lottery winner's year of spend, spend, spend)*. They all make stories reminding readers of what happened, quoting those who were involved, and asking questions about what, if anything, has happened since.

AND YOU...

Reporters are expected to work off-diary and generate their own stories. How good you are at this depends on what you see, what you hear, and who you talk to. The more you get out of the office, the more contacts you make, the more likely you are to come across potentially newsworthy items – the notice announcing a business is going to close, the bus-shelter full of used syringes, the shop-window photo of

---

👍 *Lists of local and notable wills are available from subscription services, and the details can make good copy.*

Look out for people who lived modest lives yet left a fortune. Don't be too surprised if affluent people leave very little: it usually just means that they had good advice on tax avoidance (not evasion, which is illegal).

It is worth looking at who the main beneficiaries are. If someone leaves a large sum to a cats' home but very little to close relatives, there's a story in it.

👍 *Spend a couple of hours getting to know the Yellow Pages. They contain far more information than you'd expect – from lists of trade associations to how the local NHS works – and a vast number of potential contacts.*

a euphonium for sale, the pub raising money for a child's life-saving operation.

Your eyes and ears, driven by constant curiosity, will find news for you.

INFORMATION SOURCES

WHATEVER the story, there will be facts you need to check and extra information you need to include. You are not expected to know everything. You *are* expected to know where to look. Your main sources of information include:

ARCHIVES

If you are working on a newspaper, start with its back issues. Records of everything published will be stored either as filed cuttings or, more probably, as an electronic data-base accessible from your computer. Look for anything relating to your subject. It is a waste of time making phone calls to track down someone's details when all the time they have been available at the click of a button. While you are at it, check if there are pictures available too.

Don't assume that every cutting is accurate. Mistakes are made and even if corrections are published there is no guarantee these are always picked up by whoever runs the data-base.

Old minutes and agendas of council and other meetings should be stored somewhere in the office for reference. The library will also have a host of local publications such as council year-books and old census reports.

You may be able to access other news organisations' archives. Many national newspapers make their stories available on the net, free or for a nominal charge, and there are searchable websites listing those available. Check with your newsdesk what you can access.

INTERNET

This is great for general background information, and it can be very useful for tracking down detail if you know what you are after. However, its greatest asset, the quantity of information available, is also becoming its greatest drawback. It is not always easy to find what you want among all those billions of entries and you may need to employ some fairly refined search techniques to succeed. Bear in mind that even the most sophisticated search engines will only track down a relatively small proportion of what is actually available, so if your search fails to uncover what you are looking for it doesn't necessarily mean it does not exist.

There are specialist search engines that concentrate on news stories, and others which offer guidance on sources and internet research. Enter *UK news search engines* into Google for a taste of what is available.

> **Lost and found ads can be a great source for stories.**
>
> *I once spotted an ad asking if anyone had lost three dogs.*
>
> *It turned out they had run off and been been picked up by a chap in a Rolls Royce who eventually reunited them with their owner. Good little story.*
>
> **LYNN ASHWELL**
> Assistant editor
> Bolton News

REFERENCE BOOKS

Don't dismiss these as out-of-date. Frequently they are the fastest route to the information you need, especially if it is detail about someone or something that is unlikely to figure high on internet search engine lists. If you want proof of this, try finding out the age of your local vicar on the net: it will take a long, long time. Pick up the office copy of *Crockford's* and you will find out in seconds.

Your newsroom and library will have a collection of the most useful reference books, and more will be available in your public library. Many are accessible online, but you may have to subscribe before you can search their contents. It is impossible to name all the reference books you might need, but there is a list at the back of this book of those you are most likely to come across.

TRADE ASSOCIATIONS & INTEREST GROUPS

Most jobs, organisations and interests have some kind of association representing them, with national offices and, in many cases, local branches as well. There are obvious ones like Alcoholics Anonymous and The National Federation of Builders; less obvious ones like the National Society of Allotment Holders; some not obvious at all (how about the Scottish Poisons Information Bureau, or the Screw Thread Tool Manufacturers' Association?).

All you have got to do is track them down. A quick Google search will probably do it. Failing that, there are publications offering guidance to information sources, listing tens of thousands of potential contacts, though some come at a price that makes them unlikely additions to small newsrooms' shelves. Many listings are available in electronic form via the net, though you may have to subscribe for access.

SPECIALIST PUBLICATIONS

There are magazines on countless topics. Some are on general sale, some available by subscription. Their editors and staff love their subject (you don't work on *Stamp Magazine* for long if philately bores you stiff) and may well point you in the right direction for background information or quotes. Check the websites of publications for contact details. Their pages are filled by people fanatical about their hobby and ads from companies selling them equipment and services. All or any of them may help.

LOCAL EXPERTS

You will be surprised how many people there are within your circulation area with useful expertise, and they are often more than happy to help. The newsdesk will know some – the doctor who loves explaining exactly what the MMR debate is all about, the retired teacher who knows everything about local history – and you will build up your own collection of expert contacts.

TRACKING PEOPLE DOWN

IF you have the person's occupation, it's not difficult. Contact the workplace if you know it and ask to talk to the person or to leave a message. If the business has a website, check it for a phone number and/or email address.

If you know only what general line of business someone is in, phone round as many companies as you can asking if the person you are seeking works there or is known to them. Try any relevant trade association or interest group. You may not be given a phone number or address right away, but you can leave a message with your contact details. It may be that you want to find the person because of some special interest or activity. Contact clubs, groups or associations to which they might belong.

Sometimes you have a name and know they are local, but that's all. Where do you start?

ARCHIVES

If they have ever been mentioned in your newspaper before, you should be able to search through these and come up with a clue to their address.

PHONE BOOKS

Still a good source even in these days of ex-directory numbers and unlisted mobiles. Often the people with the information you need are just a phone call away. If the person you are looking for is not listed, don't stop if the surname is fairly unusual. Try phoning others with the same name. They may well be related. Your newsroom will have local phone books; you can do nationwide searches on the net.

ELECTORAL ROLL

Every newsroom used to have an up-to-date copy showing names and addresses of everyone registered to vote, listed by addresses. Nowadays you have to pay for a copy, and not all office budgets stretch to it. It is still available to consult, free, at town halls and public libraries, or you can search all the electoral registers in the country on the net. Bear in mind that registers do not include people below voting age or those who have not bothered to register, and they are not up-to-the-minute because people move house.

Bear in mind that not everything on the net is genuine or accurate. Be sure of the authenticity of your source and check if you have any doubt.

INTERNET

Put the name into your search engine and see what comes up. If it is unusual enough you may identify the person you seek or find a link to their blog. If you are overwhelmed with suggestions, try one of the people-search websites. There are scores of these – Google *Find a Person* for lists. Armed with a name, these sites trawl phone books, electoral registers, births, deaths and marriages records and any other data-bases they have managed to link into.

Try the contact websites: almost half the adults in Britain are listed on Friends Reunited, for example, and you can search by name. You are unlikely to get their home address but you will be able to email them and there may be clues that could lead you to them. If you are after relatives of someone who has died, try one of the tribute sites.

CONTACTS

Ring round (or, better still, visit) to see if anyone recognises the name. Corner shops, village stores and post offices come into contact with many people in their area; if they are newsagents they may deliver their newspapers. Pub landlords and cafe owners hear a lot of what is going on and know who lives where. So do postmen. Garages know car owners. Don't forget the churches: vicars may not see their flock often, but they know who is in their parishes and remember names from weddings, funerals and christenings. The better your contacts, the more likely you are to find one who can help.

LAST RESORTS

Stick a small ad in your newspaper and a message on its website, asking the person you seek to ring your number. Impossible to resist if they read it, and even if they don't, it may be spotted by someone else who can help.

Email the name @ hotmail, yahoo, fsnet and as many other ISPs you can think of. Cross your fingers but don't hold your breath.

Four

A DAY IN THE LIFE

YOUR job as a reporter is basically the same whatever the medium you work in: to follow up news items, delegated to you or self-generated; to gather facts and opinions through research and talking to people; to match them with illustrative material; and to produce clear, concise and well-worded reports to a given length within a given time.

As a trainee, you will almost certainly start off in the main newsroom, the hub of the news-gathering operation where you and the other reporters are based. You will be given a desk with storage space, a computer and, with luck, a phone of your own. Somewhere nearby will be files of recent newspapers, a shelf or two of reference books, maybe a television tuned into a news channel.

Working in the same building will be dozens, maybe hundreds of other people. Who they are and what they do depends on the size and nature of the organisation. Here we look at a couple of examples, a small weekly newspaper and a large regional daily, and follow two young trainees through a typical day in their working lives. The newspapers and people below are fictitious, but based on working practices in the real world.

- The Fernwood Express
- The Midthorpe Telegraph

Many journalists think working for a weekly is an easier life than working on a daily.

Wrong. The increase in internet use by all newspapers has led to the necessity of daily uploading to weekly newspaper sites.

No matter what paper you are working for, get into the habit of regular copy flow and daily updates on stories.

The days of leaving it all until a Tuesday for Wednesday publication are long gone.

ANDY DOWNIE
Editor
East Wales Weeklies

THE FERNWOOD EXPRESS

THE NEWSPAPER

The *Express* is a small independent weekly, selling around 7,000 copies a week in the rural town of Fernwood and its surrounding villages. It is based in the centre of town, with offices above a newsagent's shop which it owns. Its one edition, out on Wednesday morning, averages 48 broadsheet pages but can be bigger or smaller depending on advertising. The *Express* is printed under contract by a big daily newspaper 50 miles away and delivered to Fernwood's newsagents by a wholesale distributor.

EDITORIAL STAFF

There are four full-time journalists: the editor, his deputy and two reporters, one of them qualified, the other a trainee. All four work in the same room, with a desk and computer apiece, three telephones, a shelf crammed with reference books, a filing cabinet full of back issues of the newspaper and a coffee machine. There is a photocopier and fax in the shop below.

👍 *Many young people who go to editors asking for jobs say they want to become journalists because they enjoy writing.*

It comes as a surprise, and sometimes a disappointment, when they discover that reporting is firstly about news-gathering, and far more time is spent finding the news than writing about it.

👍 *Meet someone who clearly recognises you, but you can't for the life of you remember who they are?*

It happens to the best of us. Be honest. Say: 'I'm really sorry, I can't remember your full name.'

They'll frown and say: 'Joe Bloggs.'

You respond: 'Bloggs, of course. Sorry, Joe…'

You've got the name, and they're appeased, thinking it was just their surname you'd mislaid.

The **reporters** do most of the routine news-gathering. Some stories are listed in the diary, a dog-eared book that lives on the editor's desk. Others they pick up themselves from emails, phone calls, people dropping into the office, or while out and about in town. They also produce features, sports stories, reviews, lists of what's on the following week, and a host of other items which fill the newspaper, including (with little enthusiasm) the occasional supporting material for advertising supplements.

A lot of material is sent in by the public. The *Express* has a network of village correspondents and other regular contributors. Some of their offerings – reports by WI secretaries, parish council clerks, cricket club captains, charity organisers seeking publicity for forthcoming events – go in virtually unchanged. There is a regular local history feature by a retired teacher, a *Voice of Faith* column by a vicar. The newspaper pays a nominal sum for these if it has to, but its budget for freelance work is very limited.

Reporters are expected to carry a camera, because the *Express* no longer employs a photographer, and they take most of the news photographs. Others (wedding pictures, for example, and photos of houses for property ads) are supplied by commercial photographers, and readers are encouraged to submit their own.

Reporters' hours are theoretically nine-till-five, but they regularly work in the evening and claim time back when they can. Tuesday, deadline day, is frantic. They take a day off during the week (usually Wednesday or Thursday, when things are relatively quiet) because both work Saturdays, busy with sport, carnivals, shows and other events. They take it in turns to be on call on Sunday.

Keeping an eye on the reporters is the **deputy editor**. He opens the post, checks incoming emails, marks jobs to be done in the diary and allocates them to the staff. He does some reporting himself, including covering the weekly magistrates court and main council meetings, but much of his time is spent sub-editing the pages and liaising with the printers. Half a dozen pages at least have to be filled, finalised and sent to the printers each day. First to go are features and other timeless material; then comes sport and early news, with the front and main inside news pages last.

At the end of each day the deputy editor updates the *Express* website, a simple affair with contact details and a summary of the main stories already published: the newspaper doesn't believe in telling its public (or any rival media) what is in its next issue in case it harms sales, and has yet to venture into the interactive world of blogs and videoclips.

The **editor** makes day-to-day decisions about what goes in the newspaper, discussing the stories of the day with her deputy at an informal mid-morning meeting. The other two chip in if they are around. She also handles the letters page, writes the editorial opinion-piece and may get involved in reporting the biggest stories of the week. She hires (and fires) reporters and has a friendly running battle with the advertising department over how much space is available for editorial. She is frequently involved in meetings to discuss budgets, circulation, promotions and other business matters.

OTHER STAFF

The **advertising manager** spends a lot of time trying to persuade local businesses to buy space in the *Express*. He is also in charge of special supplements, promotions and other circulation-boosting operations. Working for him are two computer operators who design the bigger ads (called display ads) and lay out the pages full of smaller ones (called classifieds or small ads) – births, deaths, marriages, lost and found, articles for sale and so on – which the public hand in over the shop counter or phone in to a copytaker. If the ad-setters have any spare time, they update the newspaper's electronic archives.

There is a **general manager** in charge of everything from running the shop to organising cleaning contracts, an **accountant** who sorts out the books, several part-time **secretaries** who double up as shop assistants when things get busy, and a part-time **odd-job man**.

THE OWNER

The *Express* has been owned by the same family for five generations. The current owner and publisher holds 96 per cent of the shares in Fernwood Express Newspapers Ltd; the rest are split equally between four directors: the editor, advertising manager, general manager and accountant. The owner knows he could probably make more money by selling the newspaper to one of the big regional publishing groups and investing the proceeds elsewhere, but holds on because he believes an independent *Express* is good for local democracy and, more important, gives him useful influence and occasional power over the community it serves.

As managing director of the company, he chairs meetings with the other directors each month to discuss finances, appointments and major decisions about the newspaper's long-term direction. He occasionally drops into the editorial room and tries to remember what the young reporters are called.

DEBBIE'S DAY

Debbie is the youngest reporter on the *Express*. She grew up in the town, did work experience on the newspaper during her schooldays, and discovered she liked it so much that after getting three reasonable A-levels she turned down the idea of university and enrolled on a six-month NCTJ course at a further education college in a nearby city. As part of the course she spent one day a week back at the *Express*, working unpaid to back up the knowledge she was gaining at college with practical experience. It meant she was on the spot when one of the reporters put in his notice to take a job elsewhere, and she was delighted to be offered the chance to take his place. She has been there now for six

> *A local weekly paper is the best training ground there is, no matter which branch of journalism you want to get into.*
>
> *If you take your first job on a major evening title, you can easily find yourself forgotten in a corner writing up endless nibs.*
>
> *Start out on a weekly and you will get the opportunity to cover major news events that would be snapped up by seniors on city papers. Every day is different and you get to work on every aspect of a newspaper, building up an impressive portfolio that should land you a great job on an evening once you've passed all your exams.*
>
> *The pay's nothing much and the hours are lousy, but life on a weekly is challenging, fun and thoroughly rewarding.*
>
> **ADRIAN BRADDY**
> Editor
> Teesdale Mercury

👍 *The first thing trainees see when they arrive for a job interview at one daily newspaper, which prides itself on its command of English, is a notice saying this:*

VISITORS PARKING
This company does not accept liability for loss or damage to, or loss of property from cars parked in this car park, however caused, or damaged or loss of property however caused, on it's premises

Five grammatical errors in 37 words.

No job applicant has yet dared to mention them to the editor. The first to do so will probably be offered a job on the spot.

👍 *Contact suggestion: crossing patrol wardens. Make friends with the lollipop ladies and gents guiding pupils into school. They'll tell you when police arrive to arrest the headmaster.*

months, and despite earning less than her best friend, a trainee hairdresser, is thoroughly enjoying it most of the time.

08.40

Debbie's day officially starts at nine, but she gets in a bit earlier if she can to read the morning newspapers. She switches on her computer and while it warms up makes coffee for herself and the deputy editor, who has been in since eight writing up a housing committee meeting from the night before. The other reporter arrives shortly afterwards, the editor close behind.

Debbie scrutinises the office diary to see what jobs she has been allocated for the day. She is down for the calls first thing. Then a visit to an infants school at 10.30 to talk to the retiring headmistress, the opening of a new exhibition in the town's art gallery at noon, a golden wedding at 2.0.

09.00

Debbie checks her emails to make sure there is nothing urgent and then phones the police voice-bank to see what has been happening overnight. Not a lot. One minor RTA (road traffic accident) in which a car skidded off the road into a tree, the driver cut and bruised but otherwise unhurt (and un-named). It will make a paragraph, and Debbie notes the time and place. Somebody smashed a high street shop window at closing time last night and there is an appeal for witnesses. The *Express* will use a par on that, too, if only to keep the police happy. And there is notice of an inquest two days ahead, which Debbie enters in the diary and hopes she gets the chance to cover, inquests being few and far between in Fernwood. Then she phones the fire brigade, which has nothing to report.

She writes up the two one-par stories and sends them to the deputy editor's computer. He will pick them up later, write a headline on each, and drop them into a page. At the moment he is checking emails and opening the post. There are four letters from readers, two worth publishing, one (anonymous) too ridiculous to print, one about a gang of teenagers causing havoc on a local estate that will be worth following up as a news story and is passed to the other reporter to investigate. There are reports from WIs, a parish council, the annual general meeting of the bowls club. There are notices of forthcoming coffee mornings, whist drives and Sunday rambles. And there is a pile of handouts and press releases from companies and their press agencies, most hoping for free publicity and destined for the bin, but some with genuine news interest.

09.30

The deputy editor hands a couple of these over to Debbie to write up. One is straightforward and just needs to be trimmed and given a fresh intro; the other is about plans to expand a charity shop, which she decides is worth a phone call. She phones the charity secretary who sent out the press release, asks what it is all about (the shop has been a huge success, she is told, and they have got a minor celebrity to open the extension next week), writes up the story and makes a note in the diary to cover the opening. There is bound to be a picture in it at least.

10.00

By now it is time to set off to meet the retiring headmistress. Debbie is still learning to drive, so it is a bus and a walk to the school. She gets the teacher's life story, asks about her plans for the future, takes a picture of her surrounded by five-year-olds, and accepts the offer of a tour round the school. On the way she sees a notice about a forthcoming PTA charity auction, and makes a note to follow it up later.

11.30

Debbie heads back into town just in time for the art exhibition opening. After a few questions about the artist (a former bus driver who only discovered he could paint when he retired, which makes a good intro), Debbie takes a picture of him among his exhibits. She is just thinking about lunch when she is collared by a local councillor who wants to explain to her in great detail why he is against the forthcoming council tax rises.

13.30

By the time she escapes, with half a dozen pages of shorthand notes she knows she won't use, she has just got time to grab a sandwich before setting off for the diamond wedding couple. They are not in, and it is starting to rain. Debbie takes shelter in the corner shop opposite and starts chatting to the woman behind the counter, who tells her the diamond wedding couple have gone off for the day with their daughter, who has turned up unexpectedly from America. That will make the story a bit different, thinks Debbie. Before she leaves she browses through the ads pinned in the window, notes phone numbers of someone trying to sell a stuffed cat and someone else setting up yoga classes, and heads back to the office.

14.45

She finds a note on her desk saying the deputy editor has gone off to solve a problem at the printers and that she is to cover a meeting of the chamber of trade he had been going to at 6.30. She sighs: so much for the early night she had promised herself. She sits down, checks her emails again, downloads her pictures from the school and gallery, and sends them to the deputy editor's photo folder (still referred to as a

Always do what you say you're going to do.

Return pictures promptly, return calls, write up paragraphs of charity news.

These things will gain you a reputation for being reliable.

basket, a left-over from the days of paper-based copy). Then she starts to write the stories to go with them. She is interrupted by a call from the shop saying someone wants to talk to a reporter about a parachute jump for charity, and by the time she has written everything up it is too late to go home for tea.

17.30

Instead, she tries phoning the stuffed cat seller. There is no answer, and she decides to join the other reporter in the pub next-door until it is time for the chamber of trade meeting. This is as tedious as she feared, and none of it is worth reporting until, almost at the end, two members start arguing furiously about how much traders should pay towards the town's Christmas lights next year. Debbie brightens up and takes copious notes. She will get quotes from other sources tomorrow and it should make a lively story.

20.30

On her way out, Debbie sees a fire engine race past and, after a brief wrestle with her conscience, she phones the fire station to ask what is happening. It turns out to be a false alarm and, not sure whether she is pleased or disappointed that there is no story, she at last heads home.

THE MIDTHORPE TELEGRAPH

THE NEWSPAPER

This is a much bigger operation than the *Express*. The *Telegraph* is a tabloid, selling 30,000 copies a day in and around the industrial town of Midthorpe. It used to be called the *Evening Telegraph* and have five editions a day, from the 10am Early to the 6pm Late Final, but falling sales and pressure to compete with the nationals, TV, radio and the web have reduced this to one main edition hitting the streets at 7am and a second, much smaller one, updating the front and back pages only, at noon. The size varies from around 48 pages on a Monday to 72 or more at the end of the week.

Its main office and printworks are on an industrial estate on the outskirts of Midthorpe, and there are district offices in half a dozen nearby towns, each with its own reporters. In those with more than one, the most senior may have the title of **chief reporter**.

REPORTERS

The *Telegraph* has a dozen news staff at its head office. Most are general reporters, covering whatever comes their way from the newsdesk or

The Audit Bureau of Circulations (ABC) collates and publishes details of newspaper circulations, including figures for free newspapers, listed by its VFD (Verified Free Distribution) section.

It has an electronic arm monitoring website hits.

Don't mix up the circulation (number of copies sold) with readership (much bigger, based on more than one reader per copy).

their own sources, but one specialises in courts and crime, another the local council. Two are trainees. All concentrate on news, leaving sport and features to their own departments, but are expected to take photographs. Most have been trained to film and edit video for the newspaper's website, which carries news as it happens – often before it appears in print – and has a rapidly-expanding interactive audience. If reporters are working outside the office close to deadline, they can take a mobile to email stories and pictures to the newsdesk.

Because deadlines are so early, most of the reporters are producing stories for the next day's edition. They operate on a shift system. One starts work at 6am, checking what has happened overnight. A couple of others arrive at seven, some at nine, some at 11, some do the late shift from two till 10 or whenever their evening jobs finish. They work five of the six publication days, plus every third Sunday.

SENIOR STAFF

The reporters are overseen by the **news editor** and the **deputy news editor**, who organise the diary, coordinate news coverage, brief reporters and check copy as it comes in.

They run the newsdesk, and are responsible for identifying the news of the day and ensuring copy flows smoothly to the sub-editors. They are in touch with the chief reporters and district reporters in the outlying offices, news agencies, freelances and other outside sources. They keep a constant eye on television and web-based news sites. From all these they draw up a schedule showing which stories are being covered and who is covering them. It is revised during the day as stories fall down and new ones appear.

The news editor is based at one of a number of desks arranged in a circle in the centre of an open-plan office. Other desks are occupied by

> *Speed is often of the essence. You never know when you're going to have to sprint somewhere to beat the opposition.*
>
> *Vital equipment: a pair of comfortable shoes.*
>
> **COLIN MOONEY**
> Former reporter
> Reuters

> *Don't bull-shit your news editor. Vengeance will be slow and painful.*
>
> **NEIL BENSON**
> Editorial director
> Trinity Mirror Regionals

> *Don't get precious: your job is not to impress your boss or other journos but to inform, sometimes to educate and always to entertain people.*
>
> **PHIL FLEMING**
> Editor
> Lancaster Citizen

EDITORIAL CONFERENCES

Senior editors on the *Telegraph* get together for editorial conferences three times a day.

The first is held in mid-morning, when news, sport, features, website and picture editors meet the assistant editor for content to discuss each area's schedule and decide the agenda for the next day's newspaper.

The second takes place in mid-afternoon, when these six are joined by the editor or her deputy, the assistant editor for production, and the chief sub to discuss plans in more detail and amend them in the light of new stories.

Representatives of other departments may be invited in to explain future advertising drives, special supplements or promotion exercises.

A final meeting of senior editorial staff is held at 6pm to confirm that everything is going as planned, and to hand over control to the assistant editor for production in his role as night editor.

👍 *Don't let pressure to get a story, however good, put you at risk.*

If you are out on a job in an isolated location at night, always think about your own safety – particularly if you are going alone or if you are a woman.

Take your mobile phone. A rape alarm could be a life-saver.

If you are in a situation where you feel threatened, withdraw at once.

If you are at all worried about a job you are being sent out on, talk it over with your news editor first. Your safety must be paramount.

It may be that another reporter or photographer can go with you, or you can switch the meeting place to a safe neutral venue, such as a pub or your newspaper office.

those in charge of running other editorial operations, with their staff behind them, radiating out in all directions. The idea is to ensure that the heads of each area know what the others are doing and can agree among themselves the best way to handle stories as they arrive. This group of senior editorial people is known on some newspapers as the **back bench**.

Among those at this central hub are:

The **Chief Sub-editor**, in charge of turning reporters' words into finished pages. He monitors where and how stories will appear in the newspaper, allocating them to the **sub-editors** (always known simply as the subs). He is assisted by someone called a **copytaster**, who does an initial sift-through of everything that arrives and gets rid of what isn't needed.

The chief sub has to make sure pages flow steadily to the printers on time: early pages for the next day's newspaper by mid-afternoon, later pages by early evening, the front page all but finished by the end of the night.

The subs design and lay out pages, check stories for accuracy, make sure they are legal, merge them if necessary, trim them to fit the space available, and create the headlines and captions to go with them. They may well query reporters about a story if it is unclear, incomplete, or needs to be wholly re-written.

The relationship between reporters and subs can be an uneasy one, occasionally even hostile, with subs regarding reporters as dangerous incompetents while reporters look upon subs as butchers eager to massacre their carefully-crafted copy. On the *Telegraph*, happily, both recognise each other's expertise and the reporters acknowledge that subs have a useful role to play in making sure their stories are accurate and readable.

The **Features Editor** is responsible for most of the editorial content that does not fall under news or sport: background features, arts and lifestyle pages, letters, opinion and gossip columns, the women's page, TV and entertainments. She has half a dozen staff, four of them full-time writers, two of them sub-editors. Some features are bought in from outside: the TV guide, for example, arrives ready-made from the Press Association. Unlike the news operation, the features desk is often working days, even weeks, ahead of publication, and the features editor spends a lot of time planning ahead.

The **Sports Editor** controls a handful of sports reporters, two of them working full-time on the town's major football clubs, the others covering the rest of the area's sporting events. Two of them help the sports sub to produce the pages. A lot of copy comes in from news agencies and freelance correspondents.

The **Picture Editor** is in charge of all the photographic material in the newspaper. The *Telegraph* has a **Chief Photographer** and three **photographers**, who liaise with the newsdesk and individual reporters on stories requiring pictures, although routine photos are regularly taken by reporters. When photographers cover events like football matches they take a laptop on which they can download pictures and transmit them back to the office from the touchline. There is a computer-based **artist** who creates graphics for all departments, and there is a constant battle between them for her services.

The **Website Manager** is responsible for putting news, sport, pictures and advertising on the newspaper's website. She is a computer expert, not a journalist, and works closely with the other editors to decide what goes on-line. She has two **web designers** working for her full-time.

Keeping an eye on everything are two **Assistant Editors**, one responsible for content, the other for production. Above them is the **Deputy Editor**, who has overall day-to-day control of the editorial operation. And above him is the **Editor,** who spends much of her time occupied by managerial duties far from the news-gathering and production scene. She is, nevertheless, legally responsible for every word that appears in the newspaper, and she is the one who could end up in court if her reporters recklessly defame someone or commit gross contempt.

These editorial people take up most of the first floor of the *Telegraph* building. In one corner is the library, home of more than a century's bound files of the newspaper and usually referred to as the morgue. Once it held tens of thousands of indexed clippings from the newspaper, 'cuttings' to which reporters could refer.

These days everything that appears in the *Telegraph* is stored electronically and accessed instantly from computers, and the bound files are used only by readers doing historical research and reporters delving into the distant past for the newspaper's 50-years-ago-today feature. The library also contains several shelves of reference books, not all as up-to-date as they should be. In charge is the **librarian**.

Also on the first floor is the boardroom and a second, less palatial, room set aside for training. There is a rest area with a coffee machine: the staff canteen closed years ago and these days reporters bring sandwiches for lunch or buy them from a van which calls by each morning.

OTHER DEPARTMENTS

On the floor below editorial are most of the other major departments helping to produce the newspaper. Reporters are unlikely to have much to do with them, but it is useful for them to have a basic idea of who they are and what they do:

Advertising

Run by the **advertising manager** and handling everything from classified ads to special supplements. Some staff spend their lives on the phone, taking ads, talking to advertising agencies, calling regular advertisers and cold-calling potential new ones. Others, usually called **advertising reps** (short for representatives), are out on the road hunting for business. Some concentrate on special areas – housing, cars, jobs. One

> *Golden rule: clear your notebook every day, while it's fresh in your mind.*

BOB DRAYTON
Deputy group editor
Somerset County Gazette

> *The best advice I ever got came from legendary campaigning editor Harry Evans: Try to change the world and take no bloody notice of the bean-counters.*

PETER BARRON
Editor
The Northern Echo

> *Listen to advice and learn from it.*

There are a surprising number of cocky reporters who think they know everything and don't listen.

They very quickly become a liability and a burden to their colleagues.

ANDREW DOUGLAS
Deputy news editor
The Northern Echo

person in the advertising department is the **page planner**, whose job is to plan the newspaper each day, deciding where the ads go and making sure they all get in.

Circulation

Responsible for delivering the *Telegraph*, collecting unsold copies, monitoring outlets, and maximising sales. Run by the **circulation manager**, with a deputy in charge of marketing and promotions – competitions, give-aways, reader holidays, scratchcards and other devices to persuade people to buy the newspaper.

The circulation department liaises with editorial for the wording to go on the posters (called bills) that go outside newsagents' shops proclaiming the newspaper's content.

Production

This is the department that turns editorial's screen pages into newspapers to be pushed through letterboxes. Headed by the **works manager**, its staff range from computer network experts to printers, electricians to ink-buyers.

GET OUT THERE AND FIND IT!

If you do a journalism course at college you will probably be sent out into the real world looking for off-diary stories.

If you go for a job interview, you may face an editor who tells you to go into town and come back in a couple of hours with something worth publishing.

How do you handle this? One editor gives this advice:

- **Don't** re-hash anything that has already been in the newspaper (which should not be a problem, if you have read it cover to cover beforehand – if you haven't, you don't deserve a job). By all means do a follow-up on an existing story if you can spot a fresh angle.

- **Don't** go for the obvious - stories from the town hall, the public library, the theatre. The newspaper will almost certainly already know about anything you find there.

- **Don't** initiate something that will take more time than you have available - an investigation that requires interviewing a lot of people to cover all the angles, for example. Aim for a story that you can cover as quickly as possible without leaving too many loose ends.

- **Do** talk to as many people as possible about anything that could be controversial, and get plenty of quotes.

- **Do** look at everything and question everything.

- **If all else fails,** do a vox pop. At least it will prove you are not afraid to talk to people.

Finance

These are the people who keep track of money coming in and going out (including reporters' pay). Controlled by the newspaper's **finance director**.

Personnel

Headed by the **human resources manager**, looking after employees' interests such as maternity leave and pensions.

General

There is a **general manager** who looks after just about everything else: the front office staff, the state of the building, security, cleaning, and so on. Other employees include an electrician, a dozen delivery van drivers, a mechanic and several general labourers.

AT THE TOP

The heads of all these departments hold regular meetings chaired by the company's **managing director**, who as the **publisher** is ultimately responsible for the running of the newspaper. He rose through the accountancy ranks and has had no firsthand journalistic experience, but makes major policy decisions, oversees budgets and decides senior appointments.

The MD answers to the **board of directors** of the company which owns the newspaper and scores of others all over the country, and which is itself part of a global media group owned by a multi-millionaire who lives in America and has never heard of Midthorpe, let alone visited the *Telegraph*.

DANNY'S DAY

Danny, the youngest reporter on the *Telegraph*, did a three-year English degree at university and thought his work on the student magazine would get him a job on a local newspaper. He quickly discovered he was up against stiff competition from scores of other hopefuls, many with NCTJ qualifications, and after a series of humiliating interviews decided, like Debbie, to get some training under his belt. That done, he applied for every vacancy going and eventually landed this job in Midthorpe, 200 miles away from home.

He has been there for nearly a year, and it has been a steep learning curve for someone who was expected to operate effectively from day one on a big newspaper in a strange town. He earns a bit more than Debbie, being on a larger newspaper, but not much more; like her, he has enjoyed the job most of the time but finds some of the routine work less glamorous than he imagined.

> *Spend as much time as you can working alongside the senior reporters, shadowing them where possible, writing up the story and then comparing it with the senior's version.*
>
> *And keep your editor supplied with copious cups of tea all day!*
>
> **DAVID HORNE**
> Editor
> Ilkeston Advertiser

08.00

Danny arrives to find the newsroom already busy, because there has been a major fire overnight and the early shift (which came in at six) has been frantically changing the front page for the first edition.

He opens up his computer and scans the *Telegraph*'s website to see what's been happening overnight. Then he checks the diary, online and available to everyone. There are three items beside his name: *School report, Sex Shop row, Theatre photocall 2.30*. He goes over to the newsdesk for clarification and is handed an Oftsed report on a local junior school. The second item sounds more fun: a florist has applied for permission to change his shop into one selling sex aids instead of flowers, and, although there isn't a row about it yet, the news editor is sure there will be once the neighbours get to know about it. The theatre call is a chance to meet a TV soap actress who is appearing next week in a touring production.

Danny is pleased with his allotted tasks. Although the Ofsted story will be dull, the other two will get him out of the office, and that doesn't happen every day. Based outside the town centre, and under pressure to produce copy quickly and often, the *Telegraph*'s reporters do the vast majority of their work over the phone.

Next is a check on his emails. There is one from a friend who has heard a rumour that one of the town's rugby club players was arrested after a drunken brawl outside a pub last night. He forwards this to the newsdesk, which passes it on to the sports desk and the crime reporter to investigate.

Danny decides to get the Ofsted report out of the way first. It is the usual mix of doing-well-but-could-do-better, and after checking the archives to see what last year's report said on the off-chance things have got much better or worse (they haven't) he phones the headteacher for a comment and writes the story.

09.30

Now for the sex shop. Danny checks the archives for any recent cuttings about them or the flower shop owner (none), and phones the council to ask how many sex shops there are in town already (two), and who licenses them (the licensing committee). He leaves a message on the committee chair's answerphone asking her to give him a ring. The newsdesk thinks Danny should get local reaction to the plans before approaching the shop owner, and tells him to drive over (he has his own car, battered and uncertain, and claims the mileage) and find out what people say.

He finds plenty who are willing to comment, all predictably hostile to the sex shop proposal and some prepared to have their pictures taken, too. He interviews the most vociferous on video, adding some panoramic shots of the shop and surrounding houses.

Then he tries the flower shop. The owner is out, due back in the afternoon, and the assistant refuses to comment. This is a pity, because Danny won't have time to come back in person and suspects he would have more success face-to-face than on the phone. He takes a couple of close-up pictures of the shop and returns to the office.

11.15

The licensing committee chair phones back with some guarded comments, and Danny spends the rest of the morning phoning other people – councillors, a vicar, the secretary of the Mothers' Union – for quotes. They are all opposed to the plan, and Danny wants to find someone who isn't.

The newsdesk suggests digging back in the files to see who defended other sex shops in town when they were opened. Danny finds the name of a councillor who voted in favour, phones him up and gets quotes saying he is all for this one, too.

12.15

The newsdesk thinks the website will want a story now, even though Danny has yet to speak to the shop owner, so he writes what he has got, downloads his pictures and sends it all over.

By the time he has finished (lunch was a sandwich Danny brought to work and ate at the desk) it is almost time to head off for the theatre. He finds the press release announcing the photocall with the actress, and does a quick websearch for some information about her life and career before setting off, armed with cameras.

14.30

The newsdesk wants a brief picture story about the actress for tomorrow's newspaper, and half a minute on video for the website. Danny chats to her, and she obligingly agrees to be filmed saying how delighted she is to be in Midthorpe. Job done, he goes back to the office, hands the video camera to the website manager because he won't have time to edit it himself, and downloads the still pictures. He writes the words to go on the web and the story for the newspaper.

16.30

This, in theory, is when Danny should be heading home. But there is still the would-be sex shop owner to interview. He phones up and he was right: the owner isn't keen to talk. It takes all his powers of persuasion to get the owner to discuss his plans, explain why he thinks there is a demand for a sex shop, and respond to his neighbours'

When I started out as a junior reporter, I was sent on a course called Getting To Know Northamptonshire Police.

The first thing I did was reverse into a police car, writing it off.

NICK TITE
Assistant editor
Evening Telegraph
Northampton

👍 *Contact suggestion: archaeologists. Every area has at least one. Apart from working on known sites of interest, they work for developers required to survey sites of possible historical interest before being granted planning permission, and get called in when builders uncover Roman remains or long-buried bodies.*

opposition. Danny writes an up-dated story for the website and a new one for tomorrow's newspaper.

17.45

Danny checks the diary to see what he is doing tomorrow (late shift, which means he will get a lie-in), and heads for the pub.

AFTERMATH

Next day, the *Telegraph* newsdesk gets an angry phone call from the sex shop applicant, complaining that Danny has stirred up a hornet's nest of opposition.

Danny is slightly worried at first in case he has got some facts wrong, but there is no suggestion of this: the applicant just wants to vent his anger at someone and rings off abruptly after a few minutes. The news editor reassures Danny, and tells him that even the best reporters get calls from people complaining about their stories. The newspaper wouldn't be doing its job, he says, if it never upset anyone.

Two days later, the retiring teacher reads the story about her in the *Express* and sends Debbie an email saying thank-you. She's quietly pleased.

HANDLING COMPLAINTS

If you receive a complaint (and you will, often), be polite, however unjustified it may be.

Get the caller's name and contact details (if they refuse, explain that your newsdesk may want to get in touch with them) and make notes of the complaint.

Don't admit that a mistake has been made, apologise, or promise a correction.

Any admission of liability at this stage could prove costly.

If you have to discuss the problem in detail, make it clear that you are speaking *without prejudice*, a legal phrase meaning that nothing you say can be later used as evidence against you. If the complaint turns out to be a matter of trivial detail and you know you got it wrong, see if a promise to get it right next time will satisfy the complainant.

If not, or if the complaint is remotely serious, say you will refer it to your manager.

Suggest the caller writes to the editor. If that fails, ask them to hold on, and consult your news editor.

Don't try to brush the matter under the carpet or bury unauthorised corrections in the guise of a new story.

Tell your newsdesk about all complaints, whether you have solved them or not.

Five

FIRST TASKS

THE days when office juniors spent the first couple of years in the job running errands and making the tea are history. When you join a newsroom as a trainee reporter you are expected to be useful from the first morning.

You will not be given a major investigative story to cover in your early days (and a good job, too: you would almost certainly make a hash of it). Your first few weeks will be spent doing fairly simple tasks while you find your way around, proving that you have the ability to do the basics and possess the potential to take on more demanding assignments.

This chapter takes a look at some of the basic tasks that are carried out from your office desk.

- Handouts
- Calls
- Weddings
- Anniversaries
- Retirements
- Deaths

HANDOUTS

ONE of the first things you are likely to be asked to do is turn some of the day's press releases into stories for the newspaper. They may be given an initial sort-through by the newsdesk, which then hands you the ones it thinks are worth developing.

Handouts are what the name suggests: press releases sent to the newspaper free of charge in the hope that they will be used as news stories. Tens of thousands of them pour into newspaper offices every week by mail, fax and email.

Most end up in the bin but that still leaves many which get into the newspapers. Some are genuine news stories; others have little real news value but are used because there are never enough reporters to go round and busy newsrooms welcome anything that fills space without much effort. They are the source of much of a newspaper's content and, if they suddenly dried up, many a newsroom would be hard-pushed to find ideas for alternative material to fill the space.

They can be divided roughly into four piles:

Information from official sources such as government, local authorities, public and private utilities, statutory bodies and professional organisations. A typical day's press releases might include council agendas and minutes, news of a White Paper proposing legislative changes, notice of a planning inquiry, the findings of a medical disciplinary hearing. Much of this will prove useful as the basis for news stories.

Information from non-commercial bodies such as charities, unions and pressure groups about what they think and do: condemnation of

If you're ever tempted to go into PR, don't. They pay you lots of money for a reason.

SIMON O'NEILL
Editor
Oxford Mail

a government decision, comment on the latest crime figures, plans for protest action, pleas for support. This makes news, too, but all of it is basically propaganda and needs handling with care.

Information from commercial operations about their products, processes and services: the launch of a new car, a warning that gas prices are going up, a company's annual report showing soaring profits, a survey claiming to prove that one cleaning fluid works better than the rest. Some of this is news; much is just advertising in disguise.

Information from local organisations about their activities: a report of a society meeting, notice of a theatre group's next production, news of a village hall offering night classes, results and league tables from a sports club secretary. This kind of information is the lifeblood of local newspapers and much of it goes in.

Watch out for spin

Few handouts should be taken at face value. The vast majority of them come from press offices, staffed by public relations officers whose task is to persuade you to print what they want you to print. That means good news about their employers, whether they are working for

NOT FOR PUBLICATION BEFORE...

Many press releases carry an embargo, a request from their originators that the contents should not be published or broadcast before a specified time or date.

There may be good reasons for this. Lists of people featuring in honours lists, for example, are sent out to the media days in advance of their official announcement so that reporters have time to prepare stories, get pictures and do interviews, which in theory (but not always in practice) should not take place until the news is released.

Other embargoes are laid down because the originators want news to be announced by all the media simultaneously at a time of their choosing. It may be to ensure maximum impact – just before the main evening television news bulletin, for example, to gain

most publicity – or just after, if it is bad news, to avoid it.

Embargoes have no legal force. It has been argued that they are in effect setting copyright permission limits, but any infringement would almost certainly be covered by the fair dealing 'reporting current events' defence.

Usually it is in the media's interest to abide by embargoes, especially if ignoring them would mean upsetting important sources.

But many are breached, especially if the story is a strong one: armed with embargoed information, reporters will strive to get confirmation from other sources to justify speculative stories in advance of the official release time.

If you are faced with an embargo, consult with your news desk before breaking it.

Whitehall or a back-street car dealer. They will try to bury bad news, spin it to look like good, or not mention it at all.

Some of them are very good at it: ex-journalists well aware of how newsrooms work and expert at manipulating the facts to their advantage. Unpopular news may be released at times when it may not get newsrooms' full attention (just after the day's main TV news bulletin, at the end of the week, or at the start of a holiday period), or on busy news days when it is likely to be submerged by bigger stories (within an hour of the Twin Towers attack, a British Government spin doctor was urging colleagues to slip out details of higher allowances for councillors).

Your job is to sift through all this information with a critical eye, identifying which press releases are no better than the spam that clutters up your email in-box and which (if any) are news. Like digging for gold, you may have to shift a lot of rubbish but there are nuggets to be found if you persevere.

Read each handout right through, looking for the news. If it is quite clearly nothing more than an attempt to get free advertising, pass it on to the advertising department. They may be able to make money from it, and ads help to pay your wages. If it is newsworthy, ask yourself whether it might have an advertising spin-off. A press release about a new shop opening in town could well lead to an ad or even an advertising supplement featuring its goods, suppliers and other traders.

If there's a story:

Develop it:

Look for a human angle for your intro. Ask yourself who is going to be affected, and how. A dry announcement of a company's plans to expand its production plant may mean a new product, more jobs, a demand for materials from other companies, a threat to the environment.

Identify which bits of the handout you want to use. Highlight any good quotes.

Check your files to see what has gone before if the information develops something already in the news. You may need background material to explain its context.

Ask yourself if the story needs to be balanced with information from other sources, giving the other side of the story, perhaps, or putting the handout's claims in perspective. It may well need reaction from people affected by, or critical of, its contents.

Ask for an explanation of anything you don't understand. There may be references to things obvious to the handout writer but obscure to you and your readers. If nobody in the office understands, ring up the source and ask.

> *More and more communication is happening by email, driven by press officers who recognise that the medium stacks the odds heavily in their favour.*
>
> *Emailed questions allow them the time to concoct weasel-worded answers that cleverly side-step the truth.*
>
> *They prevent reporters from speaking directly to the main man or woman who, untrained in the dark arts of PR, might tell you the whole truth.*
>
> *Emailing is seductively easy: no stressful telephone interviews, no pages of badly-written shorthand to decipher.*
>
> *When the answers pop silently into your inbox, all you have to do is cut and paste.*
>
> *But it is a pact with the devil.*
>
> SEAN DUGGAN
> Editor
> Surrey Comet

👍 *If you are getting details of traffic accidents, take care when describing the people involved and what happened.*

Police may tell you the name of a car owner, but that doesn't necessarily mean that was the person driving at the time.

If they talk of two vehicles being involved in an accident, that doesn't always mean one car hit another: one may have crashed, the other swerved into a tree to avoid it.

👍 *Contact suggestion: junk shops. Every so often they get an item that's unusual enough to make a story, or turns out to be rare and worth far more than the shop owner paid for it.*

Look round the local antique dealers' and pawnbrokers' for the same reason. Charity shops are worth keeping in touch with, too.

Seek more information. If there are unanswered questions posed by the press release, phone the person who wrote it. This may lead to a better story or at least give you a slightly different angle to the one taken by rival publications relying on the handout alone.

Writing it up

Snippets of information from local sources – news of a forthcoming jumble sale, reports from WIs – may need little more than tweaking to make them read clearly and conform to the style of your newspaper. It may be better to let the words of village correspondents go in largely as written, even if their prose is a little ungainly, than to demoralise contributors by altering everything.

Very few other handouts can go in the newspaper unchanged. Even the best of them, created by professionals trained in news-writing, need to be checked, trimmed, added to, re-structured and re-written. They may need drastic re-writing, or can be used only as a source of facts and quotes as you write an entirely new version.

When writing your story:

Make sure, if you are lifting bits from various parts of a handout and running them together in a different order, that you don't distort the sense of the original or leave out something which should go in to give a balanced picture.

Get rid of the jargon and simplify the language. Government, councils and many other information sources revel in bureaucratese, issuing press releases couched in what looks at first glance like sheer gobbledegook (and sometimes continues to do so however often you read it).

Use quotes. Many press releases include some ready-made from a named person, but you can turn other material into quotations. If a press release says *Midthorpe Electronics has invented a thrilling new mousetrap which will revolutionise rodent control*, you can write *The mouse-trap 'will revolutionise rodent control', the company claims.* (Don't say it is thrilling, though: it really isn't unless you're a mouse).

Check every fact, figure and spelling that you copy from the handout to be sure they are accurate.

Think about illustration. If there are pictures or graphics accompanying the handout, consider if and how they could be used. If there are none, ask yourself whether the story deserves some.

Remember the website. If the story is strong enough, it may go online and deserve audio or video to go with it.

Update the office diary if the story is about a forthcoming event or has follow-up possibilities.

THE CALLS

EVERY newsroom has a list of people it contacts regularly to get updates on what is happening. Top of the list are the police and fire service; it may also include hospitals, the ambulance service and other emergency services, such as coastguards, mountain rescue, river and transport police.

Weekly newspapers may be satisfied with one call a day or just two or three a week; dailies make calls every few hours, from early morning until late at night. In busy newsrooms covering a wide area with a large number of police forces and emergency services, making the calls can be almost a full-time job, carried out by reporters on a rota basis. Whoever's name is in the diary to do it will phone all the numbers, note anything of interest, and then start again at the beginning. It can be a chore, but it is vital.

Who and how

Journalists who have been in the business a long time recall fondly the days when they visited the local police station in person to see what was going on, meeting the duty inspector face-to-face to go through the daily incident book. It took time, but reporters built up solid relationships with senior officers who learnt to trust them and became readier to give as much information as possible. It was also an opportunity to meet police officers of all ranks, some of whom might turn out to be useful contacts.

There are still a few newspapers where this happens, but these days, with fewer reporters and increasing pressure to fill more and more pages, calls to police and other services are almost always done by phone. Your first contact is probably with an automated voice-bank, which has a tape running with the latest information being released to the press. If there is something of interest to you, you then contact the press office.

Phoning is quicker than making personal contact, but usually less productive. You get fewer details, many voice-banks are not updated as often as you would like, and you well have to wait while press officers contact the people they represent to check the facts and whether they can let you have them. Voice-banks are available to everyone, of course, so you are unlikely to get exclusive information.

Whether you are in contact face-to-face or by phone, remember that your newspaper's relationship with the police and other emergency services is an extremely important one. They are often your first port of call and best source of information. They don't have to help you, but they are usually happy to cooperate and know there are many times when you are useful to them in relaying information to the public.

Go through the minutes and agendas with a fine-tooth comb.

Hidden in them, sometimes, are gems of stories that organisations are trying to bury.

HELEN STANLEY
Sub-editor
Daily Echo, Bournemouth

Talk to the people you're making the calls to. Pass the time of day, crack a joke, make them realise you are human.

NICK NUNN
Assistant editor
Lancashire Evening Telegraph

You don't have a responsibility to PR people, you have a responsibility to readers.

SHARON GRIFFITHS
Feature writer
The Northern Echo

👍 *Ask if you can visit press offices so that each side can match names to faces.*

You will get an insight into how they work and they will be happy to explain the pressures they are under and why sometimes they are less helpful than you would like.

What to ask about

The **police** will tell you mainly about accidents, crime and traffic. They will probably advise you about forthcoming inquests. Sometimes they want to give information to the public: details of road diversions, publicity about crime prevention, pleas for help in tracing missing people, warnings of conmen preying on pensioners or fake fivers found in the area.

The **fire service** will tell you about fires and other rescue operations, and they too seek publicity for activities such as fire prevention initiatives.

The **ambulance service** will know about accidents, including those that don't involve the police – people injured at work or at home, for example.

Hospitals are usually reluctant to volunteer information unless you have names for the people you are inquiring about. Even then, many flatly refuse to discuss named patients unless they or their relatives have given written permission.

Preparation

Your newsdesk will supply a list of sources and phone numbers, and tell you when to contact them. Check when the calls were last done, because there is no point taking down information somebody has already got. Ask the newsdesk if there is anything in particular it wants you to listen out for or ask about.

Have your pen and notebook ready. Put the date, time and name of the person or organisation you are calling at the top of the page before you start.

Voice-banks

When you listen to a voice-bank tape, you hear the latest message first, the one before that next, and so on, which can get a bit confusing if you

---

SERIOUSLY, WHAT'S THAT MEAN?

If you succeed in getting details of injuries and conditions from a hospital, you need to be clear what the various descriptions mean.

Chronically ill refers to someone suffering a long-term illness which may or may not be life-threatening.

Comfortable means they are not giving cause to immediate concern.

Satisfactory often means much the same but is a wide-ranging description that can be applied to anyone responding to treatment, even if they remain seriously ill.

Serious means what it says, *critical* means very serious indeed, *dangerously ill* means they could die at any moment.

Stable means their condition is unchanged, not necessarily that they are out of danger.

People *in intensive care* are obviously undergoing treatment to keep them alive and you may be justified in talking about them *fighting for their lives*, though no hospital would say so.

hear updates to stories you have never heard of. Listen as the story unfolds backwards, making notes about each item on a separate page and leaving space for additional details you might get later.

A depressing number of messages left on the tape will be along the lines of *'3.40pm on Tuesday October 3rd and there's nothing of interest to the press'* (even though you know there has been mayhem on the motorway and a town centre bank was robbed at gunpoint that morning). Other messages may be out of date or about events that have happened outside your newspaper's circulation area.

Some, however, will be useful. Those detailing minor incidents will make a brief paragraph. Others will be worth following up, and you will find yourself regularly phoning press officers for more detail.

Press offices

A good working relationship with the emergency services' press officers pays off, even if it is conducted wholly over the phone. Make sure you say who you are each time you phone, to get your name known. Note who you are talking to, so you can ask for them in person if you need to phone back later. The better the rapport, the more likely they are to help.

Be friendly and cheerful, professional and positive. Asking *'What's been happening today?'* encourages people to give you information; *'Nothing for the press, I suppose?'* doesn't.

Extra information

Ask if there is any additional material available – background statistics, pictures of missing people, photofits of wanted criminals, CCTV coverage of robberies or car chases – and if there is, arrange to get it.

There are stories to be had about the police and members of other services themselves. Promotions, resignations, retirements and bravery awards are news. This kind of material is usually sent out as press releases, but if you have built up a good relationship with the press office they may give it to you in advance.

Tell the newsdesk about stories you pick up on the calls. It may want you to write them up, or pass them on to someone else to develop.

Problems

There are times when you cannot get all the information you want. It may be the person at the other end of the phone simply doesn't know, or has good reasons for not releasing details at this stage: the next of kin of an accident victim may not yet have been informed,

Always be prepared with a few early questions.

The first question I ever asked as a journalist, on my first assignment to interview a golden wedding couple, was: 'So how long have you been married?'

NEAL BUTTERWORTH
Editor
Daily Echo, Bournemouth

I cut-and-pasted an emailed wedding report without checking it through.

It included a description of the bride's going-away outfit: a green suit with white accessories.

The sender abbreviated this and I didn't notice.

It went in the paper as 'The bride left for the honeymoon in a green suit and white ass.'

ANONYMOUS
Reporter
Weekly newspaper

Wedding reports are usually written up as a batch – frequently before the actual wedding day.

It is vital that you confirm that the wedding took place, by phoning the vicar or bride's family.

The day you are lazy and forget to carry out this important duty will be the day the wedding had to be cancelled at the last minute for some reason – the groom ran off with the organist, the bride slipped and broke her neck, the vicar fainted during the service – and you missed the story of the month.

OTHER CALLS WORTH MAKING

As well as making daily calls to the emergency services, most newsrooms will contact a number of other people on a regular basis, perhaps once a week – the magistrates clerk's office, for example, the coroner's officer and the town hall.

Others worth keeping a check on include local MPs, council leaders, press officers of major local industries, and union leaders.

You will build up your own list of routine calls to people in your area. Regular contact, in person if possible, with post offices, pubs, churches and schools will bring in the stories.

for example, or publishing details of a crime might hamper the hunt for criminals.

Getting names and addresses is a frequent problem. Some police forces ask people involved in accidents whether they want to be identified to the media and refuse to give you their details if they say no (which, not surprisingly, they often do). Others hide behind the Data Protection Act, arguing (mistakenly) that it would be illegal to divulge information held on their computers.

If you have difficulties like this, refer them to your news editor to see if the problem can be raised at a higher level.

WEDDINGS

SOME daily newspaper journalists may raise an eyebrow at the inclusion of these in a textbook for trainees in the 21st century, but there are still plenty of weekly newspapers that report weddings in detail.

They recognise that every bride has family, friends, former classmates and current work colleagues who want to see her on her big day and admire (or criticise) her choice of gown, bouquet, honeymoon venue and, of course, husband. Equally, people want to know about the groom.

Altogether, hundreds of readers will know the happy couple and be interested in the event – far more, probably, than ever turn out to watch the town's cricket team, which nevertheless gets half a sports page to itself every week. Weddings are news in a small community and deserve their place on the news pages.

That said, nobody expects reporters to actually go to them (unless the wedding is out of the ordinary – a pair of 90-year-olds splicing the knot, maybe, or a couple making their vows during a parachute jump – and the story needs colour and quotes). Most newspapers provide the participants with a standard form on which to fill in the details, and your job is to turn this into readable copy.

When it comes back, it should be checked for authenticity (hoaxing a newspaper into announcing non-existent nuptuals is some people's idea of fun). Phone the sender – there should be space on the form for them to leave a contact number – and while you are at it check any dubious spellings, follow up interesting angles and see if there is other useful information.

Find an angle

Weddings should be written up just like any other news story – with careful scrutiny of the information supplied to find a decent news angle for the intro. Too many reporters think weddings are beneath them and take the easy way out.

The result is a succession of turgid intros on the lines of *The wedding took place of a Midthorpe teacher to a hotel receptionist at St Mary's Church on Saturday...* or *The bells of St Mary's Church, Midthorpe, rang out on Saturday for the wedding of a local teacher to a hotel receptionist* (what else are the bells supposed to do?) or *A honeymoon in Hartlepool was the destination for a Midthorpe teacher and a hotel receptionist following their wedding on Saturday* (unless the happy couple are to spend their time ascending Everest, honeymoon venues rarely make interesting angles).

All wedding reports must include names, addresses, occupations of bride and groom; names of the church and the officiating clergy; names of both sets of parents, dead or alive; and names of best man and bridesmaids. Be careful about relationships: parents may have remarried and there could be step-people about.

You might also include the name of the matron of honour, a description of the bride's outfit and accessories, the honeymoon plans, and details of relatives travelling from afar. A well-designed wedding report form will leave space for 'anything else of interest' to glean extra information, such as any special music being played during the ceremony.

However mundane the wedding may seem to you, remember that for those involved it is one of the biggest days of their lives. Write your story with sensitivity.

IF THE MAYOR'S LOOKING SEEDY...

Some newsrooms prepare obits in advance, ready for instant use when someone important gets to the age when there is a fair chance they will die before long.

Writing them is not a reporter's most exciting job; nor is updating them every so often as the subject lingers on. You'll be grateful for them, though, the day the mayor keels over just before your deadline.

A warning: under the Data Protection Act, people have the right to see certain material stored on your computer. If an advance obit is uncomplimentary, you might be wise to keep it somewhere else.

👍 *Many weddings are held in registry offices (note the spelling: not register) and more romantic venues – hotels, castles and stately homes – are increasingly popular. Ceremonies at these must be non-religious.*

These venues have to be approved by the local authority and applications to become approved should be advertised in the press. Look out for them.

There are also, of course, a wide range of marriage venues and ceremonies for members of non-Christian religions.

👍 *Don't even hint in an obituary that the deceased was disliked or a problem when alive, however many people say they are glad to see the back of him.*

By all means mention quirks and eccentricities, but leave his wife-beating and alcoholism out of it.

Get rid of the jargon. Avoid hackneyed phrases like *happy couple* and *radiant bride.*

Check spellings: brides rarely carry bouquets of anything simple like roses. They go for flowers with names like freesia and hydrangea, easily mis-spelt.

Make sure your reports tie up with the pictures, often supplied independently by local wedding photographers. Wedding pictures all look much the same if you don't know the people in them, and it is all too easy to link a report on one couple with pictures of another.

Keep the wedding form for reference in case there is a complaint about incorrect detail.

ANNIVERSARIES AND RETIREMENTS

LARGER newspapers may ignore these unless there is something very much out of the ordinary about those involved – a couple celebrating 80 years together, perhaps, or a prominent member of the community calling it a day after a lifetime of public service. Many local newspapers, however, still carry reports about golden weddings and the retirement of everyday people – teachers, shopkeepers, police officers, lollipop ladies. You may be asked to cover these minor events over the phone, but you will get a much better story if you meet your subjects face-to-face.

Find out what, if anything, has been written about them before. Check the files. If you are covering a couple's 60th wedding anniversary, a story may well have been done on their golden anniversary ten years ago. Much of your work will have been done for you and all you have to do now is update it with a fresh intro.

You need basic information about the people involved: names, ages, education, family, career, hobbies, interests, membership of clubs and organisations.

Ask anniversary couples how, where and when they met and got married; their advice for newly-weds; what they think about the way the world has changed; how they are celebrating and who has been invited; plans for the future; and what they think is the secret of a happy marriage (a hoary old favourite, but it still occasionally brings the unexpected answer – see the quote on the opposite page).

Ask the newly-retired to compare their job now with what it was like when they first started; what their proudest achievement has been; what they were presented with as a farewell present by their former colleagues at work; what they plan to do with their spare time.

Be patient. Remember that older people don't move at the pace you do and need handling sensitively if you are to get the best out of them.

Try to talk to them when another relative is present – a spouse or daughter, perhaps. Let them prompt each other's memories. They will mention things your subject has forgotten, thinks unimportant or, perhaps, is too modest (or embarrassed) to mention.

Remember, if you are talking to men born before the 1940s, that they will probably have done national service or even fought in a war. It may seem a long time ago to you, but they will have vivid memories of their experience which may make good reading today.

Take pictures. Persuade your subjects to do something rather than just stare at the camera: anniversary couples looking through their wedding album, retired people trying out the gadget they were given as a retirement present. Not all older people are photogenic, but at the very least get couples looking as if they are happy together. Borrow pictures of them on their wedding day for a then-and-now contrast. Promise to give them back, and make sure you do.

Don't print anniversary stories until the event has taken place. Either or both of those celebrating may keel over with the excitement of it all before the big day. Watch the death notices and ring afterwards to check everything went as planned.

DEATHS

FEW newspapers carry formal obituary columns these days. Deaths are covered as news stories, though still usually referred to as obits. On larger newspapers someone's passing will be mentioned only if they were well-known, unless of course the manner of their death is newsworthy. They merit a few paragraphs summarising their life, boosted by a tribute or two from family, friends and colleagues.

Local weeklies, on the other hand, may devote considerable space to recording the death of less prominent members of the community: shop-keepers known to everyone in town, farmers who have lived all their life in the area, and teachers who taught hundreds of readers.

News of a death may come from friends or family, from funeral directors or from keeping a close eye on your newspaper's death notices: newsdesks usually have a system for ensuring that they know about such advertisements as soon as they arrive so that important deaths aren't missed or stories about them delayed.

If you are asked to write about someone's death, you need to know about their family, career, achievements and interests. This background information may well be on file; if not, you will have to make a few phone calls. Problems arise if you have to contact the immediate family, especially if the death was unexpected, occurred in tragic circumstances or was that of a young person or child. In such cases you need to handle any inquiries very sensitively: see the section on Death Knocks (page 89).

Make sure all details are accurate. This is an emotional time for those involved, and they will react badly if you get their names wrong.

The worst quote I ever got came at the end of a trying interview with a Fife pensioner about her golden wedding.

Me: 'So, what's the secret of a happy marriage?'

Old lady: 'I've nae idea, son, it hasna been happy at all.'

JACK SHENNAN
Editor
Linlithgowshire
Journal & Gazette

👍 *Many newspapers cover funerals only when those who have died were well-known (civic dignitaries, local celebrities) or died in unusual circumstances (murder victims, children losing their battle against illness).*

Even then coverage will probably be restricted to pictures of grieving family mourners and a general colour piece.

There are, however, some weeklies that give more detail and even carry a full list of mourners. If you are lucky you can arrange for this to be provided by the family; if you aren't, you stand outside the church, notebook in hand, taking the names of everyone who goes in.

It is a nightmare if there is more than one entrance. Check every spelling and be prepared for people who say they are representing a string of others unable to make it: their names need to be in, too.

Avoid cliches such as *well-known* (if he was, why say so?), *popular and highly-respected* (not everyone will agree), and *passed away* (leave that to the gravestone: stick to *died*). Don't start off *A town was in mourning this week…* because you know darn well 99% of the population don't care that someone who was the mayor half a century ago has finally kicked the bucket.

Remember to include details of the funeral and burial/cremation, if they are available.

Six

OUT AND ABOUT

YOU will spend a lot of your time as a reporter working from your desk, but it won't be long before you are sent to cover events in the world outside. Whether you are off to cover a speech, report from a meeting, or interview someone face-to-face, there are some basic preparations to make before you set off.

Get as much information as you can about the event and the people involved. There may be a press release with details. Check the office files for previous stories. If you are covering a speech or a meeting, you need to know the name and position of speakers. If you are interviewing someone, you want to know their age, address, family, job, career and anything else that might be useful. They may figure in local reference books or be mentioned on the internet. Ask colleagues if they have heard of them.

If you can't find out all the essential details in advance, make a list in your notebook of the information you need as a reminder when you arrive.

Find out what is expected of you. Ask the newsdesk how long a story they want, when the deadline is, whether you need to take photographs or video. Check if there is a picture on file that can be used if you can't get a new one.

Check you have all the equipment you need. Notebook and pens, obviously, and your list of questions. Tape recorder if you are using one, with spare tapes and batteries. Camera. Address of where you are going and map of the area. Money for phones, bus, taxi, parking. Contacts book. Mobile phone. ID. Business cards. A pencil for marking pictures. Umbrella if you may end up outdoors.

- Public events
- Demos & parades
- Speeches
- Meetings
- Press conferences
- Pictures

Never, ever play the 'Don't you know I'm a reporter?' card in trying to gain entry into nightclubs when you should be tucked up in bed.

You look daft in front of your mates and the bouncers will just itch to fill you in.

Even worse is: 'Don't you know I'm the editor?'

JOHN McLELLAN
Editor
Edinburgh Evening News

PUBLIC EVENTS

CARNIVALS, shows, galas and garden parties, pageants and parades, festivals and fetes, jubilees and jamborees, centenary celebrations and Remembrance Sundays – local newspapers report on them all.

Covering them is sometimes exactly what you imagined life as a reporter would be when you weren't chasing fire engines and exposing town hall corruption: sunny afternoons spent idly watching egg-and-spoon races, chatting to the crowds and asking the vicar how much the event has raised towards his church restoration fund.

👍 *Tell the newsdesk what you are doing and you will help the management of the office.*

If you have three good stories on your book and don't tell anybody, extra work will come your way.

If the newsdesk knows you are working on things they can try to leave you alone to complete them.

District offices and specialist reporters should produce weekly schedules of their anticipated work/stories. Any reporter can do the same.

👍 *Never agree to be a judge at a local event. You will delight the mother of the baby you name bonniest in the show, but make lifelong enemies of the rest.*

More often, however, you will find yourself with several events to cover on the same day and be rushing from one to the next, grabbing information, results and pictures as best you can. As with everything else, a bit of preparation helps.

Most of these events take place annually. Go into the archives and see how your newspaper reported them the previous year. You may pick up background information and possible angles. If it was wrecked by bad weather last time, for example, success this year might be critical if the event is to survive financially. You may spot the name of a prize-winner who swept the board, someone worth looking out for this time to see if he or she does it again.

Most events have an organising committee. The secretary will probably have sent details in advance, and a call to him or her beforehand will identify the best time for you to make an appearance – when the main parade takes place, for example, or when the prizes are to be presented. Ask for a programme to be sent to you. At the same time find out a bit about the event: its history, current prospects, whether there are any new sections or activities, who the judges are going to be, what the prizes are and who is sponsoring them, what the money raised will be spent on.

If you are expected to include results and prize-winners' names in your report, find out when and where these will be available. If they will not be ready when you make your appearance, check when you can collect them or arrange for them to be sent to you as soon as possible afterwards. Explain carefully what information you need.

On the day, contact the secretary to find out more: how many entries there were (more or less than last year? a record? anything unusual?), who the entrants were (oldest? youngest? oddest animal in the pet section?), what the attendance was (up or down? a record? a disaster?) and how much money has been made (a healthy profit or a financial disaster?) Ask if anything unusual has happened or whether there have been any special difficulties. Get a quote or two, and more from the chair and the treasurer if you can find them. Talk to the prize-winners.

Get pictures if required: bonny babies, toddlers in fancy dress, pensioners holding prize onions, the vicar in the stocks being pelted with wet beanbags. Get all the names, because names sell newspapers, and get them right.

Don't promise anyone that their picture will definitely be used – you may well end up with far more than your newspaper can print.

When you write your story, make sure you follow your newspaper's style for results. Subs hate reporters who get it wrong and force them to go through the whole lot changing commas to semi-colons.

Use the event as an opportunity to make new contacts and refresh old ones. You will build up goodwill for yourself and your newspaper if you hang around and chat for a bit instead of rushing away the moment you have got the bare details.

SAFETY PRECAUTIONS

Take a police-recognised press card with you when covering events like these.

However peaceful the organisers' intentions may be, demos can turn nasty and you want to be able to prove that you're a reporter if trouble starts and arrests are being made.

Look up the route of a march on a map beforehand and identify possible ways to escape if things go wrong.

You don't want to end up trapped in a cul-de-sac facing police with CS gas canisters.

DEMOS, MARCHES AND PARADES

THESE range from silent vigils by a handful of individuals to noisy rallies involving thousands of people. You may come across political marches, sit-down protests at development plans, anti-hunting demonstrations, and pickets of GM food crop sites.

Unless they are spontaneous eruptions of public anger, your newsdesk will almost certainly know about them well in advance. The organisers are anxious for publicity, and for a gathering of any size will have been required to give the police notice of their plans, timing and (if a march is taking place) the route.

Beforehand

As for any public event, do your homework first to find out about the people and issues involved. Look up the files. Contact the organisers to find out what they hope is going to take place, who the speakers are going to be, whether anyone prominent is taking part, where the participants are coming from and how. Identify whether the event is a one-off or part of a series so that you can put it into context when you write your story.

On the scene

Note the time a march sets off and when its leaders arrive at its destination. Somewhere along the way, stand still and count the number of people passing you in one minute. Multiply this by the number of minutes it has taken the leaders, knock a bit off because they probably march rather faster than the rear-end stragglers, and you can make a fairly good guess how many are there.

Join in marches if you can and talk to people taking part. Find anyone unusual – the mother wheeling twins along, the veteran of other protests. They will give you colour for your story and lively quotes. Judge the mood of those taking part before you reveal that you are a

> The words I would like on my grave are 'He took me there'.
>
> Every piece of journalism, however short, needs to take the reader to the event being reported.
>
> Ask the fireman how high the flames were when he arrived at the scene, how big the cloud of smoke, what he could hear (crackling timbers, exploding shells), what it smelt like (burning rubber, chemicals, flesh); ask the police the height of the window through which a burglar gained entry, where he got the ladder from, what obstacles he scaled.
>
> If the reporter hasn't been to the event and the press officer doesn't know, then insist on speaking to someone who has been at the scene.

MIKE GLOVER
Editor
Westmorland Gazette

👍 **Never go on a job without telling** somebody in authority where you are going, for your own protection as well as for operational reasons.

If you leave the building for lunch, tell the newsdesk just in case there is a fire drill in your absence, or they'll be searching all over for you.

reporter. It may encourage people to talk, but if they regard the media as hostile to their cause they may clam up or worse.

Get to any final rally in good time to find a good vantage point from which you can hear speakers and take pictures.

Cover any speeches (see below), note the audience reaction, and talk to speakers afterwards if you can.

Afterwards

Ask the organisers how successful they believe the event has been, how many they estimate took part, what they hope to have achieved, what they plan to do next. If there has been trouble, get them to comment. If they lay blame on outsiders who gate-crashed the demo, attribute their claims and get a response if recognisable individuals or groups are said to be at fault.

Talk to the police and get their estimate of the numbers taking part. This may well differ from the organisers' figure: if so, say so in your story. Ask about difficulties the police faced.

If there have been any violent incidents, find out about casualties. If the event passed off peacefully, that may be news in itself.

SPEECHES

LOOK through old copies of newspapers and you will be surprised how many columns of tightly-packed tiny print were once devoted to reporting speeches verbatim.

The national press carried pages of parliamentary proceedings. Local newspapers recorded the utterings of local worthies word for word, from the opening *Good evening, ladies and gentlemen* to the final *God bless you all*. As recently as a generation ago it was not uncommon for reporters to attend occasions such as the weekly Rotary Club lunch and report guest speakers at length, even though they rarely had anything of interest to say.

Not now. Speeches are still made, though nowhere near as many as in the past, but few people have the time and even fewer the interest to read everything that has been said in them, however important the topic. Newspapers reflect this in their coverage. Speeches by the great and the not-so-great make news only if the content justifies it, and only a fraction of the words spoken appear as direct quotations.

Nevertheless, trainee reporters are still expected to be able to cover speeches, and a test of their ability to do so is part of the NCTJ's final examinations. Most editors regard the exercise as a useful one because there are still many occasions when people stand up and say something newsworthy. It may be at an election rally, a school prize-giving, the opening of a new building or the launch of a new product. It may be a

👍 **Listen for clues that indicate when the** speaker is coming to something they think is important.

It may be a significant pause, a different tone, a change in the speed of delivery or, if you are really lucky, a preamble along the lines of 'And now I come to the point of my being here today...'

lengthy tirade from a councillor in a heated meeting or a judge's measured summing-up to a jury. Whatever the situation, the demands on your reporting talents are much the same.

Beforehand

Some speakers provide the press with an advance copy of what they intend to say. This is very welcome, as you can work out beforehand what the story is all about and write it up, ready to go as soon as the speech has been made.

Note that it is an advance copy of what they *intend* to say: you still need to check the words actually spoken. Speakers leave bits out and add new ones. Sometimes these changes are important and make the story. If an MP says something in his advance copy but omits it when he comes to deliver, it may be worthwhile asking why: has he changed his mind – or been put under pressure to shut up?

It is common practice to write advance stories on speeches whose content is known beforehand, especially if the timing of the speech doesn't fit neatly with deadlines and a report of it would not otherwise be published until some time later. Care needs to be taken to make it clear that the speech has yet to take place: *MP Ken Green is expected to tell party workers later today...*

Many speakers keep their speech to themselves until its delivery; others ad lib from brief notes scrawled on bits of card or bulletpoints displayed on overhead projectors, and you are unlikely to get a copy of these. Some speeches are spontaneous and there is nothing you can do to prepare for them. If the leader of a protest march suddenly delivers an impromptu condemnation of whatever he is protesting about, all you can do is grab your pen.

When you arrive at the venue, you may find a press table provided for you near the speaker, but don't bank on it. If you arrive at the last minute, you could end up sitting at the back of the room, straining to hear what is being said. Get there in good time. If you are using a tape recorder you certainly need to be at the front and be able to set it up and check sound levels before the speech starts.

Talk to the organiser and/or the speaker beforehand if you can. Ask questions and collect any background material on offer. Exchange contact details in case you want to get in touch later. You may not have a chance to do this after the speech if you are on a tight deadline or the speaker disappears as soon as he or she has finished.

During the speech

Don't try to take down every word that is said. It isn't a shorthand test. Treat it like any other story, making notes of points as they arrive, recording facts and figures, and only making a verbatim note when the speaker says something that will make a good quote. In a story of two

Always be suitably dressed for every occasion.

I once wore high heels to cover an agricultural show. I never did it again.

FIONA PHILLIPS
Editor
Western Telegraph

Keep some respectable clothes in the car.

Sent to cover the Great Yorkshire Show in torrential rain, I wore jeans, wellies and waterproofs.

Then I was suddenly sent to the opening of a double inquest – middle-aged lovers in suicide pact.

Difficult to get the right tone of respect and professionalism at the court, when covered in mud and smelling of cow shit.

SHARON GRIFFITHS
Feature writer
The Northern Echo

If you cover a lot of meetings of the same organisation, the time may come when they decide you are doing such a good job getting their activities into print that they invite you to become their press officer.

Don't do it, however much you may applaud their aims.

You would end up with a conflict of interests, torn between your duty to report adverse news and your loyalty to the group.

Deadlines are a busy time. Don't burden the newsdesk with questions or problems which can wait until a quieter period.

But never be afraid to raise something later which you do not understand or is causing you difficulty.

or three hundred words you will probably only need three or four paragraphs of quotes. The rest will be in reported speech. Listen to what is being said and be selective.

Don't over-do it, though. If you wait for an earth-shattering announcement and the world's greatest quote before you put pen to paper, you will probably end up with an empty notebook.

When you do take something verbatim, put a note in the margin so that when you come to write it up you know the words were actually spoken, not a summary.

Many speeches follow a similar pattern: opening formalities with general remarks, an introduction to the central topic, more detail, the main point, a recap and then a round-up of it all, often finishing with a good quote. The main point may be made right at the start, however, or left as a climactic ending. What the speaker thinks is the most important part may not, of course, be the most newsworthy. Listen for anything else that might make your intro.

Note the mood of the speaker (sombre? excited?), the reaction of the audience (enthusiastic? angry?) and whether the room is packed or hardly anyone has turned up.

If the audience is invited to ask questions, note what they say, how the speaker responds to them, and find out who they are. They may have useful comments to make or even provide you with a better angle than the speech itself.

Afterwards

If you get the opportunity, talk to the speaker. They may expand on what they said, giving you additional information, and produce better quotes off the cuff than they were prepared to give in their prepared address. Explore any angles that were not developed during the speech.

Back in the office, decide if you need to do any follow-up work. You may need more information about what you learned from the speech, or reaction from people affected by what has been said.

When you come to writing it up, the most important thing to recognise is that someone making a speech is not in itself news: what is important is its content. It must contain newsworthy information or opinions. The fact that you got these from someone speaking out loud in public is usually no more indicative of their worth than the fact that press releases arrive on paper or by email. If your intro even mentions the word *speech*, it probably needs re-writing.

Ask yourself what will make the best angle. Is it new information revealed in the speech? Is it plans for future action? Or is it the opinion and attitude of the speaker? If you have a choice, action probably makes a better intro than words – but make sure you still have a strong quote early on.

Don't string several quotes from different parts of the speech together to give the impression that they were delivered consecutively. The speaker may object that you have distorted what was said. Break them up with a *he said* or a sentence of reported speech.

Don't take quotes out of context in the search for a strong intro. Your story should be a balanced report of the speech. If the speaker qualifies a statement, say so. *Mr Jones said police should be armed* is unfair to Mr Jones and misleads your reader if his full sentence was *The police should be armed only in the last resort if law and order collapses.*

Remember that speeches made at public meetings should be covered by qualified privilege. Those made at private gatherings will have less protection and anything said outside meetings probably none at all.

MEETINGS

THOUSANDS of public meetings take place every week. Some are covered by the press because they are of sufficient public interest and have news potential.

They range from formal council meetings covering a wide range of topics to one-off assemblies of residents protesting about a single issue. In between come meetings of organisations such as social groups, recreational bodies and residents' associations, and meetings open to the public at large, held, for example, to give information affecting them all. Some meetings are packed with potential stories; others produce nothing but one or two extra names in your contacts book.

Some meetings you have a statutory right to attend, some you can go along to because they are held in public or are discussing matters of public interest, some are private gatherings to which you are invited. Others may exclude the press but provide details of the proceedings later.

Council meetings merit a section of their own later in this book. This chapter looks at the rest, the ones you are most likely to cover in your early reporting days.

Much of what has been said about covering speeches applies to meetings. The big difference is that you have to deal with a number of people talking. If the meeting is about one central issue and it is very well run, speakers may be restricted to one contribution apiece, which makes reporting fairly straightforward. Sometimes, however, meetings are a controlled free-for-all, each participant speaking several times about unrelated topics. If tempers flare and arguments get heated, it can be a job keeping pace.

Beforehand

Get as much background information as you can. Find the press release giving details of the meeting and the agenda if one came with it.

Remember you are not just there to cover the meeting itself. Something else might happen.

I went to a meeting and found the council chamber TV screens – normally used to show plans and documents – stuck on EastEnders. It made a great nib.

And I recall a trainee reporter who went straight home from a meeting when he was told it had been cancelled because of a suspicious package in the building.

DAVID JACKMAN
Editor
Epping Forest Guardian

HOW MEETINGS WORK

A one-off meeting may be run alone by the person who decided to call it, with those attending working out the rules as they go along.

The organiser will outline the topic to be discussed and throw it open to the floor.

Debate begins, different points of view are aired, arguments take place and eventually, perhaps, a decision is made to take action of some kind.

It can all be a bit haphazard, which is why one of the first things most new organisations do is establish rules of procedure, known as *standing orders*.

Among them will be what constitutes a *quorum*, the minimum number of people required to attend for a meeting to be valid.

The rules will identify officers to be elected: a *chairman*, a *secretary* or *clerk*, a *treasurer* and so forth.

If you see one of these referred to as *honorary* it means they get paid (and it's sometimes worthwhile finding out exactly how much, and whether they earn it).

There may be a *president*, often a local person perceived to be of sufficient standing to lend authority and support to the organisation (although they may rarely if ever attend its meetings).

Sub-committees may be set up to handle specific areas of interest.

These may be given powers to act on their decisions, but will usually make recommendations that need approval by the main body.

Organised meetings begin with initial formalities: apologies for absence, approval of the minutes of the previous meeting and discussion of any matters arising.

Minor correspondence may be dealt with, and the treasurer may present the latest set of accounts for approval (known as *adoption*).

Then comes the business of the day, each issue dealt with separately.

A *proposal* or motion on the first subject will be proposed, seconded and debated.

If an *amendment* is proposed and seconded, it will be discussed and voted upon. If it succeeds, it becomes what is called the *substantive motion*, replacing the original one; if not it falls by the wayside.

Whichever motion remains is then voted upon, and if passed becomes the meeting's *resolution*.

If votes are tied, the chairman or woman may have an extra *casting vote* to ensure a decision is made.

Should the motion fail, that is probably the end of it (until the next meeting, when it may well start all over again) and discussion moves on to the second item on the agenda.

This goes on until all topics have been dealt with and everyone can go home.

Otherwise, contact the organising secretary or association chairman and ask what is going to be discussed.

Check the files for information about the organisation and for stories of previous meetings. If it is a routine monthly get-together there will be on-going issues that speakers will talk about on the assumption everyone knows the background, but you may be hearing about them for the first time. Try to identify possible participants and see if there is anything on file about them and whether pictures are available.

You may well be able to do one or more stories in advance, announcing that the meeting is going to take place and explaining why. Armed with quotes from the organisers and other people affected, you may cover so much beforehand that your story of the meeting is little more than confirmation of what your readers already know, and you can use it to move forward to what happens next. Don't be tempted, if you know a good story is in the offing, to leave it until the meeting: some other reporter may beat you to it.

At the meeting

One of your first problems is knowing who the speakers are. If you are very lucky you will be provided with a map showing where various people are sitting. Otherwise it helps to get there early enough to have a quick word with those in charge, confirming who is in the chair (you probably know already, but it could be a deputy standing in) and getting the names of other officials as they arrive.

After that you need a system for identifying people as they become involved. As each starts to speak, jot down a quick description *(glasses, bald* or *red hair, green dress)* and maybe give each a code letter (A for the one on the chair's left, B for the next one, and so on clockwise round the room) for use when they speak again later. Approach them at the end to get their names. Don't let them see your descriptions if they are less than flattering.

Take notes about each topic, and quotes from speakers with something interesting to say. Note how the rest react. Leave space after each item so you can add anything you get later.

Afterwards

Often the best story emerges after the meeting. It may have been decided to take some kind of action, and plans for this could give you a strong forward-looking intro. People who have disagreed may intend to take matters further.

Talk to the main participants, the most important first. Ask others to wait to have a word with you: they will, in the hope of getting their views in print. If several items have been discussed, decide which three or four are going to figure prominently in your story and concentrate on them.

Decide if you are going to do one composite story or several, each on a different subject. If just the one, decide which topic is the most newsworthy and deal with it first before moving on to the rest in descending order of importance. Don't just start at the beginning and record the meeting as it took place chronologically. There may be a number of minor items which deserve a place in the newspaper as single-paragraph stories (called *shorts, briefs* or *nibs,* an abbreviation for *news in brief*).

> *Never answer a question you haven't asked, such as: 'He won't want to talk to us.'*
>
> **JOHN MURPHY**
> Editor
> Evesham Journal

> *Keep notes of important dates, such as murders or bad accidents. The anniversary of these occasions can make good copy.*
>
> **MICHAELA ROBINSON-TATE**
> Deputy head of content
> Westmorland Gazette

> *Make sure you get THE story, not just A story.*
>
> **IAN MURRAY**
> Editor-in-chief
> Southern Daily Echo

Nobody calls a press conference without a motive.

They are usually after publicity and want to put themselves in the best light possible.

Be sceptical. Ask yourself what they want you to know and why – and what they might not want you to know.

Check the spelling of every name, however obvious it may seem.

For every ten thousand Smiths there's a Smythe, and you're bound to come across them one day.

Check first names, too: is it John or Jon? Jonathan or Johnathan or Johnothan? Antony or Anthony, Geoffrey or Jeffrey, Clare or Claire?

Few things irritate readers as much as seeing their names mis-spelt.

Get them right.

Enter in the diary the dates of any future action decided upon – a protest march, a confrontation with the council, or just another meeting.

PRESS CONFERENCES

THESE are a mixture of speeches and meetings, with a bit of interviewing thrown in. They may be given the more accurate name of media conferences, because not only newspapers are involved.

Most follow the same general pattern: somebody with something to tell the public invites the media to a meeting, where they make an announcement and answer queries. You may get plenty of notice and time to prepare, but there are times when press conferences are called with little warning – at the scene of a major incident, perhaps, or outside a court at the conclusion of a case.

Most press conferences are called because their organisers are eager for publicity, but some take place only as a result of media pressure for answers to embarrassing questions.

If the story is big enough – a government minister explaining why he is resigning over a sex scandal, perhaps, or police giving details of their hunt for a serial killer – a press conference will be packed with reporters from the press, radio and television, backed up by photographers and television crews.

On the platform to answer (or fend off) the questions will be those in charge, press officers, minders and officials. The minister's wife may be there, stonily declaring that she is standing by her man. The parents of a murder victim may make a tearful appeal to the killer to turn himself in. It is an event full of drama, and a challenge to experienced reporters.

The press conferences you cover most often will attract rather less attention. An announcement by a company that it is building a new production plant may draw only a couple of local reporters; an invitation from a theatre to meet and take pictures of its pantomime stars – hardly a press conference at all, and often referred to instead as a photo-call or photo-op (short for opportunity) – may be attended by a lone photographer. There are some press conferences that nobody at all bothers to go to because they just don't sound newsworthy enough to justify sending someone out of the office.

Beforehand

Get the press release announcing the press conference and any briefing material that came with it. Dig into the files for background. Prepare a list of possible questions. As with meetings, it may be possible to make inquiries straight away and run stories in advance.

Once there

If there are a lot of reporters attending, you may have to battle for a place where you can see and hear everything that goes on. TV and radio people often seem to think that just because they have brought a load of cumbersome equipment they are entitled to the best positions. Don't be bullied. If you are in a room, aim for a seat near the front. If you are in a scrum outside a court, tuck in behind the most muscular cameraman around.

Proceedings will start with an opening statement, backed up, perhaps, by screen projections. You may be given a hard copy of this statement: check it against delivery. There may be further statements from others involved before the media are invited to ask questions. Reporters take it in turns, each standing up, identifying themselves and their news organisations, and putting their query to the panel. They will probably be given the opportunity to ask one or more follow-up questions before giving way to the next questioner. You may sometimes see a group of journalists working as a pack to put their target under pressure, firing a series of coordinated questions in pursuit of something they have agreed beforehand is important.

Take notes of the questions as well as the answers, or you could end up with a list of responses to queries you can't remember when you come to write the story.

Get some verbatim quotes.

Be in control. Those in charge will have an agenda and may do their best to impose it upon you. Don't be manipulated.

DON'T TRY THIS YOURSELF

There is no precise definition, legally or otherwise, of what constitutes a press conference.

Some argue that it has to be pre-arranged, be delivered by someone in authority, and involve more than one media representative. This clearly isn't so: some press conferences are called at very short notice (by a fire chief at the scene of a motorway disaster, for instance), some are called by ordinary members of the public (residents angry about plans affecting their area), and many are covered by only one reporter.

One day an enterprising newspaper may chance its arm, send a lone reporter to meet an indiscreet royal family servant in a pub, and splash his highly-defamatory revelations across its pages with the claim that the meeting was, like a public meeting, lawfully held on a matter of public concern and that reporting it was therefore perfectly legal.

Don't try it yourself. Leave it to the nationals, who can afford the ensuing court case. You would probably be done for invasion of privacy and breach of confidence, anyway.

The point remains that press conferences are easy to set up, and there is no reason why you should not suggest that someone calls one to give you protection if you want to air potentially libellous information.

Two words should be nailed to a plaque over every journalist's bed: Never assume.

Ninety-nine Michaels out of a hundred will be 'ael' towards the end, and if you check they may well ask you abruptly: 'How do you think you spell Michael?'

But you can bet your life that the one spelling you don't check is a Micheal of east European descent.

In a world of Jaysons and Leesas, it is not worth the risk to guess. Just ask.

GAVIN LEDWITH
Assistant editor
Hartlepool Mail

You can never have too many pens, pencils and notebooks.

SHARON GRIFFITHS
Features writer
The Northern Echo

👍 *Contacts suggestion: catteries, kennels, dogs' homes and animal refuges.*

Readers love animal stories, animals make great pictures.

On a quiet day, you can always find one forlorn puppy facing the gas chamber unless a new owner comes forward soon. Put its picture in the newspaper and save its life.

Don't forget the vets: good for cats surviving horrendous injuries, dogs swallowing wedding rings, and two-headed calves.

Asking questions

This takes a bit of courage the first time you do it, especially if you are surrounded by seasoned journalists who seem to know so much more than you. Don't be intimidated. Take a deep breath, stand up, say who you are and go ahead.

Be tenacious. If the person you are questioning says they don't know the answer, you may have to accept that as the truth, but don't be afraid to ask whether they think they should know, or whether they are going to find out. If they are clearly waffling to avoid giving a straight answer to your question, ask it again. Be polite but persistent: *'With all respect, you still haven't answered the question and my readers will want to know...'* They may well give in eventually, and meanwhile the sight of them wriggling to evade your inquiry will amuse the rest of the audience and do your reputation no harm.

Don't be afraid to ask for explanations if you don't understand everything. Better to look slightly foolish in front of your peers than extremely silly in front of your news editor when you confess you have no idea what the story is all about.

Do ask for opinions as well as facts. Force them into a corner: *'Wouldn't you agree this is a disgraceful state of affairs?'* forces them to agree (good quote) or disagree (prompting your reaction *'Really? How can you defend it?'*)

Don't hang on too long before asking your question in the hope that someone else will raise it for you. You may be too late. Those in charge decide when a press conference ends, and they will bring it to a halt when it suits them, especially if they think it is turning awkward.

Press conferences have obvious advantages over a one-to-one interview. There are a number of reporters asking questions, so important angles are unlikely to be missed. You have time to think about your next question while others are asking theirs. You can cross-check information and agree the accuracy of quotes with colleagues afterwards.

The downside, of course, is that you are unlikely to get anything exclusive from a press conferences unless you are the only one there. If you think you have spotted an angle nobody else is pursuing, you face a dilemma. You have to weigh up whether to raise it during the press conference and lose a potential scoop, or keep quiet in the hope that you can get hold of those involved for a private interview afterwards.

If you think there will be an opportunity to do this, and you have time, go for it. Radio and TV often set up their own interviews after a press conference, and if they do there is no reason why you shouldn't ask for the same privilege.

Otherwise, ask the question. You may have lost your exclusive, but revealing a shared truth is better than no truth at all.

Afterwards

Don't leave straight away unless you have an urgent deadline to meet.

Check details, facts and spellings with the organisers.

Find out if here is to be another press conference, and, if so, put it in the diary.

Stick around a bit. Press conferences are a good opportunity to make fresh contacts and meet follow journalists.

Writing it up

When you come to write your story, remember that the press conference itself isn't the news. The fact that someone has stage-managed a publicity event is of no importance. What matters is what has been revealed. You may well be able to tell your readers what this is without even mentioning that a press conference took place.

In the eyes of the law, press conferences are public meetings and share the same qualified privilege. So do any associated press releases dealing with the same subject matter even if their contents are not actually read out, once the press conference has taken place (but not beforehand).

PICTURES

MANY of the stories you write will have pictures with them. They help to identify the kind of people and places you are writing about. They explain the story, put it in context and lend it authenticity. They can add impact to pages and help in their design.

They may be dramatic snapshots for a major news story: the moment firefighters grab a trapped child from a blazing bedroom, a politician is hit by a protester's egg, an athlete breasts the winning tape. They may be creative works of art, pictures that stand on their own and need no more than a few words to explain their content and credit their creator.

Most, however, are more mundane. Newspaper pages are full of photos taken to accompany routine assignments such as presentations and celebrations, each with its accompanying story and caption.

All are important and deserve to be done well. People whose faces appear in print will treasure copies of the newspaper; the rest of your readership expects even the most commonplace of pictures to be interesting enough to merit inclusion in pages for which they have paid good money.

> *On my first daily paper my news editor dispatched me with a photographer to collect the name of everyone attending a local worthy's funeral, saying: 'Don't miss out a single one, and get every name right.'*
>
> *Nervously hugging my notebook, I approached mourners one by one, and then the coffin drew near.*
>
> *I advanced with courage and halted the sad procession – then the photographer suddenly yanked me away by the scruff of my neck, growling: 'We can get the names of the pall-bearers later, laddie.'*
>
> **KEITH STAFFORD**
> Former training editor
> Reuters

Don't ask photographers to do the impossible.

You can't get pictures of deserted town centre streets on a Saturday afternoon, and the best snapper in the world can't make two acres of barren land with nothing on it look interesting.

Until the 1990s pictures were taken almost exclusively by staff photographers. The invention of the digital camera, cheap, portable and requiring little or no knowledge of photography, ended all that. Today, reporters on most newspapers are expected to take everyday pictures for publication both in print and on the web, and many smaller publications have done away with staff photographers altogether. You should think visually in everything you do, asking yourself whether there are picture or graphics possibilities in each story and, if so, how they might best be realised.

Handling video is dealt with in a later chapter. This section deals with still photographs taken for publication in the newspaper or on the web. It assumes you know how to use a simple digital camera.

Working with photographers

If you are working for an organisation that employs photographers, you need to be clear where the demarcation lines are drawn. Find out whether you are expected to take pictures or play only a supporting role, advising on content and providing the words.

If the latter is the case, teamwork is essential. Too often reporters work blind, writing stories and captions for pictures they know nothing about until they appear in print. It makes it difficult to do the story justice, and can easily lead to errors. Liaise with the photographer. If you are making arrangements for pictures to be taken, make sure first

If you are using photos from your archives, be sure they are accurate (captions may have been wrong when first published), up to date (people's appearance can change very quickly), appropriate (don't show a laughing husband on a story about his wife's murder), and legal (you may not own the copyright – bear this in mind, too, when looking for pictures on the internet).

THINK GRAPHICS, TOO

Graphics are a very handy way to show a lot of complex information in a relatively small space.

They are frequently used to present data and statistics that readers can glance at to get an instant overall impression of trends or pore over at leisure to find specific details.

They should be fairly simple and self-explanatory. The most common forms include tables (information displayed in rows and columns), line charts (lines on a grid showing changes over a period of time), bar charts (blocks of varying sizes contrasting different quantities), and pie charts (circles divided into segments, each representing a percentage of the whole).

Graphics can be used in various other ways. Maps are an obvious example, though any but the most simple may require copyright permission if they are based on atlases or downloaded material.

If you are working in a newsroom that employs a graphic artist, drawings can be produced to show, for example, a sequence of events, geographical distribution, a production process or how a machine works.

Think about graphics whenever you have a story that deserves illustration, and especially when handling stories involving numbers.

One chart can save you a great deal of time listing information that would otherwise clog up your copy and bore your readers.

that he or she is available and that the time and venue are suitable. Don't organise photos to be taken outdoors in poor weather or when the light is bad. Pick daytime if possible, because daylight makes for better pictures than artificial light or flash.

Make sure the photographer has precise guidance on venue and time, and knows what the story is about, how many pictures are required, and what might make the best illustration. Explain whether you want close-ups of people or shots of them on site, and what portrayal might be appropriate: cheerful if the story is good news for them, for example; serious, upset or angry if it is not. Share ideas. Suggest appropriate backgrounds and props: lottery winners with bottles of bubbly, golden wedding couples with photo albums, environmental protesters at the scene of a proposed development.

See the picture once it is taken, to be clear about its contents. The photographer will supply a list of names, but check all spellings yourself. If you are going to refer to the picture in your story, confirm with the subs that it is going to be used and will show what you are writing about.

Going it alone

If you are taking your own pictures, life gets a bit easier. You can make most of the decisions yourself: where and when pictures are taken, what they contain, and how they are composed. Good pictures reflect the story, adding information and interest. They should almost always include people, who bring life and scale to photos, and that means people doing something rather than simply posing. Avoid clichéd shots of people staring at the lens as they exchange prizes and long-service awards, rows of children standing to attention, groups of charity workers lined up glassy-smiled behind their stalls.

There are editors who argue that static group shots cram in the faces, and faces sell newspapers. Others believe that for every interested reader there are thousands more who find such pictures a tedious waste of space. In the days when only one picture could be published, the temptation to show as many faces as possible was understandable. Now that we have the internet, many newspapers prefer to print one worthwhile photo and point readers to their website where many more pictures and faces are available.

If you have to take group shots, make them as attractive as possible: it can be done if the subjects are arranged imaginatively, appear to be doing something, are armed with props, or photographed from an unusual angle.

Whatever you decide to include in your picture, you need to know how to get the best results. The picture that goes in the page is unlikely to look exactly the same as the one you took. It will be edited by the subs, who will decide its shape, crop it to fit, and cut out extraneous background. The result may not be quite what you intended. Although

I dropped my pen under the press bench in my local council chamber, bent down to get it, and got a clear view of two highly respectable councillors playing footsie under the table. They do it every meeting and I'm the only one who knows.

NAME WITHHELD
Reporter
One of the weeklies

👍 *Contacts suggestion:
bank managers.
Boring, maybe, but good for
a local quote on the Budget
or other financial matters.
And you never know when a
friend with millions in the
vault to lend might come in
handy.*

you cannot dictate precisely how a photo is used, you can help yourself, and the subs, to some extent.

Square pictures are boring, and will be cropped to give a more interesting shape: bear this in mind when framing your shots.

Pictures work best when the focus is off-centre. Think of your picture divided into thirds, horizontally and vertically, and place your main subject on one of the dividing lines (most great works of art do this). Don't put a key feature right over to one side unless you are aiming for a special effect.

Make people look into the picture, not out of it, but not always directly at the camera. If they are doing something, leave space in front of them into which they appear to be moving.

Don't chop arms off at the elbows or legs at the knees. It looks awful, and the subs will only chop them further to get rid of arms and legs altogether. Leave them all in if they are important.

Use natural light if possible. Work out where shadows will fall and whether they will spoil or enhance your picture. If you are using flash, tell subjects not to stare straight at the camera to avoid the red-eye effect (which can be put right on computer but is an irritation).

Think about contrasting backgrounds, tones and colour. Someone in a black suit photographed in front of a dark wall may appear as a disembodied face. A woman in green may merge into a red background if the picture is printed in black and white. Aim for contrasting primary colours (red, blue, yellow) for strong pictures, secondary colours (purple, green, orange) for a softer feel.

Once you have taken your pictures, make accurate notes of who is where on each one and make sure you get all the names right. Download them while they are fresh in your mind. There are tips on putting words to pictures in the chapter on writing.

Seven

TALKING TO PEOPLE

YOU will spend a great part of your reporting life talking to people, almost as much as you will listening to them. Your conversations will range from chats over the phone with regular contacts to tough interrogations of uncooperative interviewees.

This section of the book will guide you through some of the conversations you are most likely to take part in, starting with the easiest.

- Vox pops
- Ring-rounds
- Surveys
- Interviews
- Death knocks

VOX POPS

A vox pop (from the Latin *vox populi* meaning *voice of the people*) is a street interview in which you ask people for brief comments about something in the news. Their views are published, with names and perhaps photos, to give a snapshot of public opinion.

Vox pops are often used alongside a main news story. There is nothing very scientific about them, and you can't do a serious story based on half a dozen quick interviews. However, vox pops can be a good read, news editors know they are an easy way to fill space on a thin news day, page designers welcome them as useful light relief on a page of otherwise serious copy, and for you they are a gentle introduction to the art of interviewing.

The questions

Vox pops can be about anything local, topical, of interest to most readers and likely to prompt lively responses. Asking about plans to stage nude ice-skating at the local theatre is likely to produce good readable comments; asking what the UN should do about the latest coup in Uzbekistan isn't. Your newsdesk will probably decide the topic, though there is nothing to stop you suggesting ideas.

Ask one main question, and keep it simple. You want brief comments, not detailed analysis. *'What do you think of the council's plan to turn the memorial gardens into a car-park?'* is fine. *'What do you think of the council's overall economic strategy, bearing in mind its need to balance environmental requirements against traffic management demands?'* will baffle them.

Make your question open-ended. *'What do you think about...'* should elicit a decent quote; *'Is it a good idea?'* gets the answer *'No'* and you have to start again.

Keep your opinions to yourself and make your questioning neutral. Loaded questions such as *'Don't you agree it's a bad idea to...?'* suggest

> *My first vox pop was a disaster.*
>
> *I looked my subject firmly in the eye, stepped forward confidently, opened my mouth to ask the question, and tripped over a dog.*
>
> *It was months before my broken wrist mended.*
>
> *It was my shorthand-writing hand, of course.*
>
> **NAME WITHHELD**
> Embarrassed editor
> Somewhere in England

👍 *Persuading some interviewees (especially older ones) to tell you their age isn't always easy.*

Don't ask people if they mind you asking how old they are, because it simply begs the answer: 'Yes, I do mind.'

Just say simply: 'How old are you?'

If they demur, try asking which age range they fall into – under 25, 25-40, 40-65, over 65, for example – and then see if you can narrow it down.

👍 *If no one wants to take part in your vox pop, move away to another place. Failure is catching.*

Then get somebody talking – even if it's about the weather, their baby or the way to the railway station.

Once one person's talked to you, others will follow.

the answer you expect to hear, and that is what you will get – whatever people really think.

Ask your news editor how many comments are likely to get published. Half a dozen will probably be enough. You will almost certainly have to do more interviews than this to make sure you get a good range of quotes.

The targets

You want to question a representative sample. Asking six similar people will get you six similar answers. Get a range of sexes and ages – a teenage boy, a mum in her twenties, a middle-aged man, a woman in her fifties, a male pensioner, perhaps.

Modify this if your question is clearly relevant to a specific section of the population: if your topic is baby-changing facilities at the town hall you will probably concentrate on mothers. Keep a check on the range of people you speak to as you go along to make sure you get the right balance.

You need a range of opinion, reflecting both sides of the debate. Don't stop after six interviews if they have all said much the same thing. Keep going until you have a variety of opinions expressed in different ways – or until you are convinced absolutely everyone is of the same mind.

Don't approach people clearly in a hurry, battling to control children, or talking to someone else. Aim for those already standing still, waiting at bus stops or window-gazing – people likely to have a few minutes to spare. Try drivers in a taxi rank, market stall-holders when they are not serving, publicans when trade is slack.

Main shopping streets are the usual starting-point. Pick a spot where you can talk to someone without blocking others. If it is raining, choose people who are sheltered. They will appreciate it, and you can't write on a soggy notebook anyway.

The approach

Look cheerful and confident. Have your notebook and pen at the ready. Don't use a clipboard: people will think you are doing market research and going to delay them for ages. Keep your camera (or photographer if one is with you) out of sight until you have got comments safely in your notebook. People will shy away if they think they are going to be pictured straight away.

Approach from the front, walking towards your potential interviewee and catching their eye before you are upon them. Smile. Let them weigh you up for a second. If you are in front it is difficult for them to ignore you without appearing rude; if you try to make contact from the side or behind they may be startled and uncooperative.

Be courteous: remember they don't have to talk to you. Introduce yourself briefly: *'Excuse me, I'm Tim Johns from the Gazette...'* and try to get your question in straight away: *'...and I'm asking people their views about turning the memorial gardens into a car-park. What do you think?'*

Avoid starting off with *'Would you mind if I asked you some questions?'* or *'Can you spare me a few minutes?'* It is inviting people to say sorry, they are too busy – and they will go on their way.

If they refuse to respond, thank them politely and try again. But you will be surprised how readily most people agree to help. They are usually faintly flattered that anyone should want to know what they think.

The quotes

Six people all saying *'Yes, it's a good idea'* isn't enough. Ask them why. You want a range of readable reasons:

'Yes – parking in the town centre is a nightmare'

'No, the gardens are the only place you can relax when shopping'

'Yes, the gardens are a tip, full of teenagers doing drugs'

'No, the gardens should stay in memory of people who died in the war'

Follow up to prompt extra detail:

'It's taken me 20 minutes to find a parking space this morning'

'My grandad's name's on the memorial, he'd turn in his grave'

There is no point in pursuing anyone who says they know nothing about the topic on which you are asking them to comment. But there is no reason why you should not include one person who says that they frankly don't care one way or the other.

Once you have a good quote, get their name and address. How detailed an address will depend on your newspaper's policy – it may want the full street name, it may be happy with a general area. You may be expected to get ages, occupations and other details (parent? student? tax-payer? driver?) if they are relevant.

Pictures

Say *'That's great – all we need now is a quick photo'* and get the camera out (or bring in the photographer). Don't waste time trying to take a fancy picture: all you usually need is a simple headshot.

If they look alarmed at having their picture taken, reassure them that everyone else you are interviewing will be pictured too and explain that without a photo it is unlikely their (excellent) opinions will be published.

Ask them to smile if it is appropriate – but remember that a cheerful grin doesn't go well with a vox pop about MRSA deaths at the local hospital.

Make sure you know which picture is which. Put a brief description (*moustache, spex, green tie*) in your notebook next to the person's comments so you can identify them later on.

Learn to use the secret word: 'help'. Few can resist it.

When interviewing someone, don't try to pressure them. They are likely to clam up.

This isn't necessarily because they are hostile. Journalists make many people nervous, even though deep down most are helpful.

If you say: 'I am a representative of the press and people have a right to know ...', they will likely give you a funny look.

If you say: 'I'm a bit stuck here, I wonder if you could help?', they'll say: 'Of course, what do you want to know?'

Never try to browbeat people. Always be friendly and polite, especially when they are being hostile. Friendliness is much harder to resist than bombast or bullying.

TIM GOPSILL
Editor
The Journalist

Finally...

End by thanking them for their time. If they ask when it will be in the newspaper, say you expect it to be in the next edition but it is up to your editor to decide which responses, if any, get published. Then start a new page in your notebook and move on to your next victim.

Writing it up

Type up your best quotes as a list, clearly identifying who said what:

> *'It's a disgrace' – Mrs Ivy Bartlett, 32-year-old housewife of Green Lane.*

> *'Best thing since sliced bread' – Mr Dan Ruddle, 67, retired engineer of South Street.*

If there are pictures, check and double-check the right quotes go with the right faces. Attributing comments to the wrong person is very embarrassing and you will end up printing a correction.

RING-ROUNDS

THESE are a version of vox pops, but done over the phone to pre-selected people. You may be after opinions – it's Budget Day, perhaps, and you have been asked to phone half a dozen service stations in the area for their reaction to a hike in fuel tax. You may just want some facts: you are doing a feature for the Christmas supplement, for example, and want to know what is selling best in the town's toy shops.

Similar trawls can be carried out by text or email, but these take longer and there is no guarantee everyone will respond.

SURVEYS AND POLLS

SERIOUS surveys of public opinion that attempt to discover what the population as a whole thinks about a matter of importance are, as we have already said, usually left to professional pollsters.

Selecting the right sample and asking the right questions is a highly sophisticated business. People tell lies, say they don't know because they are embarrassed to admit how they really feel, or give questioners the answers they think they want to hear. Even the best polling organisations frequently make mistakes (think how many pre-election polls of voting intentions contradict each other). Conducting your own survey, whether through face-to-face street interviews or by selected telephone calls, is time-consuming, needs a lot of people to ask the questions, and is fraught with the peril of getting it embarrassingly wrong.

Using professionals, however, can be very expensive. As a result, few local or regional newspapers attempt serious surveys, relying instead on lifting the results of those carried out by national media organisations with larger budgets.

On the other hand, surveys about inconsequential matters are commonplace, especially those whose accuracy cannot be checked. Hardly a day goes by without some tabloid inviting its readers to let them know what they think about the frothy news of the day (*Should Corrie star Jayne leave love rat Danny? Ring or text us now...*), encouraged by the popularity of interactive television shows in which viewers decide which wannabe reaches the next round of *Pop Idol* or minor celebrity gets booted from the *Big Brother* house. Reader polls should be honestly reported, even if the results don't fit in with the newspaper's own views. Not all are.

Local newspapers have not been slow to follow suit, especially those with thriving websites. Not only do the results of these text-and-tell-us surveys make a good read (though it is hard to describe many of them as news stories) but they nurture readers' feeling that they are part of the newspaper and, what's more, the newspaper can make money from all those calls and texts.

INTERVIEWS

INTERVIEWS are a mix of conversation and interrogation, a form of controlled dialogue in which one person (you) asks the questions and the other (you hope) does most of the talking.

They may be little more than gentle conversations – a chat, for example, with an elderly couple celebrating 60 years of what they claim has been married bliss. They may be tough interrogations, confronting a public figure with claims that could destroy their reputation. They may be impromptu or well-prepared, face-to-face or on the phone.

DON'T GET TAKEN OVER

Surveys can be hijacked. Supporters of one point of view can swamp phone lines or send multiple texts to skew the results.

Radio 4 asked listeners which law they would most like scrapped and more than half of respondents named the fox-hunting ban after hunt supporters got their act together.

This sort of thing doesn't matter much if they are voting on something trivial (though it may be embarrassing) but can be important if the subject matter is of consequence and the poll result taken seriously.

Ask your readers if a new supermarket should be built on the outskirts of town and most may not feel strongly enough about it to vote; meanwhile, town centre traders who see their livelihoods threatened will respond en masse and you end up with 87% *of residents oppose superstore plan* if you are not careful.

Handle surveys like these with caution and a large measure of scepticism.

> *Always remember who you've interviewed, because they'll always remember you: it is probably the biggest thing that happens in their life.*
>
> *I'm sure being interviewed by me is still imprinted on John Prescott's memory!*
>
> **GRAHAM PRATT**
> Deputy editor
> The Journal, Newcastle

> *Don't pretend you understand something if you don't.*
>
> *You are likely to make mistakes, miss the point of the story and totally confuse the reader.*
>
> *Ask the person to explain it to you: 'Is it possible that you can put that in a way that the average person in the street would be able to understand?'*
>
> **MALCOLM POWELL**
> Editor
> Lynn News

👍 **Don't try to get an interview by pretending to be anyone but yourself without a very good reason, approved by your newsdesk.**

Subterfuge, except in cases of serious investigative journalism with a genuine public interest, is condemned by the journalists' code of conduct.

Whether phoning or meeting people face-to-face, say who you are and who you represent right at the start.

Some come out of the blue. The phone rings and reception tells you there is a pensioner at the front counter who wants to talk to a reporter about her cat killing the Rottweiler next door... It's two minutes to deadline, and the newsdesk tells you phone up a vicar – any vicar – for a quote about same-sex marriages... You're on a routine visit to the town hall and find everyone in the housing department swilling champagne because they have just won the lottery...

In cases like this, there is not much you can do to prepare yourself apart from grab your pen and notebook and start thinking fast. Usually, though, you have time to do some planning.

Preparation

Carry out some research before you contact your subject. If you are uninformed, your interviewee may be irritated, lose confidence in you and become unhelpful. Even if they remain cooperative, you will find it difficult to detect what is news and what is not, and your interview will be less productive. Ask yourself:

Who is the subject?

Find out all you can. The basics – name, address, age, family, job – and anything else that might be useful. See if you can identify any special interest or experience. Nothing breaks the ice better than a common pastime, shared experience or mutual acquaintance.

What is the story?

Have a clear idea what it is all about. Is your story essentially about the person – a profile of a bank manager who is retiring, for example? Or is it about information they possess – why his bank is closing down and putting a dozen people out of work?

What are the questions?

Make a list of the essential information you need to know. Ask the newsdesk for guidance if necessary. You will need full name, age, address and occupation for almost anyone you interview; other essentials will vary depending on who you are going to meet and why. If it is a profile, you will want to know about family, education and career. If it is a harder news story, these details may not matter: you are after the facts and opinions.

Make a list of questions to be answered. Number them so you can identify which one goes with which answer. Don't draw up a rigid plan of attack, though. You will need to be flexible during the interview, reacting to what you learn. Following a strictly-defined path may mean you miss important angles.

Do all this before you contact your subject, whether you plan a phone interview or a face-to-face meeting. You might get no further than this initial call – it may be they are about to set off on holiday, and this is the only chance you have to talk to them – so you need to be prepared to do the interview there and then. You will sound very foolish asking

👍 **Keep an eye open for the vox pop victim who you can turn into a full feature.**

It never does any harm to come back with more than you were asked for.

if you can phone back in ten minutes once you have got yourself organised. Have pen, notebook and questions ready just in case.

Phone or face-to-face?

The vast majority of interviews are conducted by phone. It's quicker, it's cheaper, the interviewee can't see what you are writing, and you don't have to worry about what you look like or whether you are smiling enough. Busy people may be more willing to talk on the phone than give up time for a face-to-face meeting. If it all goes wrong you can always disconnect suddenly and blame the switchboard.

But there are major disadvantages. Telephones are impersonal. You can't greet the interviewee with a smile and impress them with your appearance and attitude. You can't use the body language of encouraging nods and sympathetic smiles to keep the interview flowing. You can't see how the interviewee is reacting to your questions, whether they are happy, worried, bemused or just plain bored. You can't see what they are wearing, what they are doing, what their surroundings are like.

A phone call takes people by surprise. They are unprepared and may feel vulnerable and uncooperative. They may be in the middle of doing something important when you phone, talking to someone else or trying to control the kids. There may be other people around they don't want listening in. Some – the elderly, for instance – may find phone conversations difficult because of hearing, speech or other problems you know nothing about.

If you are calling from your desk there may be background noise or interruptions from colleagues that hamper your conversation and confuse or irritate the person you are trying to talk to. And if you pause for more than a couple of seconds they wonder if you are still on the line.

All you have is your voice, your persuasive manner, your judgement of how the interviewee feels from what they say and how they say it, and your ability to listen to answers, write them down, and think of the next question all at once.

Sometimes, of course, you don't have a choice between phone and face-to-face. No news editor is going to send you off an hour before deadline to meet someone living 200 miles away. But if you have the luxury of choosing how to carry out an interview, go for it face-to-face almost every time.

Face-to-face

We will assume it is a quiet day, your deadline is a long way away, the interviewee lives in town, and the news editor is in a good mood. You are going to meet someone in person.

How?

Turning up on the doorstep unannounced is sometimes unavoidable, but make an appointment if you can. People appreciate knowing that you are coming and it will help to avoid interruptions.

I phoned someone whose shop was closing and my first question was: 'Why?' They instantly froze on me.

Now I always start with: 'Sorry to hear about the business closing, would you like to thank your loyal customers at this time?'

ALEX CAMERON
Chief reporter
Chard & Ilminster News

Be careful about accepting the offer of a cup of tea: you'll have to drink it, even when it's a soiled mug from the sink and contains strange floating debris.

SIMON FERNLEY
Production editor
Cornwall & Devon Media

If you have the choice, sit at an angle of about 45 degrees to your subject.

Facing each other head-on is confrontational; side by side on a settee leaves you twisting around and hampers your note-taking.

Contact suggestion: druids, white witches and other off-beat cults. There are more of them about than you'd think. They may have curious dawn ceremonies to celebrate solstices or even dance naked in the moonlight. Tracking them down might not be that easy, but it's a fair bet they use the local health food shop.

Who?

If you are not sure exactly who you want to talk to – you are after information about a company's new contract, for example – start at the top and ask for the managing director. You may end up talking to a secretary and then get shunted to the press office, but it is worth trying.

Those in command know the value of good publicity and want to be sure the facts are right and the story reflects well on their company. If you are getting nowhere, try the deputy. They will recognise the importance of getting it right, too, but if they don't want the responsibility of answering your questions they may put you through to the boss.

If the person you want isn't there and nobody else will do, ask when they will be in and phone back later. By all means leave a message asking them to phone you, but don't bank on them doing so. Leave your office number and times when you will be at your desk. Leave your mobile number, too. If you have an answer-phone, make sure your message on it is professional.

If they don't reply and you can't get through after several calls, track down their secretary or PA and ask bluntly whether the person you want to talk to is deliberately avoiding you. *'It's not going to look good if I say your company refused to say anything despite repeated calls, is it?'* might work.

What?

Explain who you are, give a general idea of what you want to talk about, and how long it might take. If they don't sound keen, emphasise that it is going to be to their benefit. Be positive: *'We're doing a story about this and we're anxious to get both sides... I'm sure you'd want us to get the facts right... People might think it odd you weren't willing to comment...'* Persevere. Some people are falsely modest when asked for an interview and most can be won round. Don't resort to threats or blackmail.

Where?

Let them choose. Most people feel more relaxed at home or in their workplace. It may be useful to see where they live or work and how they get on with their family or work colleagues, but you may feel at a disadvantage on their home ground. They may suggest neutral ground, a pub or cafe. This may be a relaxing venue but you may encounter problems with privacy, noise and interruptions. Food and drink get in the way, and it may not be easy taking notes. If they say they will come to you, identify (and book, if necessary) an appropriate place in the office where you can carry out the interview in private.

When?

It may depend on when your interviewee is available and what it is about. If it is a personal matter, it may have to be lunchtime or evening for people working during the day. Evenings are bad times for publicans (trade is at its busiest then) but good for mothers (the children are in bed). Night-shift workers won't welcome you first thing in the morning. Vicars are pre-occupied at weekends.

And...?

If you are driving to meet someone at their home or workplace, ask about parking. Check the name and the arrangements, put them in your diary and the office diary. Liaise with the picture desk if you need photographer.

Opening steps

Be punctual. Give yourself plenty of time to get to the venue and, if you are driving, to find somewhere to park. If you are running late, phone ahead and warn your subject. When you arrive, keep your notebook and camera out of sight for the moment.

First impressions count. If you look competent and act professionally you will impress your subject and enhance your chances of a good interview. Greet them appropriately – a warm smile is fine on most occasions. Offer congratulations if they have just won the lottery, but look serious if you are about to ask the head of an old folks' home why half her residents have been wiped out by salmonella.

Check you have got the right person and introduce yourself. *'Mrs Brown? I'm Tim Johns from the Gazette, thanks for seeing me.'* Use their title until they invite you to do otherwise or call you by your first name. Be ready to shake hands but let them make the first move. Sit down when you are invited to.

Put them at ease

If you are meeting someone who is used to dealing with the media, you can probably get straight to the point. If not, it is worth spending a few moments in small talk to put your subject at ease and create a rapport. They may be quite nervous about talking to you.

Comment on the weather, traffic problems, the great view from the window, the painting over the fireplace, what a lovely cat they've got. Try to find some common ground, something you share. If there is a car in their driveway, ask if it is as economical as the adverts boast. If there is a football scarf hanging in the hall, discuss the team's latest result. If you know they were born in Blackpool, say what a great holiday you had there once (but don't make it up – you will be caught out straight away). Show them you are a friendly and interesting person, not the foot-in-the-door ogre they feared.

Accept the offer of tea or coffee if you have plenty of time and there is somewhere to rest the cup while you take notes. While they are putting the kettle on, you can have a look round and maybe spot things worth asking about – the photo on the mantelpiece, the picture on the wall. Decline alcohol, however well you can handle it. If the interview goes badly and your subject complains about your story, the first thing they will say is that you were drunk. Don't smoke.

Often the most daunting thing for someone new to interviewing is learning how to handle people whose views differ from his or her own.

Some people retreat into avoidance, while others adopt the opposing view.

Let curiosity be your guiding value: curiosity in its best sense – a genuine interest in the world around you – rather than plain noseyness.

This will drive your interest, reassure your interviewees and bolster your efforts to remain objective.

SUSAN GREENBERG
Ex-reporter, Reuters
and The Guardian

Be a first class listener. Always show interest and never stop an interviewee in full flight.

ALAN KIRBY
Editor
Coventry Telegraph

Try to vary your responses as you listen to an interviewee.

Saying 'Uh-huh' at the end of every sentence they utter can be very irritating.

You may not realise you are doing it. Tape-record yourself doing a mock interview with a friend and listen to what you say.

And ask the friend to tell you truthfully whether you do anything else that is distracting or annoying: gesticulating oddly, scratching your ear, chewing your lip or biting your pen-top.

Little things like that can annoy (or amuse) your subject and affect the way they respond to you.

Keep plenty of eye contact, but don't stare at them all the time. It is unnerving. Watch their body language and copy it unobtrusively. If they sit back in a relaxed position, follow suit; if they are bent forward over their desk, stay upright.

To the point

After a couple of minutes, ease the conversation round to the reason for the interview. *'Well, as you know, we're interested in your plans to climb Everest on a camel...'* and bring out your notebook. People expect you to take notes and will be unhappy if it looks as if what they are saying isn't worth recording. Don't try to remember everything and write it up later – you can't.

Rest the notebook on your knee if you can: it is less obtrusive than on a desktop, and your subject can't read what you are writing. You don't want them to do that, especially if your shorthand is a bit ropy. Watching you struggle to record disconnected words in longhand makes you look unprofessional and they will worry whether their words are being accurately reported or, worse, start arguing about what you have written. If your Teeline is immaculate, on the other hand, by all means let them catch a glance of your notes occasionally: it impresses them. If you are using a tape recorder, keep it as far out of sight as possible.

From here on you have got to be in control, gently steering the questions in your chosen direction. Be in charge; you are the professional and it is your interview. The alternative is letting them ramble on or start dictating what they want you to publish (which, if they have been trained in handling the media, they will do their best to achieve).

Asking questions

Don't be too abrupt. Begin with basic questions they will have no problems answering: *'Can I just check a few facts to start with?'* Ask for the spelling of their name, their job title if any. It will help them relax and reassures them that you want to get things right.

Don't get bogged down in detail at this stage. Ask an open question: *'Can you give me a general idea of what it's all about?'* and let them tell you. Cover the past, present and future, building up a picture of what has happened, what is going on now, what might take place later. Build up a chronological picture of events. Make a note in the margin of angles you want to come back to later.

Encourage your subject to keep talking with the occasional nod. *'I see...uh-hmm... and then?'* Don't be worried if for the first few minutes you seem to be asking *'And then...?'* a lot of the time. A frequent comment by interviewees in NCTJ examinations after poorly-performing candidates have walked out is: *'If only they'd just kept asking me what happened next.'*

Take notes in a relaxed fashion. Scribbling frantically, however good the quote, not only reveals that your shorthand is not up to much but may make them realise they have said more than they intended and try to withdraw or qualify it. Don't leap up and down when you get a great quote saying *'Hey, that's fantastic!'*

Keep going until you are up-to-date and got a clear general idea of what has taken place. Then go back for the detail. *'You said the alarm was raised by a guard. Who is he? How old? Where does he live? What did he do? Was he hurt? How long has he worked for you? Where is he now?'* and so on.

When you have covered the facts, ask for opinions. *'How do you feel? What sort of people would do this? What sort of person was the victim?'* This is when you may well get your best quotes. *'I'm horrified... the burglars acted like animals... he was a lovely man, do anything for anyone...'*

Do...

Ask one question at a time. If you pose three at once, the third will be answered; the other two get lost.

Use a mix of closed and open questions to get facts and opinions: *'Were you first on the scene? What did you see? How did you feel?'*

Prompt them to be specific. If you ask a lottery winner *'How will this change your life?'* the odds are they will say they haven't decided yet. Ask them whether they plan a holiday, if they will give some away to relatives, what is the one thing they have always wanted and can now afford.

Keep the interview flowing. Avoid long silences while you make notes and wonder what to ask next. If your mind goes blank, check your advance list of questions or ask for more detail about something you already know. Brief pauses – a few seconds – are okay, and give the impression you are being thoughtful.

Try to manoeuvre your subject into saying what you want them to say. Putting words into the interviewee's mouth – *'Would you say that you were absolutely gob-smacked?'* – is frowned upon by some, but it is a common and useful technique if interviewees don't come up with anything worth recording on their own.

LAST IMPRESSIONS COUNT TOO

Leave as professionally as you arrived.

Thank your interviewee for their time, shake hands, and make sure they remember you as someone they will be willing to talk to again. You never know when they might be useful.

There is an oft-repeated story of an old lady who hit the headlines and was besieged by reporters.

She sent them all away, but when they returned she let one in for an exclusive interview.

'Why me?' he asked. She told him: *'Last time, you were the only one who bothered to shut the gate behind you.'*

> *Always look interested. Practice it.*
>
> *If people think you share their passion they get a little carried away – always good.*
>
> *Don't fill in the silence after a short answer, because everyone hates awkward silences and they usually start filling them – sometimes saying things they shouldn't!*

FIONA HEAVEY
Reporter
Leitrim Observer

> *Take all the photos available – not just because your picture editor will want to see which reproduces best, but to stop rival reporters getting their hands on any.*

PETER AENGENHEISTER
Editor
Rugby Advertiser

Listening to other people's conversations in public places is not illegal, though they may object to it strongly.

Listening at keyholes is not acceptable unless you have very good reason.

If you are left alone in someone's office or livingroom, there is nothing to stop you examining anything on open display, but opening diaries, searching drawers, or photographing documents would be a breach of privacy and contravene the code of conduct unless there were good public interest reasons.

Removing items without permission would be theft, though the code says it might be excusable in the public interest.

Always appear interested in what they are saying, however tedious it may be. If you look bored they will be affronted, and any rapport you have built up will be lost.

Be alert if your subject goes quiet or starts speaking more slowly or quietly. It may just be that they are trying to find the right words, but they may worried about saying the wrong thing – or wondering how best to lie.

Check every spelling.

Don't...

Don't interrupt. Let people finish what they are saying before you pose your next question. Breaking in halfway through their sentences will irritate them, and you may cut them off before they say something important.

Don't ask the blindingly obvious. *'How do you feel about your daughter being trampled to death?'* invites an angry response of *'Bloody awful – how do you think I feel?'*

Don't ask the impossible. *'Why do you like sky-diving?'* will stump them. *'What is it that makes sky-diving so exciting?'* or *'What's the most frightening sky-dive you've ever done?'* will work.

Don't be afraid to ask for explanations. Far better to feel slightly ignorant in the interview than try to write later about something you don't understand.

Don't ask loaded questions based on your own opinion: they can backfire. *'You must think it's a disgrace'* may get the response *'What makes you think you know how I feel?'* Stay neutral. Use phrases like *'Some people might think...'*

Don't deliberately deceive, but equally you don't have to reveal everything you know. You can legitimately imply you have more information than you actually do.

Finally...

When you think you have covered everything, check through the lists you made beforehand for any essential details you have missed or questions you haven't asked.

Do a final recap. Go through the facts as you understand them. Your subject will correct you if you have got anything wrong, and maybe add some extra detail. Ask if there is anything else they would like to see in your story.

If you need to take pictures, now is the time to get the camera out or arrange for a photographer to call. Treat it as a routine operation – *'All we need now is a quick picture of you with your collection of cheese labels... have you got a favourite we can show the readers?'* – so they don't have much opportunity to object.

There may be other material you could use to illustrate your story. Ask if you can borrow any relevant photos. Try to get pictures showing people in action: holiday snaps of children playing are far better than static school line-ups. Promise to return them and make sure you do. Write the name of the subject, the date, and to whom it should be returned in pencil on the back.

Before you leave, hand over your business card and explain where they can contact you. Ask them where and when they will be available if you want to get in touch later. Afterwards, if you haven't recorded everything during the interview – perhaps because the subject was unhappy having their words recorded in front of them – write it up as soon as you can while it is still fresh in your memory. Notes written immediately after an interview are usually acceptable in court. The police do it all the time.

Reluctant interviewees

If you interview a public relations person about a new product you will be received with charm and possibly a free lunch. If you track down a confidence trickster you may have the door slammed in your face and will conduct the interview, if there is one, through the letter box. Between these two extremes there is a wide range of response.

Reluctance to be interviewed does not necessarily indicate that the person has something to hide. It may be that they believe they will derive no advantage from being interviewed. They may be keen on their privacy and view a reporter, however discreet, as intrusion. Many people are a little frightened by the media. You will often have to use your powers of persuasion and your approach will vary from case to case.

Salesmen say you should never ask a question that invites the answer no. Avoid *'I don't suppose you could tell me...'* because the easy reply could be *'Sorry, no.'* Attempt to appear confident that you will be listened to and your questions will be answered.

Be persistent. The longer you keep people talking the more likely you are to win their confidence and persuade them to agree. Even with a reluctant golden wedding couple, you can point out that their friends would be disappointed not to read about their anniversary. Don't become aggressive or give them cause for a complaint of rudeness or harassment.

With a person involved in controversy you can be more outspoken. If polite requests fail, you can point out that you already have in your notebook some viewpoints on the matter and that if the person you are approaching declines to comment his or her view will go by default. Or you can point out that you already have your information and are seeking confirmation. That may well provoke the person approached to say, *'No, it's not like that at all,'* and give a different version of events. If the person still refuses to comment, note the fact in your story. Otherwise readers will blame you for not giving a balanced account.

Halfway through interviewing the family of a 16-year-old athlete who had died suddenly, I asked precisely what had happened.

As the mother sobbed, the father leapt up and began staggering dramatically from the door to the sofa.

'He came in and was like this,' he told me, clutching his chest and twisting his face into a stage contortion of agony.

'Then he fell – like this,' he said, collapsing to the floor. 'Then he were twisting and turning, twisting and turning like this' (wails from family and friends) 'and then... that was it.'

He let out an awful, rattling gurgle, and lay still, his eyes staring into space.

I beat a hasty retreat.

ANTHONY LONGDEN
Managing editor
Newsquest,
Herts, Bucks & Middlesex

Be careful about your choice of language when talking to teenagers.

They will be affronted if you ask them for a child's point of view, for example: it is better to refer to them as young people.

Once into the interview, you may find the going difficult. The interviewee may be reluctant to answer a specific question. Don't be easily put off. Try re-phrasing the question. If that fails you can point out again that you can give the interviewee's side of the story only if he or she tells you.

In a difficult encounter it may be wise to keep the contentious questions, the ones they may well not want to answer, until last. By that stage you may have gained their confidence. If not, and they decide to halt the meeting, you have at least something in your notebook.

Interviewing children

Quotes from children can make good copy: refreshing, uninhibited, original, often funny. But be careful.

There is no reason why you should not do a vox pop among kids in the town centre about what they think of plans for yet another megaburger joint. However, the PCC Code of Conduct says you must have permission from parents (or guardians, teachers or other adults in

Smile as you speak on the phone, and nod in agreement when people respond.

They can't see it, but it shows through.

If you are being given a hard time by an interviewee on the phone, try standing up.

It is said to boost your confidence and add authority to your voice – though taking notes is not so easy.

ON AND OFF THE RECORD

You will come across people who say they will talk to you only if what they say is off the record or unattributed. There is a vital difference between these two, which not all interviewees (or reporters) appreciate.

Off the record is information you are offered on condition that it is not published.

It is very tempting to accept, but beware. You may learn something that you simply cannot ignore. You – or somebody else on your paper – may get and publish the same information later from another source, in which case your first informant will think that you have broken your promise to keep quiet and will probably never speak to you again.

If you are offered something off the record, make it very clear to them that this might happen. Be certain about what is covered. It is up to your subject to tell you if they want to go off the record, but if you have any doubt, check early in the interview with a positive 'I assume I'm okay to use this?'

If you promise not to publish something,

keep your word – and that means making sure nobody else knows, not even your news desk, which can be difficult.

Unattributed quotes are ones that your informant is willing to see published so long as the source is not revealed. Avoid them if you can. They raise doubts in your reader's mind about whether they are genuine, and once that happens they will wonder whether the rest of your story is authentic.

If your subject insists on anonymity, ask if they are prepared to be disguised as *an un-named source, a close colleague, a member of the council.*

If all else fails, ask if you can put them down as saying 'No comment', which can be revealing. Then ask if there is anyone else who might be prepared to speak and be named.

Occasionally you will face the problem of a naive interviewee who says at the end of an interview: 'Of course, this was all off the record.' You are not morally bound by this, but should think carefully about ignoring it if it means sacrificing a valuable contact.

charge of them) before you interview or photograph youngsters under 16 (under 18 if they are in local authority care) about anything affecting their welfare or that of any other child. The code is not keen on you interrupting them at school, and says you should not publish details of their private lives simply because their parents are in the news. You must not identify children who are victims or witnesses in sexual offence cases.

Treat children as equals and take their opinions seriously, but remember they are children. They don't always tell you the truth. They may lie deliberately because they think it is fun; they may tell you what they think you want to know because they are intimidated or anxious to please or reluctant to admit they don't know; they may simply be mistaken.

Death knocks

There will come a time (unless you are very lucky) when you will be sent out to interview the grieving relatives of someone who has just died. It is probably the worst job in journalism.

If the deceased person had reached a ripe old age and their death was not unexpected, it may not be too bad. But if you are going to meet the parents of a child killed in a horrific accident, you need to have your wits about you. The Code of Conduct urges sensitivity and discretion and will condemn unwarranted intrusion into grief.

This is one of the few times when phoning up to make an appointment may not be a good idea. The call may well be answered by someone whose instant reaction is to say they want nothing to do with the media and slam the phone down. If that happens, you are unlikely to get much further.

Get all the information you can up front. Name, age, address and the circumstances of the death should be available from the police. Check the files so you don't waste time asking for details you should already know.

There is no good time to call. Make sure it is not on the morning of the funeral. Try knocking on a neighbour's door first (choose the ones on the same side of the road so you are not seen). They may well be prepared to talk to you, especially if you tell them it will minimise distress to the family. If they are on good terms with the family, you might even be able to persuade them to accompany you nextdoor: arriving with someone familiar will make you more acceptable.

Your attitude is crucial: you must be serious, sympathetic, understanding, professional. Offer your condolences, explain why you need to talk to them: *'I'm so sorry to disturb you at a time like this, it must be dreadful for you... I wonder if I could just check a few facts...?'*

They might slam the door in your face, but you will be surprised how often they will welcome you. They are in shock, and having someone, anyone, to talk to is cathartic. They want reassurance that the dead person's life will be remembered, and that maybe it was not in vain. If

My first death knock was interviewing the parents of a little boy run over by a lorry.

I was so frightened and ill-prepared that I was physically sick on the way. But they were eager to see me. They wanted me to speak out in support of a local campaign to ban lorries taking shortcuts through the village, so that their son didn't die in vain.

It's my answer to accusations that reporters have no right to intrude on private grief.

PETER BARRON
Editor
The Northern Echo

👍 **Bear in mind, when emailing,** that many people are lax about computer security.

Your emails may be read by third parties, and you have no easy way of checking that the person replying to you is the person you think it is.

their child has died in an accident they may be angry or bitter, and seek publicity as a means of condemning those responsible (beware of libel) or at the very least making sure a similar tragedy does not happen again.

If they are reluctant, try explaining that *'we'd like to pay tribute to your son – he deserves the best we can do...'* and say you are sure everyone who knew him will want to read something about him. If it is a big story, you can point out gently that there will be other reporters arriving later (some from the nationals, perhaps) and it would be better to talk to you now than have to face all the others, who may not be as understanding as the local newspaper. You might give the impression

---

COULD HAVE DONE BETTER...

1. Phone rings

DAVIS: *Andrew Davis.*

REPORTER: *Hello, can I speak to Andrew Davis?*

DAVIS (thinks): *I just said who I was, are you deaf?*

2. Phone rings

DAVIS: *Andrew Davis.*

REPORTER: *Hello, can I talk to you about your lost giraffe?*

DAVIS (thinks): *Who is this? What's it got to do with you?*

3. Phone rings

DAVIS: *Andrew Davis.*

REPORTER: *Mr Davies, I'm Dave Hackett from the Gazette...*

DAVIS: *It's Davis. No E.*

REPORTER: *Yeah, that's what I said, Davies. About your giraffe...*

DAVIS (thinks): *If he can't even get my name right...*

4. Phone rings

DAVIS: *Andrew Davis.*

REPORTER: *Hi there, Andy, it's Dave Hackett from the Gazette here...*

DAVIS (thinks): *Never heard of him, but he calls me Andy, the presumptuous little –*

5. Phone rings

DAVIS: *Andrew Davis.*

REPORTER: *Hello, Dave Hackett from the Gazette here. It's about your lost giraffe...*

DAVIS: *Okay, how can I help you?*

REPORTER: *How old are you?*

DAVIS (thinks): *Hang on, what's that got to do with it?*

6. Interview on-going

REPORTER: *And are you married at all?*

DAVIS (thinks): *Eh? How can I be not all married? Prat.*

7. Interview on-going

REPORTER: *So do you do anything or are you too old to work?*

DAVIS (thinks): *Too old? I'm in the prime of life, you young –*

8. Interview on-going...

DAVIS (sobbing): *So you see, I'm totally devastated.*

REPORTER: *Really, what a great quote, that's terrific.*

DAVIS: *You heartless little –*

9. Interview ending

REPORTER: *Well, thanks, we'll send a photographer round.*

DAVIS: *Photographer? No one said anything about pictures, I'm not having that.*

10. Interview ending

REPORTER: *Just give us a bell if you hear anything, yeah?*

DAVIS (thinks): *No chance.*

that you will share your story with the others to keep them away, and you might even mean it.

If they resolutely refuse to talk to you, accept it. Don't harass them. Ask if you can come back later at a better time, or if there is someone else from the family you could talk to.

If they are willing to see you, question them as gently as possible. Let them talk and encourage reminiscences. Ask if there is anything your newspaper can do to help (unlikely, but they will appreciate the offer). Suggest they choose their favourite picture of the dead person to go in the newspaper. Exit with more sympathy.

Remember to ask about the funeral – when, where, any special arrangements (are colleagues forming a guard of honour? will they play the departed's favourite songs?), who is going (are relatives flying in from Australia?), and who is officiating.

PHONE INTERVIEWS

MUCH of the advice above about face-to-face interviews applies equally to interviews conducted on the phone, but in the absence of visual contact, your voice becomes even more important. Your subject has to be persuaded from the start that you are someone worth talking to. You have got to sound friendly, courteous, articulate, on the ball and professional.

Timing can be important. If you want people to spend time talking to you, avoid phone calls at the start of the working day, when people are checking their post and emails and generally sorting themselves out, or at the end, when the last thing they want is the phone ringing for the umpteenth time that day. That said, it is worth bearing in mind that in many businesses, especially smaller ones, the boss gets in before the rest of the staff and stays back later in the evening – and you may catch him or her then. Don't ring people late at night without very good reason.

Be very well prepared, your list of questions beside your notebook. You can't afford gaps while you ponder what to say next, because they will wonder if you have rung off. Don't waste time on small talk. Get straight to the point.

On the phone people tend not to talk but to answer questions, giving you responses rather than statements. As well as their answers, write down your questions or at least an identifying key word or two, or you may be unable to remember them when you come to write your story.

Listen very carefully, to be sure of what is being said. You can't see them. Be alert for jokes or ironic responses: if in doubt, check that they really mean it.

Check spellings. Some letters – S and F, M and N, for example – sound very similar over the phone.

Persevere, even if you think you are making a hash of it. Unless you are being downright rude to them, few people will actually put the phone down on you.

> *Never take an umbrella with you on a death-knock, no matter how hard it's raining.*
>
> *They're more likely to let you in if you look like a drowned rat.*
>
> **DAVID SUMMERS**
> Editor-in-chief
> Bucks Herald

Contacts suggestion: railway employees. Station staff know about accidents and other incidents, and when security is tightened because of terrorist threats or the arrival of big-name politicians.

Do an annual check on the most unusual item of lost property – and do the same at the bus station and every cinema and theatre in town.

EMAIL INTERVIEWS

THESE are useful if you are seeking answers to factual questions. You can take your time planning your questions and you don't have to think on your feet; equally, your subject may feel happier about responding thoughtfully via the keyboard rather than having to give an instant reply on the phone.

What they do tell you can be easily copied into your story, saving you typing time and avoiding transcription errors. There is no chance of you being accused of misquoting what they have sent in an email.

Emails are less productive if you are after analysis or good quotes: you can't develop your subjects' answers or lead them into saying things off the top of their head that, with reflection, they might not have said. Emails take time. There is no guarantee people will read them or reply straight away (or at all) and you can't follow up what they say without sending further emails and awaiting further replies. More effective are two-stage interviews – an email first, with initial questions breaking the ice, followed by a phone call to expand and clarify what you are told.

Eight
THE UNEXPECTED

ROUTINE diary assignments make up a lot of your life as a trainee reporter. Every so often, though, there comes the unexpected breaking story that tests your ability to think quickly, plan effectively and operate under pressure.

Some people describe all these as 'off-diary' stories, because they cannot be forecast. Others restrict the term to items that reporters find for themselves. This chapter takes a generous view and covers stories which have not been on the diary, whether they are hard news breaks or human interest stories, originating from the newsdesk or the result of a reporter's own initiative.

- Major incidents
- Weather stories
- Phoning copy
- Human interest

MAJOR INCIDENTS

AT the top of the scale are terrorist attacks, air disasters, earthquakes and riots, events of such magnitude that it is very unlikely you will come across them on a local newspaper, let alone have to handle them on your own (though one day, if you move up the career ladder and become a news editor, you will be expected to coordinate such coverage).

Incidents that you may well encounter include accidents (fires, motorway pile-ups, train derailments, drownings), crime (murders, rapes, robberies, bank raids, armed sieges) and searches (people missing at sea, on mountains, underground). Information about them may come from routine calls or tip-offs from the public. Reporting them may include actually witnessing the incident – a fire, a siege, a rescue attempt, for instance. In other cases, such as traffic accidents, it is a matter of getting to the scene afterwards and obtaining eye-witness accounts of what happened.

In a large office you may be one of a team handling news breaks like these; in a smaller organisation it may be up to you to cover them from start to finish. It can be daunting. Look upon it as a challenge.

FIRST

Phone the police and/or other emergency services to get a general picture of what has happened. Then let your newsdesk know about it. They may well want a story straight away if deadlines are looming, or a summary to put on the website as breaking news.

Always be alert for the unexpected. A reporter of mine sent to interview an 'adult' film star was very nervous and unsure about the line of questioning, and it would have been very easy for him to miss the local councillor sneaking out of the building just as he arrived – but thankfully he didn't.

ANDY DOWNIE
Editor
East Wales Weeklies

The media are sometimes used as the channel for warnings about bombs, product contamination and other threats to public safety.

Most organisations have established procedures for dealing with such calls.

It is vital, if you receive one, that you record fully what is said (it may include a coded message to demonstrate authenticity) and inform your newsdesk and the police immediately.

They will advise whether calls should be taken seriously.

If they are hoaxes, the media usually refuse to publish details unless they result in major public disruption.

Even then, they tend to be referred to as security alerts rather than hoaxes.

You may be expected to treat it as a running story – producing an initial version and then updating it regularly with fresh information and a revised intro.

Have a clear idea how you are going to tackle the story. Make a quick checklist of what you need to know. Most incidents have past, present and future angles. You need to cover what has gone before (any similar incidents or warnings), what is happening now (who, what, where, when and so on), and what will happen next (the effect on the public, inquiries, reaction).

If you have time, check the files for background: it may save you asking questions about information already available. But your main priority is getting to the scene while things are still happening. Make sure you have your phone, camera and press card with you.

On the scene

Find the person in charge: a senior police or fire officer. Press officers may be around to help, and they know you have questions that need answers. If they can't or won't speak straight away, ask for a press conference at the earliest opportunity.

Don't get in the way of the emergency services or waste time asking police officers, firefighters or ambulance personnel what is going on. They won't have an overview of the situation and will almost certainly be forbidden to talk to the media.

Talk to survivors, eye-witnesses, neighbours. Ask how the alarm was raised, what they saw happen, who was involved, how they felt at the time and feel now. You need facts about the drama and plenty of colourful quotes to go with them.

If you are talking to friends or relatives of people killed or injured, be sensitive to their needs and feelings. Remember the code of conduct's strictures on intrusion into grief or shock.

Keep in regular touch with your newsdesk, especially if you are providing copy for immediate website use.

DON'T LAY THE BLAME

Beware of reporting eye-witness claims about anyone or anything being to blame for an accident or fire.

They can't possibly know for certain, and it might be legally very dangerous to repeat their allegations if they are defamatory or if court cases are a possibility in the future.

Police and fire officers will be wary of attributing blame, too.

By all means ask police if they think bad weather caused a pile-up, for example, or fire officers whether they suspect arson, and if they say they do, report it.

If they merely say it is one possibility of several they are investigating, the best you can say is that they have not ruled it out.

Sources of information

Police will have details of timing, casualties, vehicles, damage, who raised the alarm and traffic disruption. They may make appeals for witnesses and release pictures or CCTV footage. There may be a special incident room and hotline numbers for anxious relatives or witnesses to call.

The fire service will tell you about the number of officers and appliances attending, the equipment used, rescue operations and difficulties. They may suggest the possible cause of a fire or issue warnings to the public about how to avoid further incidents.

The ambulance service will have details of its people and vehicles, doctors and paramedics on the scene, whether an air ambulance was called in, how many casualties have been taken to hospital, how many have been treated on the spot.

Hospitals will give details of deaths, injuries and the latest condition of patients. If there are many people affected, press officers will release regular casualty lists and bulletins on victims' progress.

Property owners may tell you the extent of damage to property, estimates of the cost of repairs, anything destroyed of special value (financial or personal), whether they were insured.

Motoring organisations (AA, RAC) will add details about traffic problems; rail and bus operators will know about disruption to public transport.

Writing it up

Go for the human angle – how many dead, how many injured, how many saved – before telling readers about damage to property or disruption to traffic.

It may be difficult in the early stages of a major incident to get accurate figures of how many are dead and injured. Don't guess. If police tell you eight bodies have been found and six people are still missing, say *At least eight died*. If they hold out little hope of more survivors being found, say *Fourteen are feared dead*.

You may well have problems getting victims' names. Police will not release them until next of kin have been informed. By all means try to find out from other, authoritative sources – relatives, friends, neighbours, workmates – but check thoroughly and consult your newsdesk before you put them in your story.

Follow-ups

There should be plenty of these. You may be able to get interviews with survivors in hospital. The cause may be announced and prosecutions launched. There will be reaction from individuals, politicians and pressure groups, calling for inquiries or improved safety. If people have died, there will be funerals and inquests.

Those magic moments never go quite as you expect. Early in my career, leaving the pub one lunchtime after deadline, I couldn't help but notice that the Alexandra Palace, on the doorstep of my London patch, was on fire. I dashed back to the office and phoned the printers in faraway Nuneaton to issue the breathless command: 'Stop The Press!'

They told me not to be so silly.

JOHN FRANCIS
Group editor
Bedfordshire Newspapers

I was sent to report a children's party, and ended the day at Leatherslade Farm – the Great Train Robbers' hideout had been discovered that afternoon. What a start for a trainee reporter!

JOHN CHIPPERFIELD
Assistant editor
Oxford Mail

People may remember you if you do a good job... but they'll remember you even more if you do a bad one.

Contacts suggestion: estate agents. Get them to tip you off about newsworthy properties coming on the market before their ad appears in your newspaper: they'll welcome the free publicity. You want to know about celebs looking for property in your area, too.

If you ask some non-journalists for information 'for a story', they think you're planning a work of fiction.

It sometimes helps if you say you are 'writing an article' instead.

WEATHER STORIES

HEATWAVES, floods, snow-storms and force-ten gales: they come round year after year and are reported, especially if they bring chaos to readers' lives.

If the weather is a big enough story, several reporters on a large newspaper may be assigned to cover it; if you are working on a weekly, you may be asked to work alone to produce a round-up of everything that has happened.

There will probably be more to it than you expect. Here is a checklist for the day blizzards sweep across your area: the list can be adapted for other severe weather conditions: just swap sun-cream for wellies and dried-up lakes for frozen ones.

First

Monitor local radio and television stations and internet news sites for the latest situation.

Contact emergency services – police, fire service, ambulance, coast-guards, mountain rescue. Find out about accidents, blocked roads, stranded villages, damaged or fallen buildings. There may be an appeal to people to stay at home. Contact the Army, Royal Navy or RAF if they may be involved in rescue operations and airlifts.

Phone hospitals if people have been injured.

Then

Work your way through all the other possible sources of information, thinking about picture possibilities all the time:

Stranded communities: Contact them for human interest stories. Try the post office, the village shop, the pub, the garage, the vicar.

Transport: Find out what is happening on the roads (AA, RAC), buses, trains, air, river and sea. Check the council about plans for road clearance operations.

Power: Contact those responsible for electricity, gas, water and sewage. Is there advice to consumers about using power or coping without it? What should people do about electric cables lying in the road, broken gas supplies or frozen pipes? Are there standpipes or other supplies of emergency drinking water? Is there reassurance for pensioners worried about heating bills?

Communications: Find out whether phones have been affected (landlines and mobile networks), and whether television and radio transmissions have been hit. Check if your own newspaper can be delivered (don't slow down if it isn't, though: there's the website to keep up-to-date). Is the post getting through or are postmen stranded? What about other delivery companies?

Industry: How are employers coping? Have people got to work, and if so, how? Anyone sledging in or using skis? Have low temperatures affected materials, machines or other production processes? Are orders and deliveries affected?

Agriculture: Contact the National Farmers' Union (NFU). How badly have farmers been hit? What about lost sheep and ruined crops? Check fish farms (are they frozen over?) and forestry (how many trees have been destroyed?)

Shops: Are they open? Is there a rush to buy anything – bread, shovels, wellies?

Schools: Have any been closed? Are there heating problems? Are teachers and/or pupils missing? Have they been sent home? Have exams been cancelled? Contact schools direct and the LEA.

Hospitals: Make another check, this time to see how the weather has affected them: have doctors and nurses made it in, or have operations been delayed or suspended?

Hotels: Have they been hit? Any stranded guests?

What's on: Or off? Have shows, sports events and other meetings been cancelled? Have a look at the listings in the latest issue of your newspaper and phone round organisers. They may want to announce that events have been abandoned – or tell the public things are still on.

Weathermen: Why did it happen? When did it last happen? Will it happen again and when? Did they expect it (and if not, why not?) Is it all the fault of global warming? Ask local amateur forecasters as well as the official meteorologists.

PHONING COPY

IF you are covering an on-going incident, such as a rescue operation or a siege, you may be expected to stay on the scene and send your story from there. There is plenty of technology about to make this possible.

There may come an occasion, however, when time pressures, physical constraints or technological problems mean you have to resort to phoning your copy directly to the newsdesk, another reporter, or someone employed specifically to do this (known as a copytaker). Mobile phones don't work everywhere. Before they and computers took over, dictating stories from a call-box was often the only way reporters could get them in before deadline, and many newspapers employed one or more copytakers fulltime; some newspapers still have them. If you end up working as a freelance or for a news agency, filing copy to a number of publications with which you have no established electronic link, you may have to use them.

This section explains how to phone copy through. If you think you might have to do this (and unless you have a very uneventful life as a reporter, one day you will), learn them. Copytakers are notoriously short-tempered and suffer fools irascibly. Before you reach for the phone:

One day there will be a really big story – the death of a prime minister or a crash killing hundreds – and you will be tempted to try too hard.

The best single tip I ever had was when I was asked to do a 'funny' and struggled too hard to make an effect.

The news editor came over with my copy, dropped it on my desk, and said: 'Just tell the story'.

Just tell the story. President Kennedy was assassinated in Dallas yesterday. Princess Diana died yesterday after a car crash in Paris.

BRIAN MACARTHUR
Former Assistant editor
The Times

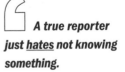

A true reporter just __hates__ not knowing something.

RICHARD DAVIES
Night editor
The Northern Echo

Go through your notes numbering each main point and highlighting each good quote.

Cross out stuff you definitely won't use.

Transcribe any shorthand outlines that may baffle you later.

Decide on your intro and write it out beforehand, in readable shorthand.

Work out exactly how your story is going to be structured, because you can't cut-and-paste over the phone (and even if you could, the copytakers wouldn't do it).

Then dial. There are conventions for dictating copy to make sure the recipient knows what you want to say and avoid all the errors latent in telephoned conversation:

Start off with your name, where you are based, who the story should be sent to, and your catchline: *Tim Hacking, Midthorpe. For Telegraph newsdesk. Catchline: Hotel.*

Dictate your story clearly at a pace the copytaker can cope with: half a dozen words at a time, no more. The copytaker will indicate when they are ready for more.

Indicate all punctuation and announce each new paragraph: *Rescue workers are battling through the remains of a hotel which collapsed [comma] killing at least one person [comma] after fire swept through it early today [fullstop, new par].*

Warn the copytaker of any proper names needing capitals and spell out any words that need clarification. Some letters of the alphabet sound much the same over the phone – F and S, for example, and M and N – and mistakes are easily made. If you know the official way to do this (see the panel below), all the better: *The Easton Hotel [that's Cap E for Echo – A – S for Sierra – T for Tango – O – N for November Cap H for Hotel] went up in flames just after midnight [full stop, new par].*

Make sure all figures are recorded accurately: repeat them numeral by numeral because many sound much the same – five and nine, for instance, or 13 and 30: *More than 40 [that's four-zero] residents were led to safety before the building [comma] built only last year at a cost of [pound sign] 17 [that's one-seven] million [comma] caved in [full stop, new par].*

TANGO-ROMEO-YANKEE THIS

The phonetic alphabet used by most emergency services goes like this:

Alpha-Bravo-Charlie-Delta-Echo-Foxtrot-Golf-Hotel-India-Juliet-Kilo-Lima-Mike-November-Oscar-Papa-Quebec-Romeo-Sierra-Tango-Uniform-Victor-Whisky-Xray-Yankee-Zulu.

Knowing this is useful in all sorts of situations. It not only keeps copytakers happy but impresses police if you use it when making the calls and comes in very handy for pub quizzes, as well.

Copy it into your contacts book: you never know when it will come in handy.

Indicate where quotes start and end: *Chief Inspector Alan [one L: A-L-A-N] Clarke [with an E: C-L-A-R-K-E] said [colon, open quotes] It's [that's with an apostrophe] a disaster area [fullstop, end quotes, new par].*

It looks horrific in print like that, but it works and the rules are well worth learning. Practice one quiet afternoon, using a tape recorder or reading to a colleague. If you don't, the first time you try it in real life you will make an almighty hash of your story and maybe undo all the good work you have achieved up to then.

HUMAN INTEREST STORIES

HUMAN interest is a term that sometimes puzzles new reporters. Surely, they say, almost every news story worth the name involves people as its subject matter or as its readers. They have a point. A story full of dry facts with no mention of human beings and nothing in it to arouse anyone's emotions is a poor story indeed.

We use 'human interest' as a convenient title for stories which fall somewhere between hard news, which is immediate, fact-based and tightly written, and features, which are timeless, descriptive and written in softer, more colourful language.

Sometimes the distinction between hard news, human interest and features is blurred, and one story can produce all three. If a report is published revealing that hundreds of children die each year for lack of kidney donors, that is hard news; an analysis of how and why donorship has declined over the past ten years is a feature; the plight of one five-year old on dialysis, desperately seeking a donor, makes the human interest story.

This is the distinguishing mark of such stories: a focus on the life of an individual human being (or a small group of them) rather than on events affecting people as a whole. They have been described as 'people journalism' and their rise in popularity – there are far more of them around today than a generation ago – has run parallel with a general move by many newspapers towards a softer, more caring, life-style approach to what they publish, inspired not least by a belated recognition that women form a vital part of their readership.

Human interest stories are often about ordinary people. They highlight their dramas, hopes, fears and achievements, satisfying our curiosity about how the rest of the world behave and think and feel. They are tales of adversity and triumph, kindness and bravery, care and compassion, despair and delight, unashamedly arousing emotional reaction from their readers. At their best they are inspirational, bringing lumps to the throats of thousands.

They don't have to be grim reading. Many are light-hearted, even jokey, dealing with the quirks, foibles, false hopes and failures of ordinary men and women. They may be far more entertaining than informative. They end up at the bottom of the front page or tagged on to the end of news bulletins, gentle relief from the more serious news which has gone before.

Human interest stories and great pictures are what make papers sing and if this could be drummed into trainees it would be great.

Some of them see it straight away, but those who don't need to know stories are not about councils or courts or hospitals, they are about the people in them.

GRAEME HUSTON
Editor-in-chief
South Yorkshire
Newspapers

Always write what you see – paint a picture with words.

IAN MURRAY
Editor-in-chief
Southern Daily Echo

👍 *Never be afraid to make a complete idiot of yourself in front of an interviewee or colleagues by asking the simplest questions.*

You'll look even more stupid if you get it wrong in print.

👍 *Scots are people, scotch is what you drink. If it's Scottish scotch, it's spelt whisky. If it's from Ireland, the United States or anywhere else it should be whiskey, though not all foreign producers take much notice of this.*

👍 *Contacts suggestion: Weather monitors. There are amateur meteorologists dotted all over the country, feeding daily statistics about sunshine, rainfall, wind strength and other matters to the Met Office. Persuade them to let you know when you've just had the hottest, wettest or windiest month on record.*

Human interest stories can, of course, be about the famous or notorious. The tabloids thrive on them. It usually means stories about sex, for which the public has an apparently insatiable appetite: there can never, it seems, be enough scandal about erring politicians and three-in-a-bed celebrities.

Sometimes such stories are no more than voyeuristic invasions of privacy, written purely to titillate and sell newspapers; but at their best they are worthwhile journalism, exposing the pompous and the hypocritical.

Keep your eyes open

Some human interest stories will be handed to you on a plate by the newsdesk, but you will be expected to find many of your own. News editors hope that you will come in every morning with at least one story or picture idea. Almost everyone has a story to tell. It's just up to you to find it. How?

Look for them wherever you go. You will see possibilities all around you – notices in shop windows, advertisements in the newspaper, people in the pub, neighbours with odd hobbies or homes or pets.

Look for the human interest angle in every hard news story you cover. Ask yourself how it affects people and whether you can find someone to tell you about their individual experience.

Ask yourself how dry reports or sets of figures could be humanised. Find the victims, the battling parents, the people who are better off, worse off, celebrating and in despair.

Identify human interest possibilities when you are writing features. You may come across people with a fascinating story to tell which can be used on the news pages.

Human interest stories should be written less aggressively than hard news. You can use slow, scene-setting intros, bring in a lot more description, let the quotes flow, and use more colourful language. They remain, however, news stories rather than features, though the dividing line between the two is sometimes a fine one.

Don't forget the pictures. The best words in the world about someone fighting valiantly against crippling odds won't tug quite as hard on readers' heartstrings as a photo of them smiling bravely on despite it all.

Nine

SHAPING THE STORY

YOU'VE got your story, checked the facts, collected some quotes, and told the newsdesk it is on its way. Now you have to turn it into something people will want to read or hear. This chapter looks at how you organise your material for publication in a newspaper.

- Story length
- Angles and Intros
- Story structure

How much?

The first thing you need to know, of course, is what is required of you. Ask the newsdesk how long a story they expect. They may tell you to *'give it what it's worth'*, which is a mixed blessing. It's good because you have flexibility and don't have to keep a constant eye on the length; a problem because the newsdesk or subs may disagree with your judgement of *'what it's worth'*, in which case the story will get cut (making some of your effort a waste of time) or you will be asked to add to it at the last minute (an irritation when you are busy on something else or just heading out for lunch).

More likely the newsdesk will suggest a length. This will probably be a number of words (*'make it about 250'*). You will soon learn how much screen space is taken up by stories of different lengths. When you first start work it is worth experimenting on your computer so you can gauge exactly where you are when you are typing up.

COLS, CEMS AND PARS

You may be asked to calculate your story length in columns (*'give us a single-col'*) or measures (*'around 20 cems'*) or paragraphs (*'four pars will do'*).

If so, you need to translate this into words so you can check what you write against the word count.

Columns and centimetres are easy enough to work out: just add up the number of words in a typical column-length story in your newspaper or how many you get to the average centimetre.

Paragraphs are not so simple. A paragraph can be as long or short as its creator wants it to be. Serious broadsheets run paragraphs many sentences long; brash tabloids make every sentence a new par.

Find out how your newspaper uses paragraphs. Don't simply write for as long as you feel like it and then just split your story into the number of paragraphs you have been asked for.

Each paragraph should ideally be a logical, self-contained section dealing with one element of the story – a new quote or a fresh piece of information. Like this one.

Whatever measurement system your newspaper uses, be grateful you are not working in the dark days of typewriters when reporters had to calculate story length without the aid of a computerised word count.

👍 *If you're doing a write-off for the front page, don't bore your readers by simply repeating the first paragraph of your story.*

Use that for the write-off and re-word it for inside.

How many?

Check that you are expected to produce just one piece of copy. Some newspapers routinely split long stories into two, a main piece and a second one, called a sidebar, dealing with another angle. It may be that some element of your story would be best presented as a separate panel – a brief biography of the central characters, perhaps, *('Who's Who...')*, a fact box *('Ten things you didn't know about...')* or a table of statistics *('What your councillors claimed in expenses')*. By all means suggest splitting your story into two sections (or more) if you think it might work.

In addition to your story, you may be asked to do an additional abbreviated version summing up the main points (known as a write-off) for use on the front page. This may be just one paragraph for use in a column of similar write-offs (sometimes known as tasters or teasers) encouraging readers to look inside for more detail. It may be several paragraphs long if, for example, your main story is the strongest of the day but too long to fit on the front page. In a case such as this your write-off becomes the lead story and is cross-referenced to your original story spread across one or more pages inside.

Check your deadline. The best story in the world is no use if it is still half-written on your screen when the newspaper goes to press.

Find out, if there are pictures to go with your story, whether you are expected to produce captions.

Make a plan

Once you know what is expected of you and how much time you have to do it, open up a new file (there is guidance on presentation later in this chapter) but resist the temptation to start typing straight away. However tight your deadline, spend some time marshalling your thoughts and planning your story.

👍 *Take an interest in the stories your colleagues are working on.*

You may have knowledge you can pass on, or they may be doing a story that links with yours.

Or you might both be unwittingly working on the same story...

Few journalists would swap today's technology for the phone kiosks and typewriters of yesterday. But the methods of the past had one advantage: they forced reporters to plan the whole of their stories before they started to write. There was no cut-and-paste if they changed their mind halfway through typing onto paper: they just had to tear it up and start again. If they were dictating their story over the phone, copytakers under pressure flatly refused to change things just because the reporter suddenly decided the intro could be better phrased and the second and third pars should be transposed. It forced reporters to have a clear vision of how their story should be, and that was no bad thing.

Now that we have computers, too many reporters leap straight to the keyboard, confident in the knowledge that they can change things at the touch of a key. Cutting and pasting wastes time and invites errors and omissions. Facts get out of sequence, names appear out of the blue, and story structure disintegrates. Make a plan and know roughly what you are going to say before you start.

Go through all your notes. Cross out all the rubbish you thought might be useful but now clearly isn't: you don't want to be reading it time and again. You are going to have to be selective, because you won't have space for everything. For each bit of information, ask yourself whether anyone is really going to be interested in it. Don't include it just because you have it, however much effort it took.

Highlight the best quotes so you can find them again easily. Transcribe any tortuous shorthand outlines you recognise now but might not be able to decipher in 20 minutes' time. You might type out one or two quotes while they are fresh in your mind, to be cut and pasted into your story later.

Don't embark on a full transcription of everything in your notebook. It is a waste of time writing down masses of material that won't be used, and it will take so long you may not get your story written in time.

Do make a rough list of what should go in your story and decide how you are going to approach the story (the angle), what is going to go in your opening paragraph (the intro, probably just a single sentence), and in what order you are going to deal with the rest.

ANGLES

DECIDING how to approach many stories is not too difficult. Nobody had any doubts when Diana died in a Paris underpass or hijacked planes hit the Twin Towers. It isn't, however, always that obvious. Even the most experienced reporters sometimes find it difficult to choose which angle to go on.

The choice

Occasionally the problem may be deciding how to interpret the story as a whole. If the bank rate goes up, is that *Good news for investors* or *Bad news for borrowers*? If council tax goes up, is that a *Blow for struggling pensioners* or a *Boost for local services*?

Sometimes these judgements will be made for you by your newsdesk. If you are working on a national, they may be determined by your newspaper's political stance. A by-election result will be a cause for celebration by one newspaper, a source of despair for another; a decision to let a controversial asylum-seeker stay in the country will be heralded as a victory for liberal commonsense by some, a proof of national decline by others.

More likely, it will be up to you to make the choice between two or more distinct elements, each of them a legitimate angle. Something dramatic happens, and there are significant consequences. Which do you concentrate on first of all?

Suppose 200 people die when the wings fall off a jet, and airlines cancel all flights for week while the cause is investigated. The crash will make excellent reading, full of drama and heartbreak. But airports at a standstill and millions of people stranded is strong stuff too.

> *Make sure everything you write is balanced – and that doesn't mean adding a paragraph of denial on the end of 14 paragraphs of claims and accusations.*
>
> **PETER BARRON**
> Editor
> The Northern Echo

> *When considering whether a story is fair and balanced, ask yourself how you would feel if the story was referring to you.*
>
> *Have you been treated fairly by the reporter and the article?*
>
> **DAVID JACKMAN**
> Editor
> Newsquest West Essex

STEW MUCH TO COPE WITH

Faced with a multiplicity of possible angles, there is a temptation to bung them all together into an Irish stew of an intro, mentioning a bit of everything in the hope that everybody sampling it finds something to their taste:

The leader of Midthorpe's ruling Mad Hatters Party yesterday announced wide-ranging plans to re-introduce public floggings, ban pedestrians from the city centre, give free cocaine to under-fives, make nudity compulsory on Fridays and replace Bonfire Night with a mass orgy in the cathedral...

It's far more than anyone can take in one go – and it still leaves you with the problem of where you go next. Chickening out and avoiding all the possibilities by going for a round-up story along the lines of *Midthorpe council leaders yesterday announced wide-ranging proposals affecting everyone in town* will send your readers to sleep.

You could and would get both angles in the intro *(Air travellers faced chaos last night after a jumbo jet broke in two)* but after that you would have to decide whether to focus on the drama of the crash or the massive disruption it had caused.

Which would grab your readers' attention the most? Easy if the plane was full of Britons and crashed in Manchester (you would go for the first) or if the victims were all from far-away countries and died somewhere obscure on the other side of the world (the second). It might be harder to decide, though, if there were a dozen Brits involved and the plane came down over Sweden.

Similar choices have to be made on many lesser stories. Plans are announced for a massive new supermarket in the centre of town: is that *Big savings for shoppers* or a *Death-blow for small traders*? The council refuses planning permission for the football club to hold weekly rock concerts: is that a *Crisis blow for cash-strapped club* or a *Triumph for protesting neighbours*? Maternity services at a small town hospital are transferred elsewhere: do you concentrate on the greater efficiency and cost-saving this is supposed to bring, or on the problems faced by expectant mothers with further to travel?

At a much more mundane level, you might cover a golden wedding and discover that the couple first met as rivals in a holiday camp talent contest, that their only child is flying back from Antarctica, and that they attribute the success of their marriage to a mutual passion for cheese. All three angles are possible, but you have to start with one and deal with the others later.

The audience

The choice may be dictated by your audience. If a pharmaceutical company in Midthorpe announces the discovery of a dirt-cheap and effective alternative to Viagra, the *Financial Times* is likely to emphasise the effect on the company's profits and shareholders' dividends while the

Sun has fun with the new lease of sex-life it promises wrinkly readers. Meanwhile, the *Midthorpe Telegraph* may angle its story on the number of new jobs created to cope with soaring demand for the product.

The timing

Sometimes your choice of angle is limited by your timescale. If lightning strikes someone sheltering on a golf course the day before you publish, you don't have to be in the running for a Reporter of the Year award to work out that *Golfer killed by lightning bolt* is a better way to approach your story than *Club's hope of county mixed foursomes trophy is dented by tragedy.* But if you are working on a weekly and your story will not be coming out for another five days, the odds are that by then your audience will already have heard about the incident from other sources and you will be expected to come up with a fresh angle.

You would probably still decide the club's trophy hopes were a pretty poor choice, but there would be alternatives: other players who escaped death, family tributes to the one who died, golfers massing for the funeral, or the golf club's decision to cut down every tree on the course to stop it ever happening again.

If in doubt about the angle, don't be afraid to ask for advice: far better than having to re-write it later or, worse, having it rewritten for you by a sub in a hurry. Make sure that, whatever you choose, the other angles are included later in your story.

Having made your choice, the next task is to decide is roughly what is going to go where. There are no absolute rules about this, and the way you put your story together may be affected by whether it is hard news or soft, serious or light-hearted. Most news stories, however, follow a familiar pattern.

STORY STRUCTURE

ONE of the first things new reporters have to recognise is the world of difference between the way works of fiction are put together and the way we write news stories.

Novels, short stories and even jokes are a bit like arranged marriages. The people involved are introduced; there is a gradual exploration of their characters and actions; then comes a detailed chronology of events; finally there is the climax when all is revealed. News stories are very different. They are the one-night-stands of the writing world, passionate affairs in which the climax comes first, the details follow later (if at all).

News stories come in sections like a novel, but in a different order. First is the intro, short and sharp, containing the latest, most important and attention-grabbing information. Next comes elaboration, a mention of other important angles and the best of the quotes. Below that is the chronology

> **What makes a good reporter?**
>
> **R**eaders:
> Remember who you are writing for.
>
> **E**xpression:
> Set the tone by words and phrases.
>
> **P**ix:
> Think about them before you write.
>
> **O**rder:
> Structure your story.
>
> **R**eadability:
> Make your copy flow.
>
> **T**reatment:
> Discuss the style with the newsdesk.
>
> **E**xtras:
> Don't forget the follow-ups.
>
> **R**ight:
> Make sure it's all accurate.
>
> **STEVE SINGLETON**
> Supplements editor
> Blackpool Gazette

and detail of what has happened or been said. Last of all come the loose ends, anything else you think worth mentioning, in descending order of importance. Readers get the main facts first and can skip the rest if they are in a hurry. Subs trying to save space can chop the story from the end, confident that they are losing nothing vital.

Pyramids and posers

One much-quoted way of looking at this sectional structure suggests that you imagine your story as an upsidedown ('inverted') pyramid, a triangle standing on its point. The wide bit at the top is supposed to be the intro, the narrow bit at the bottom the left-overs.

Not everyone finds this an easy concept. Literally-minded trainees have been known to object that the base of a pyramid is the big boring bit nobody sees because it is underground, while the pointy part – short, sharp and, well, pointy – is the bit you look at straight away. If, they argue, the bit at the bottom is cut out by the subs because it is the least important, the whole thing would fall over. You may prefer to visualise the pyramid the right way up, or choose another analogy. Some see a story as a pile of building blocks; others have likened it to a train: driving force at the front, VIPs in first class close behind, standard passengers next, a couple of parcels vans bringing up the rear ready to be left behind if necessary.

You don't have to have a picture at all, of course. Another way of looking at how a story is put together is to see it as posing a series of questions and answers. You write your intro and ask yourself how the reader would react and what they would want to know next. Then you tell them, raising fresh questions that you go on to answer, and so on till everything has been explained. A bit like this:

A Midthorpe schoolgirl is flying across the world for a night out with chart-topping mega-group Desert Penguins.

Reader: Lucky girl. Do I know her? How did she manage that?

Gemma Gumley, 17, won the dream trip in a fanzine competition.

Reader: Dream trip? What's going to happen?

She will stay in a five-star hotel on the group's exclusive Caribbean island, be wined and dined by all five Penguins, and then dance the night away with the star of her choice.

Reader: And all she had to do was enter a competition?

Gemma, a sixth-former at Midthorpe Comprehensive, came first out of 12,000 contestants challenged to guess the group's combined weight.

Reader: I'll bet she's over the moon.

'I'm over the moon,' said Gemma after hearing the news yesterday at her home in Grimsdyke Close, Midthorpe...

And so on. Try it.

AND BUT SO NOW AND MEANWHILE

There is a tabloid variation of the question-and-answer approach, called Consequences after a Victorian parlour game in which players write consecutive sentences that, put together at the end, reveal a story.

This version anticipates minimal reader reaction and assumes they have to be dragged from point to point:

Pop Idol Wayne Bucket is splitting up with his wife Jolene after eight turbulent years.

Yeah?

And last night she launched a multi-million divorce suit against him.

Uh-huh?

But the star said he would fight her every inch of the way.

And?

And he added that he would be demanding custody of children Gozo and Dandelion.

So?

Now lawyers for both sides are preparing for a long legal battle.

Uh-huh?

Meanwhile, Wayne is due to start a nationwide concert tour next week.

Problem?

But fans fear he may have to cancel...

Note the need to rely heavily on link-words (*and, but, now, meanwhile*).

And think how tedious it would be if every story in a newspaper was written like this.

Whatever way you imagine a story being structured, the message is the same: the most important information comes first, the least last.

THE INTRO

YOUR intro is the moment in this literary love affair with your readers when your eyes meet theirs across a crowded room and – if it works – tell them instantly that this is the start of something irresistibly good.

It has to be exciting, urgent, tantalising, full of promise. You have only seconds to sell yourself before they turn elsewhere, and they almost certainly will if your opening sentence fails to grab their attention. They might possibly read on past a poor intro if the headline is intriguing, the subject matter is close to their heart, or there simply isn't anything better for them to do, but most of the time what goes in the first paragraph of your story is vital.

With a straightforward hard news story, choosing what to include in the intro should not normally be a problem. If five people die in a house fire and you are the first to report it, there is unlikely to be much question about what goes in: *Five people died when fire swept through their home this morning.* Everything else – rescue attempts, other people injured, damage to the building, disruption to traffic, the cause of the fire, neighbours' tearful tributes to the dead, plans for funerals and inquests – will come later. But it is not always that easy.

Here come the Ws

Take a simple story about a man dying in a car accident. The intro could just be:

What happened: *A man has died in a car crash.* That's not enough, though. It could be any man, anywhere, any time. We need more. Maybe:

Who, if the victim is someone well-known or there is something about him or her which is unusual: *Councillor dies in smash, Champion leek-grower killed, Driver (94) in death crash.*

Where, if the place it happened is relevant or different: *Blackspot claims eighth victim, Car hurtles into supermarket, Driver dies on level-crossing.*

When, if the timing is out of the ordinary: *Bonfire Night tragedy, Day trip ends in death, Bridegroom dies on wedding eve.*

Why, if the cause is known (not very likely yet, but possible): *Death car hit black ice, Driver blinded by sun, Faulty traffic lights blamed for pile-up.*

These five possibilities, **Who, What, Where, When** and **Why**, have been affectionately known to generations of journalism trainers as *The Five Ws.* They are essential elements of every story, the answers to the questions that must be answered. You can often add another to the list:

How: *Crash victim burnt alive, Driver blown to pieces, Car somersaulted eight times.*

You may not know the answer to the How question, of course, but even so you will see stories that, usually for want of anything better, kick off with How as the central peg on which to hang the rest: *Mystery surrounds the death of...* or *Accident investigators are trying to discover how...*

You may be able to add a seventh question, because many stories have consequences or implications for the future:

What next? *Town blacked out by car crash, Motorists warned of brakes defect, Murder probe after car body found.*

In a simple car crash story, you can probably state what has happened as fact. The man is dead, the police have confirmed it, and unless you have reason to doubt them you don't need to give the source of your information in your intro. But if your facts are uncertain, there is an eighth question:

Who says? *A driver who died when his car hit the town hall was doing more than 90mph, eye-witnesses claimed today...*

Attribution of sources in your intro is important if you are writing about someone saying something you don't know for certain yourself or making an allegation or accusation that may be disputed. You must make it clear that it is the speaker making the claim, not you. It is vital in court cases.

The same applies to any story about someone saying something controversial or outrageous. If you write *The world will end at midnight*, readers have the right to know immediately whether this is a serious warning from the world's top scientists or merely a prediction by the leader of a lunatic doomsday cult.

Sometimes, of course, what is said is news only because the person saying it is well-known, and their name is central to the intro: *I love deep-fried garlic sprouts* won't raise many news editors' enthusiasm if the speaker is a tramp; add *the Queen told Parliament yesterday* and watch them leap for the phone.

Leave some till later

Which of these eight Ws you choose to include in your intro (we've made How an honorary W because *The Five Ws and an H and two more Ws* doesn't sound nearly so neat) depends on your judgement of what is most newsworthy and most likely to get your readers hooked.

Don't try to answer all the WWWWWHWW questions in the first sentence. Once in a blue moon you may get near: *A one-legged tightrope-walker* [who] *died* [what] *in his blazing car* [how] *after hitting a runaway elephant* [why] *on the Midthorpe bypass* [where] *yesterday* [when], *prompting demands for a ban on travelling circuses* [what's next]. But usually that is far too much to squeeze in and it leaves the reader floundering in a sea of ideas, uncertain what the main point of the story is supposed to be.

Identify the most important elements and leave the rest until later. Most of the time you will choose the Who and the What, because most news is about people doing or saying things. If you haven't got a person (or a group of people or at least an organisation) in your intro, look at it again.

If in doubt, ask yourself what you would shout across the newsroom if your news editor asked what the story was all about, or imagine what would go in the headline if you only had a few words to play with.

Short and simple

Your newspaper may have a limit on the number of words allowed in an intro. Some newspapers ban opening sentences longer than 20 or 25 words and intros of more than 40 are rare in even the most serious nationals.

Don't bog your intro down with unnecessary detail. Trainees writing news stories for the first time are often tempted to get in as much as possible. It is a mistake. Unless the person involved is well-known, use labels instead of names. Avoid precise times and addresses. Don't do this:

Father-of-two Albert Fothergill, aged 34, of Peasbody Gardens, Midthorpe, who worked for a butchery business in the town's High Street, was drowned in a vat of fermenting beer at 3.43pm yesterday while trying to rescue his two-year-old white chihuahua Fang who had fallen into it during a guided tour with his owner of the Midshire Brewery Company's premises in Gas Lane, Midthorpe.

HOUNDED TO DEATH?

Don't try too hard to be clever or, worse, funny. It can lead to artificial, contrived intros that are meaningless, superfluous or in downright bad taste:

Curiosity killed the cat. But it applies to dogs, too, as Arthur Fothergill discovered yesterday, when wondering how his favourite beer was made led to his death...

...is awful.

☞ *Most of the media follow the recommendation of the Press Complaints Commission that house names or numbers should not be published, to avoid errors and to protect the occupants from criminal activity.*

There are some people whose occupations put them at risk if their names and/or addresses are publicised: police and prison officers, for example, and members of the armed forces.

Be wary of giving detailed addresses of vulnerable people living alone, children, judges, relatives of people accused of serious crime, major prize-winners and sanctuaries for victims of abuse or violence.

That gives far too much detail, slows the story down and leaves the reader not only breathless but wondering which bits out of all that are important (what, for a start, has Albert's ability to sire two children got to do with anything?) and uncertain what it all means (does Albert own the brewery?). All you need is:

> *A Midthorpe butcher drowned in a beer vat yesterday while trying to rescue his pet chihuahua.*

The reader has the guts of the story, and even if he or she reads no further they know who has done what, why, and roughly when and where it happened. If they want to know which butcher it was and exactly when and where he met his doom, they will find out in the next couple of sentences.

Even if they don't care about those details, they will read on to find out what on earth a chihuahua was doing in a beer vat. Good intros tease, giving just enough to whet readers' appetites and make them hungry for more.

Don't pare your intro down too far, though. *A man died yesterday trying to save his dog* is not enough. Make sure you have included the key words and out-of-the-ordinary details that make the story different and bring it to life *(butcher, drowned, beer, chihuahua)*.

When to use When

Know your newspaper's policy on whether When goes in the intro. Daily newspapers want to appear as up-to-date as possible, and will probably encourage you to put *today*, *yesterday* or possibly *tomorrow* in the intro whenever you can.

Weeklies will do the same if they are handling late news, but much of their content is days old by the time it is read and they do their best to disguise this by burying *last Thursday* well down the story. The result can be intros that end too abruptly: *A butcher drowned while trying to save his pet* is screaming out for a *yesterday* time reference. You may have to tinker with the wording to get round this, even though changing the tense to *A butcher has drowned...* loses much of the urgency.

A common solution, if you have the quotes, is to intro on someone's account of what happened days beforehand: *Brewery workers told yesterday how they watched a man leap to his death...*

This can, however, lead to you getting ahead of the real story, a common error by reporters desperate to find a *today* intro. *Workmates were today mourning a man who...* or *A pet chihuahua is recovering today following...* or *Police are investigating today after...* suggest that the grief or recovery or investigation are more newsworthy than the accident itself. (In any case, almost every story involving the police could start with *Police are investigating*. That is their job. It would be a great intro, of course, if you could write *Police are not bothering to investigate...* or *Workmates were laughing today after...*).

If you find yourself writing *An inquest will open tomorrow on a man who...* stop and ask yourself whether the inquest really is the most exciting way into your story. If the first verb in your story is not the one describing the central, most important action, start again.

Wherever you put it, the date something happened must go in. Don't use the term *recently,* because everything in the news must be recent. If you are looking ahead, be specific too. Don't write *next Thursday* because the *next* is unnecessary or inaccurate. If your paper appears on Tuesday, say *on Thursday* if you mean in two days' time, *on Thursday next week* if you mean nine days away.

Where to put Where

Know, too, whether your newspaper expects you to put the Where in the intro. Newspapers with wide circulation areas may prefer to leave information about where something happened until well down the story because they think identifying the place immediately will discourage readers living outside that area from reading on.

Many smaller newspapers work on the assumption that their readers expect everything they read in their local press to be local, and conclude that putting the town's name in every intro is unnecessary (apart from leading to a tedious multiplicity of stories starting *A Midthorpe man...*).

Not all agree. Some insist on place-names in every intro so that readers can readily spot items of interest to them and avoid being irritated reading stories that turn out to be irrelevant to their lives.

THE ESSENTIALS

WE'VE got our intro:

> *A Midthorpe butcher drowned in a beer vat yesterday while trying to rescue his pet chihuahua.*

Now you can start answering some of the other WWWWWHWW questions to give the reader the rest of the essential details of the story. Basic identification can come in the next few paragraphs as you expand on the drama and cover the main points of the story:

> *Horrified workers watched 34-year-old Albert Fothergill dive to his death during a guided tour of the Midshire Brewery in Gas Lane, Midthorpe.*
> *He leapt into the 50,000-gallon vat, full of fermenting bitter, after his dog fell in. It was later rescued unhurt.*
> *The brewery has confirmed claims that safety barriers around the vat were not in place at the time. Health and safety officers say they are investigating.*

That's the who, what, why, when, where, how and what-next covered, plus attribution for the safety barrier claims – a strong secondary angle to the story that you will return to later. You might well be wary of using claims like this without firm evidence from witnesses and comment from the brewery, and any rebuttal should be high in the story.

Check every single figure. I did a story about a charity calling for people to donate old computers, and transposed two of the numerals in its phone number.

The number I gave belonged to an old lady who was inundated with calls.

My editor had to go round personally with a bunch of flowers to apologise.

He's never let me forget it.

HELEN ROSSITER
Reporter
Somerset County Gazette

A wellspoken lady rang me up and said it was a good job she was speaking to me on the phone because if she could see me she would jolly well slap my face – and that was just over a women's institute report.

BRIAN TILLEY
Deputy editor
Hexham Courant

👍 **Save what you have written every couple of sentences, before an accidental keystroke or computer gremlin wipes the lot off your screen and you have to start again.**

Most computers have an auto-save function, but it is still good practice to save manually just in case.

Hardbitten hacks have been known to cry when their 600 immaculately-crafted but unsaved words vanish because they hit the delete button by mistake.

👍 **Contact suggestion: Traffic wardens.**
It must be worth a try: they can't all be heartless ogres. A feature on their experiences, looking at things from their point of view, would be different – and they may be so grateful somebody's actually treated them as human beings that they turn a blind eye when you next deserve a ticket.

We need one more par to give the remaining essential details about the dead man:

> Mr Fothergill worked for Midthorpe Co-op in the town's High Street. Today relatives were comforting his widow Joanne and their children, five-year-old Darren and Kylie, two, at their home in Peasbody Gardens, Midthorpe.

QUOTES

TIME to have somebody saying something. Don't leave this too late. Quotes bring stories to life and you need well-chosen ones scattered through your account. If you have managed to talk to somebody who saw what happened, you will probably choose quotes about the drama and the onlookers' reaction:

> Amy Muckle, the tour guide leader, said Mr Fothergill jumped into the vat the moment he saw his pet was in trouble. 'He didn't hesitate,' she said. 'I couldn't believe my eyes.'

If you haven't got eye-witness accounts, you may have good quotes from elsewhere:

> Friends said the dead man was devoted to the dog, a two-year-old called Fang. 'He loved that animal like a child,' said neighbour Martha Holgate. 'He took it everywhere.'

or perhaps:

> Police described Mr Fothergill's death as a tragic waste of life. Insp Malcolm McCrowe said: 'Once he was in the vat he stood no chance.'

or, better than nothing:

> Today friends and colleagues paid tribute to the man they called Midthorpe's finest butcher. 'He made amazing black puddings,' said workmate Gary Morritt. 'The place won't be the same without him.'

Quotes should move the story smoothly forward, introducing fresh information. Make sure they say something new rather than merely repeat what has gone before. Don't do this:

> Workmate Gary Morritt said Mr Fothergill made excellent black puddings. 'He made amazing black puddings,' said Mr Morritt.

Pause a moment

Check your word count. You should do that almost as regularly as you hit the save button. Every word you write over your limit is time wasted typing it in and more time wasted getting rid of it later.

You have written around 150 words about Mr Fothergill's demise so far. The bare essentials have been covered, and if that is all the space available that is the best you can hope for. Whether you have room for more or not, this is a good time to stop for a moment and check whether you have omitted anything vital – personal details of the central characters involved, angles that must be in. Ask yourself if your story so far would stand up on its own if it had to be cut to a few pars. If not, go back and put in what is missing.

THE CHRONOLOGY

IF you are still well within your word-length, now is the time to tell the whole story. Start at the beginning and work through it logically, adding detail as you go:

> *Mr Fothergill, vice-president of the Midthorpe Butchers' Federation, was one of 14 people visiting the Victorian brewery. They were halfway through their tour when his dog broke free...*

and so on until you have covered Mr Fothergill's pursuit, the fatal plunge, the rescue attempts, the arrival of emergency services and the recovery of the body – not forgetting to mention how the dog got out, what state it was in, and where it is now.

Slip in more quotes along the way. Make them work for their place, each one saying something different and moving the story forward. Don't include four eye-witness statements all saying much the same thing, just because you have them in your notebook. Pick the best or use a little from all of them, each quote covering a different bit of the story.

ROUNDING IT OFF

FINALLY, add any other bits left over. These may include more tributes, background about Mr Fothergill (local man, educated in the town,

---

IF YOU THINK WE MADE IT UP...

It is unlikely you will come across a story quite like that of Mr Fothergill and his dog (though Google does come up with an astonishing 38,300 suggestions if you do a search for 'butcher + chihuahua + drown + beer').

However, many of the stories you cover as a reporter can be handled in much the same way. You will find that most of the scenarios dreamed up for journalism examinations follow this pattern, too.

And if the next thing you're going to do isn't hop into Google to check if that 38,300 figure is true, you aren't the sceptical reporter we hoped you were.

> *If there was just one piece of advice I would like every reporter to take on board it would be to take two minutes, just two minutes, to read through what they have written before handing it on.*
>
> *It would relieve so much stress along the line.*
>
> **DAVID DUFFY**
> Deputy editor
> Oxford Times

> *You only really need to ask a person why and how they did something.*
>
> *Other people can usually fill in the other details such as where and when, but only the main protagonist can tell you why.*
>
> **TOM MALLOY**
> Editor
> Kilkenny People

Heard about the hold-up man who put his mask on back to front?

An intro like that defies you not to read on.

You can often get away with asking a question in the intro on a soft news story, something you never do in hard news where your role is to answer questions, not pose them.

Somewhere in every newsroom – on a peg behind the door, in the news editor's bottom drawer behind the forgotten draft of a new house style book – there's a black tie, ready for instant use when a male reporter is told he's off to a funeral or on a death knock.

There is never an office umbrella when you need one.

butcher all his life, played cricket in the local Sunday league, loved his pint) and information about what happens next (inquest, funeral, the investigation, the brewery abandoning guided tours, maybe the possibility of a posthumous bravery award from the RSPCA). There may have been other tragedies at the brewery in the past. And what happens to those 50,000 gallons of beer in which Mr Fothergill expired – is it ruined or will Midthorpe's beer-drinkers be expected to swill it down, dog-hairs and all?

Give the most important bits first and keep each element together rather than hopping back and forth. This round-up section of your story can easily become haphazard if you are not careful. Think of it as a washing line, with all the different items pegged out next to each other in descending order of importance: sheets at one end, socks at the other. If space is tight the subs can lift all or part of an item off the line without affecting the overall structure.

FINISHED?

SAVE it. Check it through. If you have the time (and access to a printer), you may find it easier run a hard copy off and work from that rather than straight off the screen: it is surprising what a difference seeing words on paper makes to your ability to spot mistakes.

Check that you have included every essential bit of information, explained the background, and attributed everything necessary. Check every fact, figure and spelling. Check punctuation and house style. Sort out the presentation. Save it again. Read it right through for a final check, trying to look at it from the reader's point of view: does it answer all the questions, does it flow easily, does it read well?

If you are writing captions for pictures or other illustrative material to go with your story, you may be expected to tag these to the end of your story or send them as a separate file. Either way, make it clear which story they relate to and make sure they accurately reflect what is in the pictures – what is included, who is on the left and right, and so on.

When you are fully satisfied with your story, add the wordcount and send it to the newsdesk. Tell those in charge that it is ready for their attention. Print out a hard copy if you are going to need one (for a training logbook, for example) – don't leave it until later when you may not be able to find it. Make a note of what it is called and where you have stored it.

OTHER STRUCTURES

THERE are other ways to approach stories, and we'll look at some of them now.

Soft news

Hard news tends to deal with recent events of a serious nature, answering factual questions about what happened and why. Soft news is usually about people rather than specific events, may not have an immediate impact on readers' lives, and is often as entertaining as it is informative.

It is less time-sensitive than hard news and although it may be written in response to a hard news event, it is often triggered merely by the fact that a reporter has come across it. Much of it comes under the general heading of 'human interest'. It includes profiles of people and stories about life style, arts and entertainment.

Soft news can be serious: a story about a baby's year-long battle against a life-threatening disability, for example, or a profile of a community scarred by unemployment. At the other end of the scale are stories so trivial – those tracking the mundane activities of minor celebrities, for example – that it can be difficult to see their news value as they descend into what serious journalists dismiss disparagingly as mere infotainment.

You can take a more relaxed approach to soft news stories, with the intro setting the scene and establishing the tone. The language and the opening detail may be more colourful. As in hard news, the main point will still be near the beginning, but the reader may be introduced to it in a more gentle fashion:

While the rest of us gather round the fireside Christmas tree this week, one young Midthorpe boy is staying well clear. Five-year-old Steven Scargill is one of only a handful of children born with a genetic disorder than makes him allergic to pine needles...

You may be able to use a quote as the intro:

'Never again!' Boris Knight threw away his car keys and made the vow yesterday after failing his driving test for the 17th time...

The drop intro

Also known as the Delayed Drop or Slow Burner, this is when the main point, which would be in the opening words of a hard news story, is left until later. The effect is to give the reader a jolt. It may just be a momentary delay, over by the end of the first sentence, as in this example:

Pensioner Sonia Bailey planned to spend yesterday doing the washing like every other Monday – but instead she was knocking back the champagne.

👍 *Unless you really want to make an enemy of the subs, don't insert messages in your copy like this:*

[subs – please check spelling of this name]

It will thoroughly irritate them, and rightly so: it is up to you to get things right first time.

and this one:

> *Britain's new heavyweight champion is frightened of nothing – until it comes to spiders in the bath.*

Handle drop intros with care. They only work if you keep the reader's interest going all the way to the point when you hit them with the surprise twist at the end.

It may take a couple of sentences:

> *By-election candidate Fred Dalton hired the biggest hall in Midthorpe for a mass rally last night. At 7.30 he was waiting on the platform, speech in hand. No-one turned up.*

Or it may take several paragraphs:

> *Toby Kirby has never worked a day in his life. He spends his days eating, sleeping, and taking the occasional stroll down the pub with his best friend.*
>
> *So it came as something of a surprise when an income tax demand for £2,000 arrived with his name on it.*
>
> *Toby is a two-year-old Highland Terrier.*

This approach rarely works with anything but light-hearted, quirky stories like this that aim for humorous effect, rather like telling a joke. It can occasionally succeed with what is essentially a serious story if you know your readers are going to react, if not with amusement, at least with satisfaction at the outcome:

> *Internet entrepreneur Maximillian McSwindler made millions selling holiday flats in Spain to eager British holidaymakers. He lived a life of luxury, owned penthouses in Paris and Barbados, and drove round in a gold-plated Ferrari.*
>
> *None of the flats existed. Yesterday, his jet-set life-style in ruins, he started a ten-year jail sentence for fraud...*

Usually, however, the drop intro is a disaster if you try it with bad news. Don't do this:

> *Widower Tommy Green lived alone in one room of his tiny unheated cottage, ate nothing but bread and cheese, and wore the same battered suit for years. Neighbours in Grubworth said he never went out.*
>
> *Yesterday he was the talk of the village after robbers broke in, tortured him to death and got away with £50,000 in gold bars hidden under his mattress.*

Readers will regard that as in very poor taste. Even worse:

> *The Dalton family were laughing and singing as they sailed off on a trip round the bay. Little did they know that 20 minutes later they would all be dead, drowned as a tidal wave swept over their yacht...*

The cumulative approach

This is another approach probably best kept for light-hearted stories. It lists a series of events leading up to the conclusion and goes like this:

Good Friday was a bad day for burglar Bill Jones. First he got stuck in a shop window as he tried to break in. As he struggled to escape, someone stole his van parked outside. Then he was bitten by a passing dog. And when police finally arrested him, they told him the shop was empty.

Yesterday he promised Midthorpe magistrates: 'I'm going straight from now on.'

Narrative

You will see this step-by-step approach in background stories when the reader probably already knows the outcome. It tells the story from start to finish, packing in detail along the way and breaking most of the hard news rules. Use it when the chronology of events is perhaps more interesting than the event itself:

It was just after midnight when the robbers struck. Dressed in black overalls, faces masked, they parked their seven-year-old white Mercedes under the streetlight outside Barclays Bank and crept into the dark.

Half a mile away, PC Harry Richmond sat yawning in his unmarked patrol car, weary for the end of his shift....

No reporter actually saw any of this, of course. It was built up from detailed research, asking a lot of questions and at times, frankly, letting imagination take over to provide minor detail (well, the copper would yawn, wouldn't he?).

Reportage

Here, on the other hand, a reporter has actually witnessed events and is writing about what he has seen first-hand:

Midthorpe dressed up yesterday for the town's Easter parade. There were dads in clown costumes, mums in crinolines, kids turned out as

My first news editor had a sign behind his desk. On one side it said: 'Sweetness and Light'; on the other: 'But not Today'.

You always knew when not to approach him.

JOHN CHIPPERFIELD
Assistant editor
Oxford Mail

KEEP ME OUT OF THIS

Radio and television go for the personalised eyewitness approach a lot.

In newspapers, first-person accounts are rare, reflecting a general feeling that print reporters should not be seen thrusting themselves into the limelight.

You may well go through your news-reporting career without once using the words 'I' and 'me' except in quotes from somebody else.

Don't assume, just because you can see a jacket slung over the back of someone's chair, that they're actually in the office.

Many an old hand has been known to bring in a spare one and leave it there while they sneak out for a quick pint.

They take a sheaf of papers with them, so that when they return it looks as if they've just been down the corridor to query something.

football stars, cartoon characters and celebrity wives. And through them rode carnival princess Alice Goodbody, undressed as Lady Godiva...

The presence of the reporter can provide the intro:

I watched as they came in their thousands, young and old, rich and poor, those who had survived and the grieving families of those who had not. All were united in their determination to see the man who had for so long ruled their lives go to the gallows...

Ten

WRITING THE WORDS

KISS 'N' TELL: keep it short, keep it simple, tell it straight. The secret of news-writing is as short, simple and straightforward as that.

Your job is to tell your story so that it is immediately understood by your readers. Every word has to count. Every sentence has to be clear. Every paragraph has to flow, taking the story forward in a logical fashion.

It looks easy. In fact, it is harder to do than writing lengthy prose. Getting all the facts, drama and human interest of a story into the fewest words possible is an art, and learning to do it challenges many new reporters, especially those whose previous writing experience has been confined to producing school essays and university theses. They have to forget much of what they have been taught, and start again.

This chapter looks at the words we use, the way we use them, and the way we string them together. It is about writing for newspapers, though much will apply equally well to stories written for broadcast or use on the web (the special needs of this are examined later). It assumes you have a reasonable grasp of the English language and know the difference between a noun and a verb, an adverb and an adjective. If you don't, go away now and find out. There is a section later on in the book about grammar, punctuation and spelling.

Much of what follows is about the need to write as tightly as possible. Readers find it easier to understand stories if they are written in a straightforward way and they don't have to waste time on unnecessary words and complex sentences. Sub-editors appreciate not having to cut and re-write copy (which invites errors) and can concentrate instead on giving your story a final polish.

You benefit because you write fewer words, saving time and effort; because you get more information into each story; and because you earn a reputation as a writer of crisp copy that needs little alteration. And that earns you bylines.

CHOOSING THE WORDS

Keep them simple, but not so simple that your story becomes boring. Readers are not stupid. Most have a vocabulary of many thousands of words and are quite capable of understanding what they read and hear in a wide range of media.

First words are vital. A story starting *A meeting of Littlecombe's Public Protection Committee last night discussed* will have readers yawning as they turn away. *Nude bathing will be banned* will have them eager for more.

- News stories
- Writing for pictures
- Presentation

Never mind if you got a first in your degree with a dissertation on Hamlet's indecision: it was never going to be read by 60,000 people.

But all those demeaning cheque presentation picture stories you spend your first months writing for your paper will be.

If you get someone's name wrong it's a fair bet your paper's reputation will plunge in the eyes of thousands.

Check every spelling.

GAVIN LEDWITH
Assistant editor
Hartlepool Mail

Don't think that writing one-par shorts is easy. They can be among the hardest stories to do.

Nibs have to be written as tightly as possible to include all the essential information in a very short space.

On the subs' desk they may well be given to one of the most senior journalists to handle because trimming them down to the bare bones while still leaving a readable story is a much-prized art.

Contact suggestion: architects. They can give you details of major developments, including drawings, and get involved in minor home alterations long before they reach the planning application stage. You want to know about it when someone decides to put a jacuzzi on their roof or a ski-slope in their garden.

ERADICATE THE VERBOSITY

Get rid of the jargon. For reasons beyond the rest of us, otherwise articulate professional people feel obliged to use long words and convoluted sentences when writing for publication.

Businesses talk of *adopting an interventional strategy to cope with ongoing operational cash-flow difficulties* when they mean they are trying not to go bust.

Council officials turn homes into *housing accommodation units* and playgrounds into *leisure amenity facilities*.

Academics love little-known words like *hegemony* and *pedagogues* when they mean *power* and *teachers*, because that is the language they speak among themselves and it makes them feel superior.

Replace all the academese, officialese, bureaucratese and any other-ese you come across with language your readers will comprehend.

And don't assume they will understand technical terms just because you do.

Use short words rather than long ones if they do the job just as well – *fire* not *conflagration, dead* not *deceased*. People *tell* you what they *saw*, not *inform* you of what they *witnessed*. They have *cuts and bruises*, not *abrasions and contusions*. Don't, however, use short words exclusively. A whole piece of text that is full of words all of much the same length can be quite dull when you read it, as you can see from this one. Conversely, a preoccupation with excessive multi-syllabic expressions appearing in precipitous succession is undeniably injudicious. Vary the number of syllables. Don't go above four unless you have to.

Use the simplest form of verbs. Say *he vowed,* not *he has vowed,* and *he will run* instead of *he will be running*. Instead of *they made a resolution* use the more dynamic *they resolved*. Write that *she was injured* not *she received* or *sustained* or *suffered injuries,* and if she *died* say so, not that she *succumbed to her injuries*. Use verbs to make your story as up-to-date as possible: *Thirteen cats vanished today* is newsier than *Thirteen cats have vanished*.

Use attention-grabbing words. Go for strong nouns and verbs – people, things and actions – rather than adverbs and adjectives. Be specific about individuals to paint a better picture – *an actor, a mother of twins* rather than just *a man* or *a woman*.

Avoid headline words. Subs with little space to work in have developed a shortcut language all their own, a world of *bans* and *bids, fights* and *fury, slams* and *storms*. They are out of place in your story. Frequently they misrepresent reality. If someone disagrees mildly with somebody else, they aren't *rapping* them or *feuding* or *blasting* them in a *row* that will end with one being *axed*.

Don't go for the obvious. There are often alternatives that may add to your description. If a man fell from a roof, did he *catapult, dive, drop, fling himself, hurtle, jump, leap, plunge, plummet, slide, slip, trip* or *tumble*?

Cut out unnecessary words. The tighter your writing, the more information you get in your story. *He is currently in town* means *he is in town*. The same goes for *now* and *at present* and the politician's time-saver *at* *this moment in time*. The phrase *told a meeting of the council* can be shortened to *told a council meeting* which can be further reduced to *told the council* and ultimately to *told councillors*.

The word *that* can often be omitted, especially when the subject stays the same throughout the sentence: *He promised he would go*. Keep *that* in if its absence might cause uncertainty: *He promised that the woman would go* is clear; *He promised the woman would go* invites the subs to stick in what they assume is a missing *he* to make it read *He promised the woman he would go*.

Don't waste words on attribution in the intro if the facts are indisputable and the source can be left until later. *Thieves broke into a cinema last night, said police* can do without the last two words. *Doctors have discovered that eating mouse droppings improves your sex life* would be much better if it started *Eating mouse droppings*.

Don't use slang outside quotes. It is sloppy English, and words familiar to some readers will baffle others. Using the latest street rap may make you popular with younger readers but alienate their elders.

Don't use contractions such as *don't, won't, wouldn't,* or *hasn't* except in quotes. They can cause problems: does *he's a dog at home* mean he owns one or behaves like one?

Stay out of it. Unless you are writing a narrative account, avoid the words *I* and *me*. Keep the newspaper out of it, too. *He told the Gazette yesterday* is a waste of words. He has obviously talked to you or you wouldn't have the story. Save it for real exclusives: *The Prime Minister told...* Don't use *The Gazette can exclusively reveal* if your revelation is no more exciting than new drains being laid in the high street.

USING THE WORDS

Be active, not passive. Say people did something, not that something happened to them. *Three people died* is more immediate than *Three people were killed*. Don't say *a woman has been bitten by her pet*, say *an eight-foot gorilla mauled its owner*.

Be user-friendly. Think of your readers and humanise your stories. Don't say *a sewerage regeneration scheme is planned* when you mean families are going to get better drains. *Midthorpe Transport has agreed working-time reductions* is council-speak for bus drivers getting more time off.

Be wary of clichés. If a phrase leaps to mind (there's one, for a start), it is probably because you have heard it a hundred times before. Think of a fresh way to say it. Promise yourself never to use such exhausted phrases as *up in arms, mercy dash* or *storm of protest*. Leave *leggy blondes* and *hellraising heart-throbs* to the tabloids. Avoid 'in' phrases and vogue words – *state-of-the-art, window of opportunity, exit strategy, leading edge technology, eco-anything*. They are by definition over-used, and usually already out of date.

> *My first news editor told me I got the job because my stories had 'nae flowery language'.*
>
> **There's no better advice than keeping it simple.**
>
> **JOHN McLELLAN**
> Editor
> Edinburgh Evening News

> *The job's not about what's best for the journalist. Always do what's best for the reader.*
>
> **LES SNOWDON**
> Editor
> Scotland on Sunday

> *If it's sin, put it in; if in doubt, leave it out.*
>
> **LYNN ASHWELL**
> Assistant editor
> Bolton News

👍 *Most newspapers ban all but the mildest of swearwords in copy, except when they are in direct quotations and justified by their context (words alleged to have been spoken by a defendant, perhaps, or by a celebrity whose use of them is surprising and revealing).*

Even then there are some obscenities that are almost universally banned.

Find out your newspaper's policy, and how to represent forbidden words in print: it may be by missing out letters, using asterisks, or simply deleting them altogether.

Be very, very careful if you are writing a story about the company whose full name is French Connection United Kingdom.

Don't exaggerate. One burnt-out room is not a building *gutted in an inferno*. Two politicians arguing are not *at war*. If you say your local theatre *faces disaster* when its lead actress gets laryngitis, what are you going to call it when the place goes up flames and 80 people die? Be careful about hardening up stories. Your description of a scuffle as a *fight* tempts your subs to call it a *battle* in their headline and a *riot* in the contents bill.

Don't try to be too clever. *Milkman Harry Jones saved a toddler from drowning* is quite strong enough without you adding that he had *plenty of bottle* or was *a gold-top hero*. There is a place for clever wordplay in lighter stories – most newspapers use it, with varying degrees of enthusiasm – but it must be done well. Firstly, it must be original. *Trains getting the green light* and *blooming good flower shows* must have been heralded as bright ideas once, but it was a very long time ago. Secondly, it must work on both levels, making sense even if the reader doesn't see the joke and takes it literally.

Use alliteration carefully. Headline-writers love this – repeating the same consonant in successive words: *teenage tear-aways, militant mums*. It can give your story rhythm and help its flow: *Ten teachers went on parade yesterday, demanding medals*. Don't overdo it. *Fearless firefighters furiously fought the flames* turns into a nursery rhyme.

Don't start stories with numerals. Spell them out: *Fourteen, Thirty-two, Six hundred*. If the figure is more complicated than that, turn the sentence round so you can use it in numeric form later on.

Don't repeat yourself again, once more and another time. You see it frequently: *The defendant, who pleaded guilty, admitted... Mr Black, prosecuting for the Crown... She said she thought... He hurried quickly from the scene...* Be wary of repeating words in the same sentence.

Don't ask questions. You are giving your readers information, not running a quiz. They will be irritated if you start a story *Will Midthorpe get new wheelie-bins? That was the question on councillors' lips last night...* – especially if they have already read the headline saying *New wheelie-bins on their way*.

GIVING DESCRIPTIONS

Use adjectives and adverbs sparingly. Make nouns and verbs do their work instead. Write *the winner fled* rather than *the winning entrant ran away fast*. *Seven people roasted alive* will horrify readers quite enough without you describing it as an *horrific fire* in which people *horrifyingly* met *an horrific death*.

Get rid of redundancies. Many adjectives and adverbs are used without thought because they have become linked automatically to the nouns or verbs they describe: *in close proximity to a violent explosion* (is there any other kind?), *he complained bitterly about the serious danger* (can it ever be trivial?). A *final decision* is a decision. Nothing can be *almost unique* (although it can be *near-perfect*).

Use adjectival phrases. *Sales director Don Brown* is shorter than *the sales director, Don Brown,* or *Don Brown, the sales director,* and gets rid of a couple of commas that slow the flow. Don't overdo it, though: *Midthorpe Council's Housing Committee's 43-year-old retiring vice-chairman and father-of-three Don Brown* leaves the reader too much work to do before being told who you mean.

Don't use subjective descriptions such as *attractive, handsome, pretty* or *popular*. Readers may well disagree with your choice of adjective. Avoid *famous, well-known* and *much-loved*. If they are, you don't need to say so; if they are not, you are saying something untrue.

Don't try to identify people in a different way every time you refer to them. Some writers have a curious horror of repeating names and instead produce stories like this:

Mr Fred Brown will try to swim the Channel tomorrow. The Midthorpe father-of-two said: 'It is an enormous challenge.' The wife of the 34-year-old, who has never swum more than 200 yards before, said the former schoolboy butterfly-stroke champion and secretary of Midthorpe Swimming Club should be certified...

How many people are we talking about here? It could be anything up to six. Stick to *Mr Brown.*

Don't be too precise with large numbers. Round up a figure like £2,997 to *almost £3,000.* Accuracy is vital, but there are times when you can be too precise with smaller numbers, too: *he was aged between 17 and 18 and between 5ft 6in and 5ft 7in tall* is silly. *About 17 and 5ft 6in tall* will do.

Explain abbreviations. You don't have to spell out those that are universally understood – BBC or DVD, for example – but readers deserve clarification if you mention something like ACPO. Use the name in full (*the Association of Chief Police Officers*) first time round and the initials later on, or talk instead of *the association.* You may be able to get round the problem of long titles with lots of capital letters by referring to *ACPO, the chief police officers' association* (or *Acpo* if your newspaper puts acronyms – initials that spell out a pronounceable word – in lower case).

Be careful with people's ages. Nobody in their 40s likes being called *middle-aged* even though, statistically, it is probably true. Sprightly 60-year-olds resent being called *elderly* or *veterans,* and *senior citizens* has become a cliché. Keep *old* for those over 80. Remember that not all *pensioners* are

---

RATHER INTERESTINGLY...

Don't tell readers how to feel. *The baby died* is tragic: you don't need to put *tragically* in front of it.

The same goes for *happily, luckily, remarkably, ironically, funnily* and just about every other word ending in *-ily*.

If it is happy, lucky, remarkable or ironic, the facts of the story should make it clear. If it is funny, readers will laugh; if it is not, telling them they should won't help.

Don't force your reaction on others who may not agree.

60-plus: people who have been widowed or retire early may start collecting non-state pensions long before they reach their 60th birthday.

At the earlier end of life's scale, keep *toddlers* for children under three: after that they start hurtling around. *Youths* (traditionally a term reserved for males, but increasingly used now to mean either sex) turn into *young men* or *young women* in their late teens, though *girls* go on well into their twenties and beyond.

FORMING SENTENCES

AIM for an average sentence length of around 20 words but ring the changes. Mix short ones with the occasional longer one to offer variation and avoid a staccato effect. Rarely go above 35 (your newspaper may have a defined upper limit) or you risk saying more than your reader can absorb in one go. Intros, certainly, should be shorter than that. Use very short (two or three-word) sentences sparingly to add variety. Like this.

Sentences usually have a verb in them. Sentences in news stories always do, unless you are aiming for special effect: *No more homeless teenagers. That was the promise...* Don't use this construction unless it adds real impact.

One thought at a time. Most sentences should stick to a single main idea with at most a single subsidiary clause. Don't connect two ideas unless they are linked or offer a contrast. It is fine to say *Mrs Green is married and has three children* or *Mrs Green is married, but her husband ran away.* It is illogical to write *Mrs Green is married and keeps pigeons* and downright daft to say *Mrs Green is married, but her dog bites postmen.*

More than three ideas in a sentence is usually too many, especially when they come in a torrent of subsidiary clauses. Try getting to the end of this example (an extreme one, admittedly) without stopping to work out what is going on:

The couple, who are celebrating with a party to which all their relatives have been invited, including their eldest daughter, who is flying from Australia, where she and her husband, who is a plumber, have lived since 1998, since when she has not seen them, on Friday, on Saturday, have been together for 50 years.

There are eight ideas buried in there: the couple have been married half a century, they are holding a party on Saturday, all relatives are invited, they have at least two daughters, the eldest has lived in Australia since 1998, her husband is a plumber, she is flying here on Friday, and she hasn't seen her parents for a long time. Broken up into three sentences, it makes sense:

The couple will celebrate their golden wedding on Saturday with a party to which all their relatives have been invited. Among those coming is their eldest daughter, who is flying on Friday from Australia. She has lived there with her husband, a plumber, since 1998, and it will be the first time she has seen her parents since then.

Put the main point first. Avoid subsidiary clauses at the start: *Police are searching woods for the body* has more impact than *In their efforts to find the body, police are searching woods*. It is five words shorter, too. If you find yourself starting sentences with time references (*Following their meeting yesterday...*) or explanation (*In a move to prevent...*) or qualification (*Despite the protests...*), think again.

The occasional sentence with the subsidiary clause at the front adds variety, but too many halt the flow and leave the reader constantly trying to assimilate one idea without having a clue what it is about until they have read further on.

Use link words such as *before, after, as, meanwhile, later* to help sentences flow smoothly from one idea to the next: *Every man in Midthorpe will be DNA-tested following the death of...* Don't use too many or shuffle the sequence of events. Readers' eyes will glaze if they read:

> *A man was rushed to hospital after being rescued from a blazing room in which he was trapped for ten minutes before later leaping to safety after being given a ladder as his wife looked on.*

Read each sentence to yourself to check that it flows easily. If you have to pause for breath where there isn't a natural break, or find yourself tongue-twisting over an awkward phrase, re-write it.

PLACING QUOTES

DON'T use quotes for the sake of them. They should add something to the story. Use them to convey what people think and feel rather than what they know. *Coun Brown said: 'I am appalled.'* is a good enough quote; *Coun Brown said: 'There has been a rise in the number of stray dogs.'* is dull, much better summed up in reported (indirect) speech: *Coun Brown said there were more stray dogs.*

Reported speech saves words. Replace *He said: 'I believe it is an accurate summary of the situation'* with *He said it was true.*

Don't start news stories with a quote. It leaves the reader wondering who has said it and unable to judge its merits until the source is revealed. *The world will end tomorrow when a Venusian spaceship*

> *It is the duty of a sub-editor to be difficult, tetchy, demanding and hormonal.*
>
> *But they will thoroughly respect any reporter whose copy is clean, tightly-written, entertaining and on the nail.*
>
> **NEAL BUTTERWORTH**
> Editor
> Bournemouth Daily Echo

DON'T DO THIS, HE BESEECHED

Stick to 'said'. Many new reporters think it necessary to find alternatives to *said*, using words like *added, revealed, commented, confirmed, stressed, explained* or, worse, *frowned, joked, laughed, cried* or the potentially embarrassing *ejaculated*.

In a flowery feature you might want to indicate how someone behaved when speaking, but in a news story *said* is nearly always all you need. Keep *revealed* for genuine revelations, *admitted* for court stories or confessions extracted under pressure.

Avoid the rest (unless they really did cry, of course).

> *Never assume, never spin, never invent – and if you do get it wrong, have the guts to say so.*
>
> **SIMON O'NEILL**
> Editor
> Oxford Mail

Don't change quotes, and never make them up.

The temptation is always there: you know what they meant to say, but they went on too long and you could phrase it just that bit better.

Resist. Leave the words alone. That is what they said and your job is to report it faithfully (it is why you spent all those long hours doing shorthand).

Otherwise the day will come when someone complains, and no defamation jury is going to look kindly on you if your shorthand notes don't accurately reflect what went in your story.

Your editor won't like it much, either.

AVOID 'QUOTES' LIKE THIS

Don't use too many 'broken quotes'.

A key phrase quoted in an intro is fine if it uses dramatic words that you would not normally use – *Midthorpe United players are 'mindless rubbish', according to their manager* – but too many 'brief phrases' scattered through 'a story' look 'untidy' and 'slow it down'.

Most, like those in the last sentence, are unnecessary. *He said it was 'a disaster'* reads just as well without the quotation marks.

---

arrives full of two-mile-high aliens is a bit of a let-down if the second sentence says *This was the warning from 63-year-old ferret-plucker Alf Brown from his padded cell yesterday.* Paraphrase what has been said and attribute it, giving the full quotation later if necessary.

There are often typographical reasons, too, for avoiding opening quotes: if your newspaper uses dropped caps (large capital letters at the start of a story) they look wrong with a quotation mark in front of them.

Some newspapers insist on attribution before every quote, others are less rigid about it. If yours is among the latter, never go beyond the first quoted sentence before explaining who is speaking.

Don't repeat things. *Asked if he agreed, he said: 'I agree.'* is silly. Drop the first four words or, if you must, follow them with a quote that takes the story further: *Asked if he agreed, he said: 'There is absolutely no alternative.'*

Trim quotes to get rid of tedious waffle. If the leader of the council says *Taking everything into account, I think we should chuck the agenda in the bin and go for a pint* you don't need the first six words.

Don't run quotes together to give a false impression of what has been said. Separate them with *he said* or some other device.

Don't miss bits out and type a few full stops like this ... (called an ellipsis) to show words are omitted, or use square brackets to put something in, as in *Mr Green said that he [Mr Brown] failed to understand what he [Mr Green] had said.* Turn the sentence round or use reported speech.

Don't run quotes from two different sources together without introducing the second speaker first. Never write *Mr Brown said he was in favour. 'I am completely against it,' said Mrs Green.*

Clean up grammar in quotes with caution. Minor errors can be altered (report *I were talking* as *I was talking*, for example). If a speaker says something nonsensical or ambiguous, collar them afterwards for an explanation in words that make sense. If their words are hideously ungrammatical, don't report them verbatim (unless you want to make a fool of them – and an enemy). Find out what they meant to say and put it in reported speech.

FINISHING OFF

Read your story through thoroughly. Check every word, every spelling, every fact and figure, every punctuation mark. Check that every sentence is a sentence and says what you mean it to say.

Read the version that appears in your newspaper and learn from your mistakes. Identify any changes made by the subs and ask yourself why (and ask the subs if you don't know).

Look at your story critically to see what, in hindsight, you might have done better. Is the intro as sharp as possible? Are there redundant words, or sentences that could be improved? Could it be better constructed? Does it answer all the questions and read well from start to finish? If your answer to all these questions is yes, go back and look again. Nobody's perfect.

Read the version in your rival newspaper, if there is one. See what they did with it. Work out why.

WRITING FOR PICTURES

PICTURES need words to go with them, and you will probably have the job of providing them. They may be simple captions or lengthier picture stories.

Captions

These are brief descriptions of pictures used to accompany a story, identifying who or what is shown. The logical place for them is beneath or beside the photos.

There are a number of different ways of writing captions, and you should know which style your newspaper uses. On single-column headshots, the caption may be no more than one word, giving the subject's name: *Jones*. It may give a name and brief phrase: *Bill Jones: Murder victim* or, in reverse, *Beaten to death: Bill Jones.* It may be extended to give a longer description: *Bill Jones, the fourth of the killer's victims*, or occupy a couple of lines of text spread out under a multi-column picture: *Fourth victim: Bill Jones, who was lured to the killer's lair by promises of cheap whisky.*

Some newspapers tag captions on to the end of short stories or, if the picture is just a headshot, avoid a caption altogether and slip a photo reference into the copy: *The dead man was later named as Bill Jones (pictured) who...* This is irritating if it comes well down the story and the reader has to wade through many paragraphs before discovering who is pictured.

If the picture is prominently displayed, its caption should act as a bridge between the picture and the story. Readers will glance at the picture first, then the caption to see what it is all about, before deciding whether to read the words. The caption should tease them into the story.

Don't state the blindingly obvious: readers can see what is in the picture and deserve to be told something new. Don't simply repeat information that will appear elsewhere. Readers get frustrated if they read a caption saying *The scene of yesterday's hotel fire in which four people died* followed by the headline *Four die in hotel fire* and then an intro beginning *Four people died yesterday in a hotel fire...*

Avoid labels. Make it dynamic. Use vivid language. Don't write *Firefighters at the scene* but *Exhausted firefighters sift through the smouldering rubble.*

Make sure your words aren't ambiguous. I wrote a headline about someone who'd spent years counselling the relatives of murder victims. It read: 'Dan helps murder families'.

He wasn't enormously chuffed.

JENNY NEEDHAM
Features editor
The Northern Echo

Preparation and forward planning are essential.

Even in my nightmare future, when all briefings become simultaneously-translated teleconferences covered in bed by reporters with their spanking new 'thumbtops', one crucial piece of advice remains: Be prepared!

COLIN MOONEY
Former reporter
Reuters

👍 *You may be handed a picture with hardly any information, and told to write a paragraph or more to go with it.*

It could be a landscape that your newsdesk thinks is worth publishing for its artistic merit, or a photograph taken many years ago and being reproduced now out of historical interest.

Let your imagination range wide. Indulge your talent for creative writing. Have fun. Don't go over the top.

👍 *Don't doctor pictures to improve their composition, tempting though it is when they show people widely apart or staring out of the page. Simply reversing pictures can be dangerous: married women are not happy if you show them with wedding rings on the wrong hand.*

Your job is to show the truth. If you must meddle with photos, tell the viewer you've done it.

If you are doing captions for several pictures that are appearing together, vary the words and content. Unless instructed otherwise, do separate captions for each one. Long captions referring to multiple photos are confusing, and you cannot blame a reader who gives up halfway through one that reads:

Pictured, clockwise from top left: Anne Burton, first in the under-fives egg-and-spoon race; judge Clara Duncan (second right) with hoopla trophy winners Eileen Forest (left) and Gareth Harris; raffle stallholders Irene Jackson (left) and Katherine Lumpett; winners of the tug-of-war trophy (pictured from back, left to right) Mike Nurse, Owen Parry, Quentin Russell, Sam Strong and Tommy Urquhart with umpire Vernon Watson (third from right, front row); scruffiest pet contest finalists Xerxes (muzzled), Yogi (in cage) and Zip....

The convention is to use the present tense in captions, as in the *Exhausted firefighters sift through* example above. If you have a time reference in the caption this can cause problems: *Hotel owner Fred Green arrives at the scene yesterday* is grammatically unsatisfactory. The solution (other than deleting *yesterday*) is to use a participle in place of the verb: *Hotel owner Fred Green arriving yesterday* or, if your newspaper style permits, to split the caption into two: *On the scene yesterday: Hotel owner Fred Green arrives in his Rolls Royce.*

Avoid caption clichés such as *Our picture shows, Looking on are* and *It was smiles all round as* (not least because you can bet there will be someone scowling in the background).

Captions may end with a credit for the photographer and/or a picture reference number for readers wishing to order a copy. Check if this is your newspaper's style and, if so, how it is worded. Make sure you get the name and number correct.

Find out from your newsdesk whether captions should be appended to your story or sent as a separate file.

Picture stories

These may be only two or three paragraphs long, with or without a headline, or full stories accompanying one or more prominent pictures. Picture stories can be written just as any other news story, with information about the photo given in a separate caption or, if the story is fairly short, dropped in along the way or added at the end.

This is often the best approach when the story is stronger than the picture – if, for example, it is merely a static shot of some of the people involved.

On the other hand, if the picture is dominant and central to the story, the words should be written to it, including immediate reference to its content. Contrast these brief examples:

Picture showing head teacher handing over cheque to charity organiser:

Midthorpe children have turned green to raise more than £300 for charity.
Pupils at Coke Lane Comprehensive converted derelict land behind their school into a garden, and made the money by selling flowers and vegetables to parents.

TOP TIPS FOR TIGHTER WRITERS

In general, it is advisable to write your story in as simple and straightforward a manner as possible:
Tell it straight.

Ensure that you do not use any more words than you need to:
Make every word count.

Although there is often a temptation to start stories in some other way, perhaps for the sake of variety, the reader hasn't the faintest idea what you're talking about if, as in this case, you begin with subsidiary clauses instead of giving the most important information at the start:
Give the main point first.

The passive use of verbs is to be avoided where possible:

Make it active.

The usage of less lengthy language is preferable:
Use shorter words.

Use phrases with adjectives in them:
Use adjectival phrases.

There would have to have been simpler ways of having this explained:
Use simple, newsy tenses.

This should bring loud cheers as it gives the best ever complete answer to the thorny problem of clichéd adjectives:
Avoid the completely unnecessary.

Eliminate hackneyed phrases like the plague and do not employ unnecessarily verbose official language:
Avoid clichés and jargon.

They did it all on their own and we're very proud of them,' said head teacher Muriel Fossett, pictured last night handing over the proceeds to Alan Gibb, president of the Midthorpe branch of Oxfam.

Picture showing pupil proudly clutching giant vegetable:

Jodie Moffatt has some of the greenest fingers in school – and she's put them to good use.

Jodie, of Gas Street, Midthorpe, is one of 30 pupils at Coke Lane Comprehensive who converted derelict land behind their school into a garden and sold the produce to parents. They made £300, handed over last night to Oxfam.

'It's been brilliant,' said 12-year-old Jodie, seen above with one of the giant cabbages she raised from seed.

PRESENTATION: ON-SCREEN

YOUR stories should be transmitted, whether as computer files or on paper, in a form that is clear, easy to read, and follows your newspaper's style.

Format

The way you present your copy when you send it from your screen to the newsdesk will depend on the computer system you are using: ask for advice on how to set out your work and what additional information to include. Some newspapers will be happy for you to transmit your copy much as it comes off your word-processor. Others may require it to be delivered in a specified typeface, size, width and line-spacing.

If you're wrong, admit it. A furious reader rang me up one day spitting venom, demanding a retraction, my head on a platter, apologies from me, the editor, the MD, the proprietor.

How could you get it so totally wrong?' he demanded.

'Sheer incompetence,' I said.

It took the wind out of his sails, he laughed, and settled for a small correction.

SHARON GRIFFITHS
Feature writer
The Northern Echo

Don't waste too many precious minutes agonising over the intro.

Write the rest of the story first and come back to it later.

Often it seems a lot easier then.

KATE HELYER
Community editor
North Devon Journal

👍 *Why bother with presentation? Well, it makes it easier to read, for a start.*

It looks professional.

And if you're doing an exam, the markers will appreciate you making the effort.

That gives you a tiny psychological advantage – and you may be grateful for that if you've made a hash of your story.

Unless you are told otherwise, paragraphs should be indented: hit the tab key at the start of each one or, neater, set your computer up to indent them automatically. You may have to leave a blank line between each paragraph.

Content

You may be expected to insert notes in your copy, explaining dates mentioned in your story, for example, or confirming that you have checked unusual spellings. The usual style for these is:

An inquest will be held tomorrow [Thursday] on Mr Fred Greene [Correct].

Some computer software has a Notes mode which enables you to type things like this in a way that automatically prevents them being printed in the newspaper; if not, your notes will be deleted by the subs before publication.

You may be expected to write *Ends* at the end of each story, or to indicate that there is more to come by typing *more, mf* (more follows) or *mfl* (more follows later). A word count may be required, too.

Essential information

Additional details to accompany your story will vary from newspaper to newspaper, but will almost certainly include:

Your name: Some newspapers put this (called your byline) on every decent-sized story you write. Others restrict it to page leads or exclusives. Some never credit their reporters at all. Your byline may get published with your email address tagged on, or on a long story as part of a separate introductory heading (called a standfirst): *Midthorpe is being invaded by rats. Jolene Hackett reports...* It may even carry a headshot (a small head-and-shoulders picture of you) beside it. Whether it is going to appear in print or not, it needs to be on every piece of copy you write.

Your newspaper: If you are working on a publication with reporters in several offices, you may be expected to add your location as well.

The date: Your newspaper may want the date it was written or the date of intended publication, in which case you would write *For publication Thursday (May 24th).* Check which you are supposed to give.

👍 *Contact suggestion: Samaritans. They keep callers' names secret and won't discuss individual cases, but they are far less reticent than they used to be and welcome publicity. Your local branch will be happy to help with a feature on their work and will comment generally on issues and problems facing the people who call on them for help.*

DON'T END UP BEING SPIKED

Catchlines to avoid include *kill, dead, old, unwanted, rubbish, hold* and *spike.*

Don't use days of the week or the names of people or places, either.

Any of these is likely to be misinterpreted and lead the recipient to put your copy aside or send it to the recycle bin instead of the place you intended.

Why *spike*? Because in the days of paper-based copy, unwanted items were impaled on a metal spike.

The name has stuck and a rejected story is still said to have been *spiked.*

A catchline: This is the name of your file. Every story written needs a distinctive tag to avoid confusion with others, so don't label a story *Fire* or *Crash* because there are bound to be any number of stories about fires and crashes in the system. Pick something unique about your story if you can, a word from your intro that will make it instantly recognisable to anyone looking for it. Don't create long amalgams like *Towncentreblazetuesday*. One word, as short as possible, is all that is needed.

And...

You may also be expected to include information about:

Destination: Which newspaper the story is intended for (in offices publishing more than one), which section (news, sport or business page, for example) and/or which edition (first, home, late final): *For Gazette arts page, City edtn.*

Context: An indication that the story is one of a number of linked items: *To go with school league tables round-up.*

Pictures: A reference to any photos, graphics or other artwork to go with your story: *With pix of prize-winners.*

Plus... Anything else that the newsdesk and subs ought to know or which might help them as they handle your story. This might be whether any last-minute checks need to be made (on the condition of people in hospital, for example), whether the story needs checking for legal problems (known as legalling), whether the story should be cross-referenced to anything else in the newspaper (*xref to letters*) or whether there have been any pleas to keep the story out of the newspaper. This kind of information should go at the top of your story, clearly marked *Note to newsdesk or subs.*

PRESENTATION: HARD COPY

THERE are occasions when you will need a print-out (known as hard copy) of your work: to put in your training logbook, for example, to refer to when out of the office, or (hopefully not too often) when there is a complaint about a story and you want to prove it was error-free when it left your screen. If you are on a training course you will almost certainly have to produce hard copy in class and when sitting examinations.

Print-outs for a logbook should ideally be in the same format as they were sent to your newsdesk, though if stories are set in tiny type or words run off the edge of the paper it is sensible to make adjustments to ensure assessors can read them easily.

For examination work, there are basic rules about hard copy presentation established in the days when everything was produced on typewriters and sent to printers to transform into metal. Although those days are long gone, the rules remain, mainly because most of them still make good commonsense. This is how the NCTJ likes to see stories presented, and why:

The best advice I was given as a trainee reporter was: 'Never piss off the subs.'

It stood me in very good stead over the years, and I always pass it on to my own trainees.

FIONA PHILLIPS
Editor
Western Telegraph

Check your copy and ask yourself: Is that right? Is that right? Is that right?

Don't hit 'send' until you know it is.

PETER BARRON
Editor
The Northern Echo

Nobody likes a smart-arse: humility gets you a long way.

NEIL BENSON
Editorial director
Trinity Mirror Regionals

Paper: A4, with about an inch of margin on each side. Most word-processing programs will set margins automatically. Type on one side only.

Typeface (font): Use one that is easy to read such as Ariel or Times Roman. Choose the latter for preference, because it is a seriffed type. (Serifs are those tiny lines at the extremities of each character in some fonts – as in this one – and research has shown that people find seriffed type easier to read in large blocks. That is why it is used in most newspaper text, and print-outs in seriffed type look that little bit newsier. Fonts lacking serifs, like the one used in the panels in this book, are called sans, from the French word for 'without'.)

Type size: Choose 12pt, big enough to be read without examiners having to reach for their glasses, not so big that it uses up reams of paper printing out what looks like a large-print novel for the visually challenged.

Line-spacing: Double-space throughout, or use 24pt leading if you work in points. (Leading is pronounced *ledding*, a throw-back to hot metal days when space was created by sticking thin strips of lead between the lines. Space between the reporters' typed lines was needed for subs to insert amendments; nowadays the space is for examiners to write their comments.) If for any reason you can't do double-spacing, at least leave a line space between paragraphs. You don't need to do both.

Indents: Start each paragraph with an indented space. A centimetre is quite enough. Without these, a paragraph ending near the righthand side of the page will merge with the one starting on the next line.

Page breaks: Put these in at the end of a paragraph, rather than letting sentences run from one page to the next. In hot metal days this was because different sheets of paper might go to different printers, and they needed them neat and tidy (there was a bit more to it than that, but it's all history now). These days it doesn't really make any difference, but the custom lives on and it does make copy look smarter.

Identification: Put your name, newspaper and the date you are writing the story at the top left of the first page. Put the catchline on the top right, with the page number after it: *Mystory-1*. Repeat this on each subsequent page: *Mystory-2, Mystory-3,* and so on. This goes on the right because it is the most important piece of information, and most people hold a wad of pages in their left hand and riffle through the top righthand corners with their right. Printers gripped sheets of papers in a special holder on their machines and did the same. If you are lefthanded, you just have to put up with this.

Space: Leave a few empty lines between your identification details at the top of the first page and the start of your story. If there are notes to the newsdesk or subs, put them here.

Continuation: Put *more* at the foot of each page, *end* at the end of the story, with the word count beneath.

Eleven
ENGLISH MATTERS

THERE is no room here for a detailed guide to using the English language. What follows is advice on how to avoid the most common errors made by trainee reporters. Take note of it. Don't rely on computer grammar-check programs. They are almost always unreliable and confusing.

- Grammar
- Punctuation
- Spelling
- House style

GRAMMAR

Watch your tenses

Most of the time you will report things that have finished, and you will work in the past tense: *He said the car hit the tree.* If an event is continuing, however, it is possible to switch to the present in the intro: *Neighbours are angry about...* or *A councillor says he will resign if...*

If you choose to do this (subject to house style: some newspapers forbid it), switch to the past tense after the intro. Don't mix tenses in the same sentence, as in *Mr Brown says he is furious and was going to resign.*

Check collective nouns

Most newspapers treat these – councils, committees, companies, groups of any kind – as singulars: *the association has agreed about its day trip,* not *have agreed about their.* Exceptions include the police (*they are appealing for witnesses*), sports teams (*Midthorpe United have sacked their manager*) and pop groups (*Local band Pink Throttle are in the charts*).

Make sure you know your newspaper's style, stick to it, and make sure collective nouns, their verbs and pronouns agree. One of the commonest errors reporters make is to switch back and forth: *the council have decided that its chairman should give them a break.*

Follow the rules for reported speech

The tense usually moves back a step:

> *He said: 'I am writing'* becomes *He said he was writing.*
> *He said: 'I will write'* becomes *He said he would write.*
> *He said: 'I was writing'* becomes *He said he had been writing.*

> *If you're not sure how to spell it or what it means, it's the wrong word.*
>
> **MARK DICKINSON**
> Editorial director
> Trinity Mirror Midlands

Be careful where you place words like 'only', 'even' and 'just'.

Moving them around can radically alter the meaning of a sentence.

Compare 'Only I went to the game' (nobody else did), 'I only went to the game' (I didn't do anything else), and 'I went to the only game' (there was only one on).

DON'T DANGLE YOUR PARTICIPLES

Swimming in the river, a boat hit him. No. The boat wasn't swimming. The man was.

Make sure when you write a sentence like this that whoever or whatever is involved in the first action is the one you mention next.

Swimming in the river, he was hit by a boat is an improvement; *A boat hit him as he swam in the river* is better still.

Problems arise when timing gets confused. If you write *Mr Jones said: 'I am a greengrocer'* you know he means that is his job, and he is still doing it. Turn it into reported speech and, following the rules, it becomes *Mr Jones said he was a greengrocer*. It is no longer clear whether he is still selling cabbages for a living, or used to but doesn't now.

To avoid giving the wrong impression (and it might be important – in a court story, for example) you have a choice: break the rules (*Mr Jones said he is a greengrocer*) or change your sentence (*Mr Jones, a greengrocer*).

Remember to change time references. *He said: 'I will do it tomorrow'* becomes *He said he would do it the next day*.

Watch theys and thems

Pronouns can be a problem for readers if they don't know which the intended nouns are in sentences like this because they don't clearly refer to them. That final *them* is supposed to relate to *pronouns*, but they are so far back that later plurals get in the way – *readers* and *nouns* and *sentences*. You see the same error with other pronouns and with possessives: *James told David he had seen his father, who said he was ill*. Who had seen whose father? Who did he say was ill?

The English language would be less problematic if it had a couple of extra pronouns: one to combine *he* and *she* (*hesh?*) and another combining *his* and *her* (*hes? hir?*). It hasn't, and to avoid accusations of genderism we write *he or she* and *his or her* (or, worse, *he/she* and *his/her*).

This gets tedious: *If a driver loses control of his or her car he or she may lose his or her life*. One solution is to change the wording to *If drivers lose control of their cars* but this not always an option (how many cars is each one driving?).

Many people take the ungrammatical way out (as we have in this book) and use *their* and *they* even though these plural pronouns relate to single individuals: *If a driver loses control of their car, they may lose their lives*. It is not always very pretty, but it works, reflects normal speech and is readily understood – which, in the end, is what we want. (While we are on the subject of pronouns, nobody says *She gave it to I*, so if there are two recipients it should be *She gave it to my brother and me*, not *my brother and I*.)

The more news stories you read, look at and listen to, the better you will become.

Study other people's work, analyse it, see how they solve problems, work out their secrets.

Every time you pick up a newspaper, view a website or listen to a news bulletin you should learn something about how to become a better reporter.

Use that that is right

The theory is that you use *that* if what follows defines something and is essential for the sentence to make sense: *Use the door that is green* (not the blue one). Use *which* if what follows is merely descriptive and could be left out without affecting the meaning: *Use the door, which is green* (a bit of optional extra information). The distinction between the two words has largely been lost in everyday speech and many writers and newspapers use them indiscriminately.

Avoid ambiguity

Does *She joined dozens of shoppers spending their money* mean she was helping herself from their purses? Does *He worked at the school where he was in charge of physics in 2004* mean he was there for just one year, or there for an unspecified number of years, during one of which he ran the physics department? Problems like these can be sorted by changing the word order or adding punctuation.

But...

Opinions differ on whether you should be allowed to start sentences with *And* or *But*. Purists argue that grammatically the answer has to be no: both words are conjunctions, intended only for use to connect two parts of a sentence. But, like here, they are very useful as a means of linking one sentence to the next and many newspapers allow them. If they are banned, you may be able to substitute *in addition* for *and,* and *however, nevertheless* or *although* for *but* – but none have quite the same immediacy.

PUNCTUATION

IF you really want to boost sub-editors' blood pressure and send examination markers' hackles soaring, just give them a badly-punctuated story. They despair at many reporters' inability to use commas, full stops, colons and the rest of the punctuation toolkit correctly.

These nuts and bolts of news-writing are among the most fundamental of our tools of the trade, and a reporter who does not understand them is as ill-equipped and potentially dangerous as a motor mechanic unable to adjust your brakes or a doctor who doesn't know where to stick his needle.

Punctuation matters because it helps the reader to understand clearly and quickly what you are trying to say. Get it wrong and they will be irritated, if not thoroughly confused.

It matters because it helps the subs. If you don't get it right first time, they waste their time correcting it, cursing you all the way.

Write tight, bright copy in simple, plain English.

If the reader has to open a dictionary, you've failed.

ROBIN YOUNG
Editor
Londonderry Sentinel

Remember, you're only as good as your last story.

MARK JONES
Editor
Basingstoke Gazette

When you've written up your story, try to make a thank-you call or send a note to contacts: they may come through with something else later.

KIERAN FAGAN
Journalist
Killeney, Dublin

135

Most importantly, it matters because the wrong punctuation can drastically change the meaning of your words. Take this example: *The verger, who was naked in the church, was sleep-walking.* With the commas, there is no doubt what is meant: one verger, naked, in church, asleep. Without them, *The verger who was naked in the church was sleep-walking* could mean three different things: there was at least one other naked person in the church who wasn't a verger, there was at least one other verger in the church who wasn't naked, or there was another naked verger, somewhere else.

Uncertainty like this can have potentially dire results. Take this sentence: *She went to the hotel, where she was sleeping, with the vicar.* Leave out the second comma (or both of them) and an innocent meeting turns into a passionate affair. Libel suits will follow, all for the want of a keystroke or two.

Here is a reminder of the basics:

Full stops

You need a full stop at the end of every sentence. A common error is to link two sentences with a comma instead: *He started the fire, it was soon well alight* needs a full stop in place of the comma, or a joining word (called a conjunction) such as *and* or *but*.

Commas

Commas separate parts of a sentence and, as we have seen above, are often vital. The main reason for using them is to insert subsidiary words or phrases.

For example, you write *The editor was sacked* and decide to name him. You could say *The editor (John Brown) was sacked,* but newspapers don't use brackets very often. Commas take their place: *The editor, John Brown, was sacked* or, turning it round, *John Brown, the editor, was sacked.* It is essential that you put a comma each side of the extra words you have inserted.

The same applies however long the extra phrase may be: *The editor, who had been found unconscious in the gutter outside the Red Lion on Tuesday night, was sacked.*

If there is more than one extra phrase, you need commas round each of them: *The editor, John Brown, who claims to be teetotal, said his drinks had been spiked.* Keep this commas-each-side idea firmly in your mind and you will get it right.

You don't need commas if the extra information is added as an adjective: *Editor John Brown was sacked* is correct; *Editor, John Brown was sacked* isn't. This rule applies to the lengthiest of adjectival phrases, ugly though they may be: *Eighteen-year-old deputy editor and former Midthorpe carnival princess Donna Clegg has taken over.*

Commas are used to separate complex sentences when the sense would otherwise be unclear. *I tried to hit the barman, and his friend stopped me* is unambiguous; if you leave out the comma so that it reads *I tried to hit the barman and his friend stopped me,* you seem to be saying that you tried to hit two people, and the last two words are a mystery.

Quotation marks

These (also known as inverted commas) can be single or double, depending on a newspaper's style. They go round the words being quoted: *He said: 'This is okay.'* Use quotation marks round single words and phrases as well as whole sentences: *He said it was 'appalling' and a 'waste of time'.* Note that, if the quote is a full sentence, it is introduced by a colon (a few newspapers use a comma instead), starts with a capital letter and ends with a full stop within the quotation marks. If it is just a word or phrase there is no introductory colon, the quote is all in lower-case, and the full stop goes outside.

In sentences where the quote comes first, there should be a comma before the end of the quotation marks: *'It is obvious,' he said.* The rules apply when you use two sentences broken by attribution: *'It is not clear to me,' she said. 'Tell me again.'* and when the attribution comes in the middle of a sentence: *'I am beginning,' she said, 'to understand.'*

If quotes run to two or more paragraphs, each paragraph needs an opening quotation mark but you don't use a closing mark until the whole quote is over:

She said: 'This is the first paragraph, without a closing quote mark.

'It comes before this one, which hasn't got one either.

'And this is the third and last, which does.'

If you use a quote within another quote, the quotation marks for the inner quote change from single to double (or vice versa): *She said: 'I have seen "The Sound of Music" seven times.'* Even more complex: *He said: 'I told her, "Never be afraid to ask."'* Avoid this if you can: *He said he told her never to be afraid to ask* is a lot easier to write and read. Note that the second quote is introduced by a comma instead of a colon.

Colons

As well as introducing quotes, a colon can be used to link two closely-related sentences: it highlights the link, as in this sentence. Newspapers employ them mainly to introduce quotes and other matter, such as results: *Prize-winners: 1 D Sutton, 2 K Beck...*

Never, ever, assume anything. We invited readers to nominate shop staff for good service awards and were sent details of a post office employee called Fyn.

He was, they said, a former member of the police force who enjoyed sorting packages and greeting customers.

I rang the post office, and the manager said Fyn didn't like talking on the phone. Thinking he must be a bit shy, I asked if the manager would get a quote for me.

He did, and I wrote the story quoting Fyn saying how delighted he was to be in our competition and how much he loved his job.

Only later, as the paper rolled off the presses, did I discover that Fyn was the post office dog.

STEPHEN TYLER
Reporter
Lincolnshire Free Press

👍 **Apostrophes are not used to make plurals,** despite a million shop signs advertising potato's, tomatoe's, chip's and (believe it or not) licensed premise's.

Most style books agree that they are not needed in MPs, 1960s or 'in his 20s'.

Note: it is six months' time and it should be thousands of pounds' worth of damage – though many style books prefer 'pounds-worth' or drop the 'worth' altogether and just say 'thousands of pounds of damage'.

👍 **Beware of foreign names.** People from some countries put their surname first: the Chinese trainee reporter Ti Ping, for example, becomes Mr Ti at second reference.

Semi-colons

These can be used, like colons, to link two sentences, usually in place of a conjunction: *He opened his eyes; the nightmare went on.* They are rarely used in newspapers except in results lists: *Scruffiest pet: 1 Bonzo, owner J Green; 2 Tiger, owner...*

Hyphens

Used for compound nouns (*bride-to-be*), compound adjectives (*red-haired*), numbers (*fifty-three*), after suffixes (*pre-war*), and to distinguish one word from another (*reform* and *re-form*).

Some are essential (think of the difference between *a man-eating lion* and *a man eating lion*); the need for others is the subject of debate. Know your newspaper's style for such words as *cooperative* and *livingroom*.

Most newspapers hyphenate ages as in *a three-year-old boy* but you may see *three year-old* or *three year old.* The first is preferable; otherwise, when you refer to *three year old boys,* readers have to work out whether you mean three boys all aged one or an unspecified number of boys aged three. Note that there are no hyphens in *The boy was three years old.*

Dashes

Used to link ideas, usually when there is contrast or surprise: *He was brilliant – and he knew it; she was even brighter – but she failed the exam.* They create a distinct pause and are often better replaced by commas. Dashes are sometimes used in place of brackets to slip in a bit of information: *He was clever – he went to Oxford – and conquered shorthand in a month.* Use them sparingly.

Question marks

Used at the end of questions, in place of a full stop. Note the difference between *He asked: 'Is it true?'*, which needs one, and *He asked if it was true*, which does not.

Exclamation marks

Don't use these (known in the trade as screamers or dogs' cocks) except in quotes, and even then only if the words really have been cried out in horror, surprise or glee.

If you put them anywhere else in your story, all you are doing is telling the reader you have just written something astonishing or hilariously funny that you think they are too stupid to understand without explanatory punctuation.

Brackets

Properly called parentheses, these are used to insert information: *The team (owned by a Bulgarian millionaire) lost its opening games.* They slow sentences down and can usually be replaced by commas. Some newspapers use them to give ages: *Tom Shaw (44) of Begonia Road.*

Apostrophes

These are the source of much confusion for some reporters. They have two main uses. The first is to show that letters are missing (*isn't, can't, o'clock*), which is simple enough. The second is to indicate possession, and this causes problems for many people.

The basic rules are straightforward:

If there is one possessor, the apostrophe goes before the *S: The dog's bone.*

If there is more than one possessor, the apostrophe goes after the *S: Two dogs' bones.*

If the name of the possessor ends in *S* there is a choice: some newspapers choose *Mr Jones' bone*, others prefer *Mr Jones's.* If the bone belongs to the whole family, it is *the Joneses' bone* or the *Joneses's.*

There are a few plurals that don't end in *S*, such as *men, women, children, people.* For these the apostrophe goes first: *the men's shoes, the people's choice,* not *the mens'* or *the peoples'.*

Difficulties arise with the simple word *its.* The rules say that if an *it* owns something, we should say *it's bone.* But we already use *it's* to mean *it is* or *it has.*

To prevent confusion, we break the rule and write *its bone.* If you are stuck, ask whether the word you want is an abbreviation of two words. If so, use *it's*; if not, *its.* Remember *it's a dog, it's got a cold nose but its tail keeps wagging.*

Don't write *The chairman, Mr Sam Smith's car.* Make it *the car belonging to the chairman, Sam Smith.*

PET HATES

WE asked hundreds of editors which language errors were most likely to set their teeth on edge. Here is their Top 20:

A local man... What is *local*? For readers at one end of your circulation area it means one thing, for those at the other end something quite different. Don't use the word until you have identified to the reader which locality you are talking about. In any case, it is a lazy way to start a story. There must be something more interesting about the person than just being from somewhere undefined.

Alright isn't all right, any more than *alwrong, alnight* or *alover.* It has crept into common use, though, and has even wormed its way into some dictionaries.

> *Dare a sub or news editor to cut your copy – write tight, make every word count, and you'll find your story may well go through untouched.*
>
> *Waffle, and you've wasted your time.*
>
> **ANDREW DOUGLAS**
> Deputy news editor
> The Northern Echo

> *Always remember there is more than one point of view (just listen to lawyers in court when defending clients – it could be you or your paper in a libel case!) and keep asking 'why' to get as close as possible to the truth.*
>
> **DAVID HETTERLEY**
> Deputy editor
> Hereford Times

21st in the list of editors' pet hates was 'hopefully'.

If you say: 'Hopefully, he went to watch the game' you mean he went with hope, just as you might say he went rapidly, miserably, or any other way. It's an adverb.

The word is mis-used when you mean you are the one with hope about something or someone else, as in: 'Hopefully, the team will win.' You mean you hope it does. Say so.

There is no known reason why some words end in -able and others in -ible. Why are you likable but forcible, teachable but invisible? You just have to learn them, or check them every time.

And what about -ise and -ize? Many words can end in either, and it doesn't help when the English prefer one, the Americans the other. With luck, your style book will tell you which to use.

Check out is *check* (unless it is at the supermarket, when it is a *check-out*).

Comprised means consists of or made up of and doesn't take *of* after it (*the chair comprised four legs, a seat and a back*). If you are not listing all the components, write *included*.

Crescendo. This means a gradual increase in loudness, not a climax. *Rising to* or *reaching a crescendo* makes no sense.

Decimated literally means cut by a tenth, but dictionaries accept that it has come to mean that a large proportion of something has been destroyed. It does not mean *wiped out*.

Due to. Money is *due to* creditors. Things happen *because of* or *as a result of*. Say *he blamed* rather than the extra four words in *he said it was due to*.

He was injured after a crash... No, *in* a crash – unless somebody thumped him as he surveyed the damage.

Imply and **infer.** A speaker *implies* something; a listener *infers*: *Coun Jones said he was an honest man, implying that others were not; Coun Williams inferred that he was being referred to and lost his temper.*

Less and **fewer.** You have *less* volume of *fewer* things: *There is less milk in fewer bottles.*

Mystery surrounds the millions of intros starting like this. If you don't know what is going on, find out – or at least say who is mystified: *Police are baffled* is so much better.

Over and **under.** These describe where something is: *over the moon, under the table.* If you are referring to numbers or quantity, say *more than, less than* or *fewer than*.

Police were yesterday investigating. Nobody speaks like that. They say *Police were investigating yesterday.*

Refute. This means to disprove, not simply reject or deny. *He refuted the suggestion* means he produced evidence clearly demonstrating it was untrue. If he didn't, use another word.

Residents. This is council-speak for people living somewhere. Humanise it if you can.

Rev takes the the definite article: *The Rev Brown.* There is no such thing as a *Rev*.

Rushed to hospital... Are you sure? If someone has died at the scene, the ambulance doesn't hurtle the body to the mortuary. If someone has serious spinal injuries it may well be driven to hospital at a snail's pace to avoid making things worse. Think before you *rush* in.

Shocked is shockingly over-used. *Villagers shocked at bus shelter litter* – really? They were in what the dictionary describes as 'a state of extreme horror, disgust or surprise'? What are they going to be when the midnight orgies start or sewage floods their front rooms?

The council is set to... What does this mean? Is the council definitely going to do something, hoping to do something, suggesting it does something or just throwing an idea about? Nobody says they are *set to do*

REDUNDANT WORDS

There are thousands of these, wasting space and boring readers. Here are a couple of dozen chosen at random to give you a (bad) taste of what to avoid:

As a result of = Because

At the present time = Now

Awkward predicament = Predicament

Building operations = Building

Car-parking facilities = Car-parks

Carried out a survey = Surveyed

Completely full / empty = Full /empty

Essential condition = Condition

Faced up to the problem of = Faced

For a period of time = For a time

In a desperate condition = Desperate

In spite of the fact that = Although or Despite

In the event of = If

Land for development purposes = Building land

Owing to the fact that = Because

Paid a visit = Visited

Raised objections = Objected

Seating accommodation = Seats

Shopping facilities = Shops

Slum conditions = Slums

Supply situation = Supply

Weather conditions = Weather

Will be responsible for managing = Will manage

> *Pay attention to detail, detail, and, for good measure, more detail!*
>
> **TONY JAFFA**
> Media lawyer

anything in real life: they say *Fred will be a father* or *is going to be a father* or *planning to be* or *likely to be*. Say *plans to* or *wants to* and leave *set to* to the subs with headlines to fit in tight spaces. A phrase like *The High Street is set to become traffic-free* is nonsense: the High Street can't plan to be anything.

Try and avoid this. You *try to* do something. You wouldn't write *He was trying and succeed.*

Whilst we are here, nobody says this any more. Use *while*. The same goes for *amongst* (say *among*) and *amidst* (*amid*).

SPELLING

SPELL-CHECKS are great for spotting words you have mis-typed and turned into gibberish. They are no good at all at picking up words that, though not spelt the way you intended, are still words in the computer's dictionary.

Type *then* instead of *them* and the spell-check will sail happily past, even though your sentence is nonsense. There is no substitute for reading through everything you write, looking at it word for word. If you don't do this, the time will come when you accidentally type *now* instead of *not* and you can lay odds it will be in a sentence that should have read *He was not guilty.*

👍 *Some words of foreign origin have odd plurals:*

Bureau/-eaux

Consortium/-ia

Curriculum/-a

Graffito/-i

Medium/-a

Phenomenon/-a

Stratum/-a

Thesis/-es

Others offer a choice:

Syllabus/-i or -es

Referendum/-a -ums

Stadium/-a or -ums

Check your style book.

Even if the spell-check is perfect, it takes time. Not a lot, but by the time you have used it to go through a 300-word story, check all the spellings it queries, put them right if they are wrong and tell it to ignore all those proper names it doesn't recognise, you'll have spent a couple of minutes at it. Do that with every story you write and it will add up to weeks of your reporting life.

Haven't you got better things to do? Learn how to spell the words that regularly cause trouble, so that you get them right first time round.

Problem words

Here, to start you off, are 30 of those that most frequently cause problems:

Accommodation	Acquiesce	Adviser
Ageing	Benefited	Cemetery
Definitely	Desperate	Eligible
Embarrass	Exaggerate	Fulfil (fulfilled)
Gauge	Glamorous	Grief
Harass	Humorous	Install
Jeopardy	Liaison	Maintenance
Manoeuvre	Miniature	Noticeable
Occur (occurred)	Professional	Seize
Separate	Siege	Unnecessary

Sound-alikes

These are pairs of words that sound much the same but mean very different things. Here are some examples to watch out for:

Advise is the verb *(he advised against it)*, **advice** is the noun *(it was good advice)*.

Affect is a verb *(bad light affected play, I was affected by it)*, **effect** is usually a noun meaning a result *(it had an instant effect, the effect was astonishing)* but can be a verb meaning to create *(the doctor effected a cure)*.

Censor is to restrict and a censor does it *(the government censor censored the report)*, **censure** is to be critical *(the editor censured the reporter for getting it wrong)*.

Compliments show appreciation *(he complimented the chef)*, **complement** means to complete *(he complemented the meal with a glass of wine)*.

Councillors sit on councils, **counsellors** offer helpful advice *(the councillors were so upset that they needed counselling)*.

Elicit means to extract *(the police elicited a confession)*, **illicit** means illegal *(he was found with illicit drugs)*.

ARE THEY ENTITLED?

Your newspaper will have a style for using people's titles on first and subsequent reference. Follow it.

Staider newspapers refer to *Mr John Brown* at first reference and *Mr Brown* thereafter.

Most make it just *John Brown* first time round, then *Mr Brown*.

Really chatty ones drop the *Mr* altogether and talk of *John Brown* and then *John*, which reads a little oddly if John is an authority figure (*John told his fellow MPs*) and leads to illogicalities (if a consultant is plain *John*, why are doctors *Dr?*)

Some newspapers don't seem to know what to do, and mix and match styles haphazardly. They bestow titles in serious stories but become familiar when they're lighthearted: *The woman who died was Mrs Emma Jones* but *The owner of the tallest sunflower was Emma Jones*. They introduce most people without a title but become deferential with those perceived to be important: *Among those present was John Brown, a gardener, and Mr Theodore Waddle, the town clerk. Mr Waddle told John...*

There is no logic to either of these approaches.

There are other problems with titles. When do young people become adult enough to earn a title? Children are always referred to by their first names, but is 19-year-old Darren Chavson *Darren* or *Mr Chavson* at second and later reference? Ask your newsdesk what your style should be.

And is a woman a *Mrs* or a *Miss*? It can sometimes be a real problem finding out, but it is important you get it right: some married women get upset and even litigious if you suggest they are living in sin.

Many newspapers now accept the use of *Ms*: check if yours does.

Don't be afraid. Find the confidence and believe you can pick up that phone, do that dreaded death-knock, talk to those who you might hold in reverence.

You are in control.

But beware that assertiveness can turn into what others may perceive as aggressiveness.

Finding the balance keeps the contact and a relationship, and that is all-important.

NAOMI BUNTING
Late deputy editor
Teesdale Mercury

Ex-patriots no longer feel loyal *(Dave is an ex-patriot of Arsenal but now follows Darlington)*, **expatriates** live away from home *(Jim is an expatriate, living in France, but still supports the England team)*.

Forebears are ancestors *(he is seeking his forebears)*, **forbear** means to abstain *(he forbore to comment)*.

Formerly means previously *(he was formerly on the council)*, **formally** means in a formal way *(the building was formally opened)*.

Insure is to protect against loss *(he insured the house)*, **ensure** means to make certain *(he ensured he paid his premiums every year)*.

Licence is a permit *(a driving licence, licence to kill)*, to **license** is to give permission *(the council licensed the dance-hall)*. Publicans are *licensees*.

Meters measure quantity *(a gas meter)*, **metres** are metric measurements *(a 100-metre sprint)*.

Ordinance is an order *(by ordinance of the government)*, **ordnance** means military material *(the army reviewed its ordnance requirements)*.

Pedal is what you do on a bicycle *(the pedaller pedalled furiously)*, **peddle** is to sell something *(the pedlar peddled peanuts)*.

NUMERICALLY SPEAKING

Turn numbers into words your readers can understand: *half* or *two-thirds* rather than *50 per cent* or *66 per cent.*

Be careful with percentages: a 100 per cent increase doubles something, a 200 per cent increase makes it three times bigger.

Avoid confusing phrases like *a two-fold increase* (which means doubled, not doubled and then doubled again) and *three times less likely* (how can a multiplier reduce anything?).

Know the difference between an *average* figure and a *norm* (if you have four people aged 20 and one aged 100, their average age is 180/5 = 36; the norm is 20).

Work out what large numbers actually mean to people.

If it is costing your council £3 million a year to clean chewing-gum off the streets and there are 30,000 households in its area, that is £100 for each family – a figure your readers can instantly comprehend.

Poles hold things up *(one of the tent poles fell down)*, **polls** are surveys and places to vote *(they polled voters as they left the polls)*.

Pour is what rain does *(he poured the milk)*, **pore** means to study *(you are poring over this book)*.

Practice is a noun *(golf practice, the doctor's practice)*, **practise** is a verb *(he practised his swing, the doctor practised from home)*.

Principal is the main thing *(the principal city, the college principal)*, a **principle** is a moral rule *(a man of principle, the principle of the matter)*.

Raised means something is above *(a raised ceiling)*, **razed** means demolished *(the building was razed to the ground)*.

Straight means undeviating *(he went straight to hospital)*, **strait** means condition *(in a dire strait)*, but note that you may be **strait-laced** or wear a **strait-jacket**.

Uninterested means having no interest *(he was completely uninterested in football)*, **disinterested** means being impartial *(the umpire should be disinterested in who wins)*.

Wave is water on the move or a verb meaning to flap your hand *(Britannia waved as she ruled the waves)*, but **waive** means to set aside *(the councillors waived the rules)*.

Write is obvious *(do you really want us to write it out for you?)*, a **wright** makes things *(he's a playwright who writes about rites the right way)*.

HOUSE STYLE

EVERY newspaper has a house style: a set of rules about such things as whether there is a full stop after *Mr* and how to abbreviate

Lieutenant-General. These rules vary enormously from newspaper to newspaper, but their purpose is the same everywhere: to ensure consistency throughout the publication. This has a number of benefits for you.

It helps your readers to understand what you write. They get used to the way you do things and understand when they see someone referred to as *DC Jones* that he is a detective constable, not a debt collector.

It gives them confidence in you. If you ignore the rules and, for example, vary the way you refer to councillors – *Councillor Smith* in the first sentence, *Cllr Smith* in the second and *Coun Smith* in the third – readers suspect you don't know what you are doing and wonder whether your facts are unreliable, too.

The rules are set out in a house style book, traditionally a paper document but now available in many offices in electronic form. It may be intensely-detailed, stretching to many pages and covering everything you could possibly want to know, with sections on spellings, trade names, words to avoid, grammar and punctuation. It may be little more than a couple of sheets of A4.

When you first join a newspaper, ask for a copy of its style book and study it. Some of what you find you may never need, but you should know it is there and how to use it. Some elements of it you will be expected to know straight away. Find out about:

Names and titles: Is it *the Reverend Thomas* or simply *the Rev*? Is it *Councillor, Cllr* or *Coun*?

Abbreviations: How do you handle *Chief Inspector, Sergeant, Station Officer*? Do you say *NATO* or *Nato*? Is it the *CBI* or the *C.B.I.*?

Capitals: Do you write *housing committee* or *Housing Committee*? Are we in the *North East* or the *North-east* or the *north-east* or the *NE*? Is it *spring* or *Spring*? Do you say *Magistrates Court* or *magistrates court* – and does it have an apostrophe?

Numbers: The first nine numerals are usually spelt out – *One two three* and so on – but after that do you write *ten* or *10*? Is your style *15th* or *fifteenth*? Is the date *December 19th* or *Dec 19* or *19 December*? Is it *%*, *percent* or *per cent*? Which is correct: *£5m, £5million* or *£5 Million*? What is the style for ages?

Measurements: *Five-foot-three*, or *5ft 3in*? *16m* or *16 miles*?

Results: How are lists of these formatted and punctuated?

Books, TV, films, etc: Is it Big Brother, *Big Brother* or 'Big Brother'?

TRADE NAMES

Many products are trade-marked and their names take a capital first letter. Some of them are not so obvious: Biro, for example. You need to recognise these names, because their owners are proud and protective

Always remember there are two or more sides to most stories.

As a young reporter I was asked to contact a man who had shot his neighbour's dog.

The neighbour branded him a dangerous psychopath, but when he was persuaded to talk he recounted a long history of dispute with the neighbour, whose dogs had repeatedly invaded his garden and killed half a dozen of his pedigree rabbits.

He had warned the neighbour what he would do if it ever occurred again.

Completely different story, and much better than the one originally presented to us.

GLEN COOPER
Editor
The Visitor, Morecambe

People are awarded or decorated with the Victoria Cross and similar gallantry awards, awarded or given knighthoods, made knights and dames, and made a GBE, KBE, DBE, CBE, OBE or MBE (Knight or Dame Grand Cross, Knight Commander, Dame Commander, Commander, Officer or Member of the Most Excellent Order of the British Empire).

There are many more awards and titles, and they should be listed and explained in your style book. Get them right: people are proud of them.

Few newspapers include the letters after people's names, preferring instead to refer to their titles in copy, if at all.

A VC is well worth a mention, probably the reason for the story, but lesser honours such as MBEs are often left out except in obituaries.

of them. If you don't, letters will arrive on your editors' desk, pointing out gently but firmly that you got it wrong and please don't do it again.

If you use one of these names you must be certain you are referring to the right product. If you write *a hoover blew up, killing its owner* when the machine was in fact made by some obscure company in China, the company that makes Hoovers is going to take you to the cleaners. If in doubt, call the machines just that: *vacuum cleaners.*

Most style books carry a list of trade names. Here are a few, with suggested alternatives: Calor Gas *(bottled gas)*, Carricot *(carry-cot)*, Cellophane *(transparent wrapping)*, Coke *(cola)*, Elastoplast *(sticking plaster)*, Fibreglass *(glass fibre)*, Photostat *(photo-copy)*, Plasticene *(modelling clay)*, Sellotape *(adhesive tape)*, Thermos *(vacuum flask)* and Vaseline *(petroleum jelly)*. And a Biro is a *ballpoint pen.*

Twelve
WORKING ONLINE

WE live in a fast-moving world with access to more information than ever before, provided by a bewildering array of outlets pumping it into our homes. The internet touches almost every aspect of our lives. Millions of us shop online, book tickets, research family trees, up-load digital photos and, thanks to eBay, trade happily with a worldwide market.

Many people have turned to the internet for news, too. The media can no longer depend on a public prepared to pay for news and advertisers willing to pay publishers to reach their audience.

This has forced content providers to re-appraise their view of the internet and devise new methods of working. The flow of advertising from print to online has concentrated the minds of publishers. Newspaper groups have recognised the potential of the internet and embraced the technology, many of them encouraging managers to push the boundaries of what was thought possible.

Almost every newspaper now has an online presence of some kind. Most, instead of merely publishing content from the newspaper, have taken advantage of the opportunities opened up by multi-media. Journalists record daily podcasts from on-site recording studios, video-on-demand casts (vodcasts) have become a daily download ritual for tens of thousands of fans, and reader interaction is enthusiastically encouraged.

- Reporting
- Writing
- Designing
- Interacting

REPORTING FOR THE WEB

ALTHOUGH some newspapers have dedicated online staff, most expect print journalists to apply their skills to the internet. Employers are looking beyond the traditional print qualifications of shorthand and good news sense.

They want to see evidence of video-editing and audio production ability, basic html skills and an understanding of web traffic and user navigation patterns. They expect reporters to work with a foot in each medium, contributing words, pictures and audio to a website as part of their daily routine.

At times it feels a bit like plate-spinning, feeding an apparently insatiable website at the same time as producing a print newspaper. Reporters are required to file copy at a breakneck pace for the web, then re-purpose the same content, adding fresh interpretation, for a print publication that may not appear until the next morning or even later in the week. Online archives, breaking news, searchable databases, audio podcasts and video multi-media have to be juggled along with print deadlines, photos, sub-editing and page make-up. The demands have never been greater.

We are in a new era, with frontiers limited only by the imagination of journalists.

NIGEL BURTON,
Northern Echo
Assistant editor,
who supplied much of
the material for this chapter
and the next

👍 *The immediacy and generally chaotic nature of the web increases the risk of making mistakes ten-fold.*

Websites that race to break news can sometimes be caught out. Hot tips by email or text can be hoaxes.

By all means rush to break the news first, but always exhaustively check reports and tips before you do.

Sources should be required to verify their identity before submitting new material.

If you have made a mistake, at least you don't have to wait 24 hours before doing something about it.

Stories can be removed from news sites with a single mouse click.

The need for speed

Working for the internet presents new challenges. Although the core disciplines for reporting are equally applicable to both print and online journalism, there are major differences between reporting for the web and reporting for a print publication. Some rules have not migrated across to the web and in other areas new standards are emerging. For a start, the online role is becoming increasingly collaborative. The work of reporters, photographers, technicians and designers has to coalesce to create the final result.

Daily newspaper journalists have to work to tight deadlines, but nothing like as tight as those for a website. Although print journalists may have to turn around a story quickly, they will probably have at least a short time to compose their thoughts and flesh out a story. That is not so with the internet, where stories are published as quickly as they can be written. So-called push technology, which allows news and information to be sent out to subscribers via mobile phone text messaging, makes it possible for people to get their news virtually as it happens.

Forget about other newspapers: when you are reporting for an online publication you are aiming to beat 24-hour TV news channels who can (and do) go live at a moment's notice.

Away from the desk

Many newspaper groups, recognising the need to be fast and first, have moved their online news-gathering operations away from office-bound hardware towards a web-based upload system. All the tools a reporter needs to write for a website are held on a remote server accessible via any PC connected to the web: a journalist can contribute copy in real time, armed only with a laptop and an internet connection. Some systems even allow a reporter to create simple news stories using nothing more than a mobile phone and text recognition software.

If your newspaper uses a web-based set-up, then you are all set to break the news almost as fast as you can type. Breaking news is what the internet is all about. The first story you write will often be completed before all the facts are known – an alien concept to reporters used to gathering facts, arranging them neatly, and crafting a carefully-written story for print. Websites cannot afford such luxury. They want the story, any story, as fast as possible.

A breaking news story may consist of only one or two paragraphs. It is a way of flagging up to website users that you know a story is developing and you are on to it. At its most simple, a breaking story could be as straightforward as:

> *Police sealed off the High Street to traffic and pedestrians at lunchtime. Shops were ordered to close and people warned to stay indoors. This story is still developing and we will bring you more news as we get it.*

This is almost the 21st-century equivalent of the first draft story for print, even down to the *'more follows later'* pledge as a sign-off. The difference now is that it will be uploaded onto a website for millions to read.

An audience of scanners

People don't access news on the web the same way they read a newspaper, listen to the radio or sit down to watch a television news programme. Viewing words on a computer screen comes a pretty poor second to reading print. It is tiring on the eyes, and the pleasant serendipity of idly paging through a newspaper doesn't exist for online readers.

In fact, a large number of them don't actually read anything at all – at least, not in the accepted sense. Researchers have found that fewer than one in five people who access the web for news actually sit at a PC and read every word. Most simply scan the main headlines, click on interesting links and generally root around looking for something to catch their attention. They cherry-pick the bits they are interested in, and ignore the rest.

Nor are they prepared to look too hard for the information they need. Many people treat internet activity as leisure time, and don't want to have to work at finding something interesting. If it isn't obvious, they will just click and move on.

A study in Canada discovered that the brain often makes snap decisions about websites almost as fast as the eye can see them. Many readers make up their mind about whether they like or dislike a site within the first twentieth of a second. Gitte Lindgaard of Carleton University in Ottawa, who undertook the research, says this means first impressions really do count: unless they instantly like what they see, 'visitors will be out of your site before they even know that you might be offering more than your competitors'.

That means spending time building an eye-catching website, filling it with compelling content, carefully selecting the right image and choosing the correct balance of material.

IT COULD BE UP THERE FOREVER

Not even the largest newspapers can compete with the internet for reach.

When it goes online, your work will be accessible to more than half the world's population.

It may remain available for years if your newspaper has a searchable archive that readers can use via the web.

This makes old stories more accessible than ever. No longer do readers face a trip to the local library or newspaper's head office to look up stories in back issues: the information is available almost instantly on-screen.

This raises some new policy issues. For instance, is it fair that a report of a minor court conviction should remain so easily accessible to the public, years after the offence has become spent?

If a mistake is made and a correction published in print, should the archived item that contains the mistake be removed or amended?

Should a correction appear on the website as well?

And what does 'contemporaneous' mean when a court story appears online and stays there?

> *Think website first. It is no longer acceptable for reporters to sit on a story for the following day's or week's edition of the paper. The website has to be seen to be an integral part of any newspaper.*
>
> *No matter what time of night or day a story breaks, it has to go on the website as quickly as possible even if only scant information is available. It can easily be updated.*
>
> **NICOLE GARNON**
> Assistant editor
> South Wales Argus

> *On-line: it's not the future – it's the now. If we recruit someone without the online skills we require, we send them off on a training course within their first couple of weeks because they are so essential. If we find people with these skills, it's brilliant.*
>
> **BARRY PETERS**
> Editor
> Bury St Edmunds Citizen

👍 *If you need to get across a complex issue, break ideas down into easily digestible bullet points that make it easier for web readers to absorb your information.*

👍 *Websites can publish newsworthy but potentially disturbing pictures – of a disaster scene, for example – behind a warning screen, something a print edition could never do.*

👍 *Contact suggestion: Music teachers. Elderly ladies offering piano tuition in their livingrooms are keen on publicity for their successes and will tell you about seven-year-olds heading for orchestral fame.*

WRITING FOR THE WEB

THE way you structure your story depends on how your website uses screens. There are four main ways sites are put together:

Single scrolling screen

The whole of your story and any associated material – pictures, audio, video – appears as a single file. If there are too many words for all of it to be seen on screen straight away, viewers scroll down to the end. It can be as long as you like, subject to any rules imposed by your site manager, but there is a limit to viewers' interest and if you go on too long they will get bored and, perhaps, click to another site.

Structure your stories as for print: an attention-grabbing intro (which web users often call the sell), a summary of the main points, expansion, lesser detail in decreasing order of importance at the end.

Many sites discourage scrolling because they believe viewers dislike making the physical effort of using the mouse and become unhappy when they are led far from the security of the top-of-file options.

Single-view screen

All your material has to be seen at once. This imposes an obvious limit on story length. Even if you have only the words and a single headline to place, 200 words is about the most you can fit in at a readable type size. If you have pictures, you may be restricted to half that many. Structure your story as for print, but write it very tightly indeed.

Multi-screen, single link

Here you have a series of screens, each containing a section of your story. The first screen carries the intro, the opening paragraphs and, perhaps, one or two pictures; at the foot is a *more* link to the next screen, which carries the next section of the story and is linked to the third, and so on to the end. Viewers are forced to read the story in the order you wrote it, clicking from one screen to the next. There is no length limit, and the structure, again, is much the same as for print, except that each screen-full needs to be carefully planned as a separate entity with appropriate headings and illustration, and each must offer viewers a *back* option to return to the previous and opening screens.

Multi-screen, multi-link

This offers an opening screen with intro, picture and self-contained story summary, followed by a number of link options to further screens carrying, perhaps, more story detail, eye-witness accounts, more pictures, a podcast, video and so on. These may be single-view or scrolling screens.

Viewers have a choice of where to go and the order in which they view screens. This has radical implications for the way you structure your story.

HARNESSING THE READERS

The web has created new methods of reporting which are very different to the fact-gathering techniques of the last century.

Among them is *open-source reporting*, where a journalist advertises what he plans to investigate and invites readers to submit suggestions and tips.

It helps small newspapers to punch above their weight by harnessing the knowledge of the local community.

This collaborative model works on the 'many hands make light work' theory: that a local community will have a broader knowledge and access to more resources than any one journalist.

The downside is that everyone knows what you are up to and there is little chance of bagging a scoop.

It is possible to take this model even further.

So-called *distributed reporting* encourages people to submit their own information, which is pooled, sifted and written up as a story.

By doing this, even the smallest newsrooms can recruit an army of enthusiastic stringers to help with major investigations and big stories.

It only works for stories and issues likely to encompass a larger-than-usual cross-section of the local community, natural disasters being an obvious example.

The potential drawback to both these methods is that too many cooks may spoil the broth, and a collaborative effort can end up as nothing more than a mish-mash of disconnected facts of dubious veracity.

> *Don't forget the internet is a source of news stories as well as a place you send them.*
>
> *YouTube, MySpace and other such sites are brimming with local content – often controversial – which will make a great spread both in print and in online editions of your newspaper.*
>
> **PAUL ROBERTSON**
> Editor
> Evening Chronicle, Newcastle

The opening screen has to sum up all the main information and each subsequent screen has to be self-contained. You have to break your story into its component parts, remembering that not all viewers will navigate between screens in the same order. You cannot make unexplained reference to something elsewhere (except the opening screen) because the viewer may not yet have read it.

The standard structure of putting things in descending order of importance goes out of the window. You have to imagine your story shaped like a family tree, each screen after the first of equal importance and each linked horizontally as well as vertically to the rest. Each screen should be as compelling as possible, and flag up what is available elsewhere as well as offering an easy route back to the beginning.

This is the preferred option for many news sites. though it does have the disadvantage that viewers have to wait for each new screen to load, breaking their concentration and tempting them to surf elsewhere. It is worth bearing this in mind before you overload a screen with items that might take some time to download.

For any of these options you may be required to write a brief summary, worded differently to your intro and carrying a link to your story, to go on your website's main news page, just as you might be asked to do a front-page write-off for a newspaper.

Keep it tight

Every story you write should be easily understood, the information imparted in the quickest, most straightforward way possible. The intro

> *A great journalist is one who seeks to reflect the variety of real life, seeking out special angles, personalities, background, local distinctiveness and significance – however tiny.*
>
> **OLWYN HOCKING**
> Multi-media producer

👍 *When a story breaks it is crucial to keep up-dating the web. Readers hate returning to a news site hours later only to be confronted with the same 'more news as we get it' pledge.*

A running story should be up-dated as quickly, and as often, as possible.

👍 *Almost every town is twinned with somewhere, lucky ones with cultural centres, the less fortunate with ecological disaster areas in Eastern Europe. Some are multi-twinned with places scattered all over the globe.*

You will get stories from the people running town-twinning in your area: ask about foreign visitors, trips abroad, and who pays for it all.

Contact the local newspaper in your twin town to generate stories. Link to the newspaper's and town's websites.

You might even get a free trip out of it all.

is crucial: you have only seconds to get the reader's attention. It should be short: 20 words is about your maximum. Good online stories should flow naturally from point to point. Those that are a mess of jumbled facts are the enemy of news websites.

The writing has to be tight and bright. Keep the words short and simple. Long sentence structures that are hard to follow are a sure-fire turn-off to a web audience. One idea per sentence is fine. That may sound depressing, all your finely-crafted sentence structure going to waste, but it is also a huge challenge.

Don't be afraid to pose questions or to address the viewer directly – something rarely done in print.

PAGE DESIGN

YOU are unlikely to be offered a blank screen and invited to design your pages any way you like: you will probably be feeding copy into templates with predetermined spaces and standardised typography. Even if you are allowed some design flexibility, your site will have style rules about acceptable typefaces, type sizes, use of colour and other matters of presentation. Follow them.

Headlines should be simple, summing up the story in three or four words. Don't be tempted to get too clever or flippant. Reader attention should be held by varying typefaces, highlighting keywords and using colour. Quotes can be used to liven up the way a story is displayed online. They can be pulled out and used as a design tool, depending on house style. Regular sub-headings should break up the text and guide readers forward.

Signposts

Confronted as they are with a bewildering array of news and thousands of news outlets, readers still require self-direction to find what they are looking for. It is part of the online journalist's job to help point the way. This can be done by:

Linking to all site content, which can be searched and categorised in numerous ways not possible in an old-fashioned newspaper contents panel.

Linking individual stories to other relevant stories on the day's news site.

Linking to a news archive so that readers can mug up on the background to a big issue

These are known as internal links because, although a reader can find more information, the content is contained within a newspaper's website. But external links can be good, too, particularly if they add value to a story. Do this by:

Linking to websites that offer more information. A good example would be a report pointing to statistics available on a website for a Government department, such as school league tables or council tax figures.

Pointing readers to official websites run by organisations mentioned in a story, such as the RSPCA, the Samaritans or the NSPCC.

Giving readers a link to sites where they can buy products featured in the story. Such links should carry a disclaimer warning that they are not under your control.

The best websites give readers everything they think they need, and lots more besides. That way a bond of trust grows between reader and website, and keeps them coming back for more.

Updates

Journalists enjoy far greater flexibility when working online. Stories are up-dated in real time. Photos, audio and video can be added if they are available, helping to make a good story even better. Unlike a print story, where your efforts are set in stone the moment the newspaper goes to bed, an online report can be polished and re-worked for as long as a journalist has the time. There are no deadlines in cyberspace.

Added value

This flexibility extends to other areas. A newspaper is always constrained by the number of pages it contains. Sometimes a journalist may have to forgo writing a background article to accompany a major news story because there simply isn't the space to accommodate it. This is not an issue online. So if you have worked on something in advance only to find it can't go in the paper because there isn't space, don't despair. The web could become home for all that carefully-crafted prose. It will never impose a word count.

This applies equally to photos. A picture editor will usually select one or two for use in the newspaper. A website can take the lot and let readers decide which ones they like best. Online picture galleries also increase photo sales if they are properly cross-promoted in the newspaper.

READER INTERACTION

NEWSPAPERS have a proud history of putting people in touch with each other and their communities. The internet offers all this, and far more. News sites are becoming conduits for a worldwide readership and portals for local grassroots information. Cinema listings, theatre show times, chemists' rotas, contact numbers and hundreds more titbits are uploaded for searching.

There are two kinds of reporter – those who make out they know more than they do on a subject, and those who make out they know less. Guess which is better.

Never try to impress people that you know all about their area if you don't – or even if you do. It's so easy, when talking to a know-all who says: 'Of course you know about this, don't you?' to mutter: 'Yes, of course.'

Big mistake. When you come to write up the story you could find you don't understand it all and be in trouble.

Don't cover up and write around your problem. Go back and check. Embarrassing? Too bad. It wouldn't have happened if you'd been honest and said: 'No, actually I don't. Could you tell me?'

TIM GOPSILL
Editor
The Journalist

There are obvious legal dangers in allowing the public open access, and some websites have been suspended after their readers posted obscene, defamatory or offensive material.

Site providers have some protection against being sued for defamation if offending material is removed as soon as it is brought to their attention, but someone still needs to keep a close eye on content.

It would take only one contributor adding a link to a hard-core porn site to seriously damage a newspaper's reputation – and possibly land it in court.

Contact suggestion: entertainers. The Yellow Pages list dozens of them: kids' party specialists, Punch and Judy men, hypnotists, conjurors and strippers. Every one has a story to tell.

Online journalism has blurred the line between a publication and its readership. The advent of bloggers (web loggers) has made the distinction even harder to determine. Many papers have blogs written by staff journalists, chatty pieces reflecting the personality of the author. Generally they work best when journalists are writing about subjects close to their hearts. They have a good deal of opinion, but usually cover events and personalities. Good ones attract reader comments, bad ones are ignored. If you have a passion or a hobby, you might try writing a blog. Your thoughts and opinions will stimulate readers to offer their own thoughts. Blogs that encourage reader interest are a great way of creating a bond between a newspaper, its website and the readers.

Many newspaper sites encourage reader interaction beyond blogs and forums, not least because it is a valuable source of tips and follow-ups. It also gives editors some idea of what readers think is important.

Readers can add comments to news stories. The pace of mobile phone development makes it good practice to encourage the audience to become a kind of co-author by contributing eyewitness reports via email, SMS, MMS multi-media pictures and video.

There is no need to wait for readers' letters online. Sites can carry a top-ten list of the most-read stories, or allow readers to vote for the best. Online polls produce stories. Lots of sites run their own forums and bulletin boards, and video conferencing allows readers to post their own questions in real time. Readers' picture galleries and tribute sites abound.

Rules on reader interaction vary from site to site. Some insist on responder registration and strictly police all contributions; others encourage a free-for-all; some allow only staff to post their opinions. Those with an open-door policy will almost certainly have a moderator to whom readers can complain if they find something insulting or derogatory.

RIGHTS FOR THE BLOGGERS

The state of blogging has come a long way. Some of the best bloggers can now be likened to investigative journalists, and the material they produce has the power to make headlines in print as well as online.

In the United States, bloggers have their own 'union', the Media Bloggers Association, and in some cases are accorded the same rights as print journalists.

They received guaranteed reserved seating during the Microsoft anti-trust trial.

They defeated Apple's argument that bloggers were not bona fide journalists, put forward when the company sought a court order to make an independent news site reveal its sources.

The California Appeals Court likened websites to print publications, ruling that bloggers and their sources were entitled to the same legal protection as print journalists' informants.

It works both ways: in 2006, a blogger and freelance journalist was jailed for contempt after refusing to disclose video footage of anti-G8 protesters demonstrating in San Francisco.

Thirteen
AUDIO & VIDEO

THE greatest area of change for a reporter working online is multi-media. Early websites simply repeated their newspaper's printed content and thought it would be enough to bring in the readers. It was a cheap and easy way to pay lip-service to the internet without investing time or effort.

Visitors want a lot more these days. The arrival of the iPod music device fuelled a growth in downloadable content, much of it free, and the public expects to see similar exciting and relevant video and audio material on newspaper websites.

At its most basic, this sort of content is material supplied by external agencies, such as the police, other emergency services and local authorities. Public relations companies send video with press releases in the hope it finds a place on the web.

However, as competition for website traffic hots up, newspapers are increasingly striving to produce polished news bulletins and special video reports to differentiate their offerings from those of less techni-cally-savvy rivals.

The ability to work with video and audio has become a highly-prized asset among editors looking for new journalists. Print-trained reporters have had to learn a host of new skills, many of them borrowed from the world of radio and television. The boundaries between traditional broadcasting and today's website use of audio and video – often referred to as narrowcasting – are becoming increasingly blurred, and reporters with web experience find they have acquired many of the basic capabilities needed to be effective in radio or television newsrooms.

This chapter looks at producing sound and vision for websites, and then examines the special requirements of writing for television and radio.

- Multi-media
- Audio for the Web
- Video for the Web
- Writing for Broadcasting

AUDIO

PODCASTS, at their most basic, are internet audio programmes that can be listened to on a computer or downloaded to a portable audio device. The name is a combination of *iPod* (the ubiquitous digital music player) and *broadcast*, although you do not need an iPod to listen to a podcast. Podcasters make music, talk shows and chat available for easy download in the MP3 audio format.

A quick search on the internet unearths a vast amount of podcast material. Anyone with a computer, an internet link and a microphone

In broadcasting, words paint pictures – and pictures tell stories.

MALCOLM WRIGHT
Managing director,
ITV Signpost,
who wrote much of the
section on writing for
radio and television

can create one. Millions of people have done so. They have been helped by the development of Really Simple Syndication (RSS) technology, which makes it possible for listeners to subscribe to podcast content and receive new material downloaded automatically to their computers. It is a fancy new version of the newspaper home delivery service, but now the content is delivered at all hours of the day. In most cases there is no charge, but as the podcast market matures and listeners grow more discriminating, some material is now of sufficient quality and popularity for users to be willing to pay a small charge.

Strangely, newspapers have not embraced audio as quickly or widely as they have video, even though, in terms of set-up costs, it is cheaper. A good podcast adds a new feature to a newspaper. Subscribers can 'read' their favourite newspaper driving to work instead of listening to the radio. Alternatively, they may prefer to read an interview in the print edition, then listen to the interviewee in their own words on a podcast.

This works particularly well for celebrity interviews. Arts and entertainments reporters are moving to a dual model whereby they interpret an interview in the newspaper and then upload the full discussion (which can only form part of the print article) as a podcast.

Perhaps not surprisingly, local radio has embraced the idea. Many stations offer two daily news bulletins, one in the morning, for listening to on the way to work, and one in the afternoon for people returning home. These bulletins are promoted as 'News to go' and offer long-form news lasting anything up to half an hour. Some stations are also offering 'raw news' downloads: press conferences and speeches presented live and in full. News reports often contain full interviews as well.

Newspaper programming varies enormously. Some simply summarise the day's news, while others go for more of a radio show feel, with interviews and reports by named columnists. Although the best have a professional radio station presentation, most are low budget, low-tech affairs made by journalists with no direct first-hand experience in the broadcast field.

Podcasts can be absolutely anything that a 'broadcaster' wants to do. Theoretically it is possible to produce a three or four-hour show. In practice, most podcasts are short-form – 15 minutes or less – which allows for rapid download times and ease of listening during a daily commute.

EQUIPMENT

Recorders

The quality of recording equipment is crucial to a good podcast. It is possible to use tape recorders, but the audio is poor. The sound the tape transport mechanism makes as it passes the tape across the recording head produces a drumming effect that can clearly be heard. Although filters can be run over a file to remove this noise, doing so is a time

RECORDERS: WHAT TO LOOK FOR

If you decide to buy a recorder, go for the best you can afford.

Aim for solid state machines capable of recording 16-bit PCM WAV files at 44.1 khz or 48 khz (the same or better quality than a CD).

Look for the ability to record stereo MP3 files at 128 kbps, a 1GB compact flash card that can hold more than one hour of uncompressed stereo sound, an operational life of up to four hours on normal AA batteries, a USB 2.0 interface and built-in microphones for operation in the field.

(and computer) intensive job. A totally digital sound recording solution is more cost-effective, and some manufacturers have designed recorders with this in mind.

Microphones

An omni-directional microphone which receives sound from all directions is cheaper, but operation beyond the quiet office environment has shown that cardioid microphones that pick up only the sound in front of it may be necessary.

Software

After the sound is recorded, sound-editing software can remove imperfections and, where needed, insert appropriate background music. Audacity is not only free but also a simple-to-learn, feature-rich sound editor. It can be used to record podcasts directly or edit sound files, and can run on Mac, PC Windows and Linux platforms. Among other things, it can record up to 16 channels at the same time, create multitrack recordings and dub over existing tracks, import and export MP3 files, offer easy cut-and-paste editing, and fade out volume.

VIDEO

VIDEO is the most exciting of all the multi-media disciplines you will learn. A movie camera will open doors, and mouths, in places where a reporter's notebook and pen are met with a firm 'no comment'. People, it seems, cannot resist the notion that they may appear on the internet equivalent of cinema or television. Everyone craves their 15 minutes of fame, or at least a few online seconds of it.

Types of camera and software vary hugely. At one end are the cheapest point-and-shoot digi-cams and editing software packages that come free with computers. At the other are high-definition equipment and professional editing suites in which some newspaper groups have invested heavily. It

When a student journalist in Washington DC, I was very nervous when I was sent to interview a congressman because he was so important.

As the interview progressed, an older woman kept coming to the door and signalling him. After the third interruption he said: 'Okay, mother, Okay', apologised to me and scurried off after her.

I have always remembered since then that no matter how famous someone is, they probably have a mother who terrorises them. It helps.

JEREMY GAUNT
Reporter
Reuters

Always turn your mike off as soon as you're off-camera. You'll be mortified the day you forget and everyone hears you visit the toilet.

SARAH COSGROVE
Reporter
Waltham Forest Guardian

👍 *Do film interviews first, get the words to go with the pictures afterwards. It's a lot easier than the other way round.*

doesn't matter that much, because the difference between a good video report and a bad one is not the equipment but the person who operates it.

Every journalist receives training before being sent out with a video camera. Some have an instant eye for what makes a good report, some don't. Video journalism is a skill and reporters usually find it takes some time to create even the shortest story in visual form. Remember, practice makes perfect. Even Steven Spielberg had to start somewhere.

Whatever equipment you are given, there are a number of rules when shooting video for the web:

Think your report through before setting out. Make notes if it helps. What is the piece going to be about? How can you illustrate it?

👍 *Don't forget to take establishing shots, and plenty of cutaways to fill the gaps when you come to edit.*

Make it quick. A 90-second report is about the maximum. The biggest mistake novice videographers make is creating reports that are far too long. The trend is for short and snappy news reports, not laborious documentaries. The attention span of the web audience is short, so it makes sense to keep videos as tight as possible. Think of them as the moving pictures equivalent of a story for the newspaper.

Shoot plenty of footage. Most of it will be discarded, but it is better to have too much than not enough. At first, you will need plenty of takes just to create an adequate report. Think along the lines of a 10:1 ratio, shooting around ten minutes of footage for a one-minute piece. There is nothing worse than getting back to the office and realising you have to go out and film again because the quality and quantity of your footage just isn't there.

Don't spend too long editing. Remember, the watchword is speed.

👍 *Don't pan for the sake of it, only when you are following something or somebody moving.*

Above all, think visually. Some of the advice given earlier in the section on taking still photographs applies to video as well: about composition, background and light, for example. Remember that pictures need people, but don't film someone talking about an event if you can film that event actually happening. Video is about moving images more than words or sounds.

The old adage that a picture is worth a thousand words could have been invented for the video news report.

EQUIPMENT

To get the most out of it, a camcorder should be like your new best friend. It is worth taking the time to investigate the ins and outs of all

👍 *It sounds silly, but always make sure your finger knows exactly where the record button is. It has to be within easy reach or you could miss a crucial grab shot.*

DON'T DISAPPOINT THEM

Be realistic about your abilities. Don't promise readers something that cannot be achieved.

If a video package is to be promoted in-paper, always build in enough time to complete the package and upload it to the web. Because of the pressures to juggle online and print requirements, that probably means telling readers that a video may not be available on your web site until lunchtime, or even the following day.

its features. When you are working, you may only have one chance to grab that precious shot, so using your equipment should be second nature. Things to watch out for include:

The lens

The most important part of any camera. An optical zoom uses optics to magnify an image, whereas a digital zoom relies on electronics to blow up the centre of the frame, to the considerable detriment of your footage. Avoid using the digital zoom if possible. If you can't get close enough, find another vantage point.

The microphone

Wind noise is your enemy on location. If at all possible use an external microphone for interviews. However, if you cannot do this, think the situation through. Try recording an interview indoors or, if the worst comes to the worst, position your subject with their back to the wind. At least that way they will act as a natural shield.

The tripod

Reporters may be reluctant to use a tripod because they feel embarrassed lugging around such a hefty piece of equipment, but a good tripod can make or break a video report. No matter how steady your hands, or how good the anti-shake electronics are on modern camcorders, a tripod will be better. Get into the habit of filming your footage with a tripod-mounted camera. A tripod is often the only way to film yourself talking to camera if you are on your own.

LCD screen

A flip-out LCD lets you film without having to use the viewfinder. It also allows you to film at different angles and see the results, or even film yourself without chopping off your head. Remember, though, that an LCD screen will use up more battery power than using the viewfinder alone.

Memory card slot

Many digi-cams come with a slot for a solid-state memory card and the ability to save stills. Unless you have plenty of time (which is unlikely) you are best ignoring this feature. If you need to, software will allow you to extract usable stills from movie footage back at the office.

> *When contacting people, especially those running businesses, make it clear that you are a reporter, not an advertising rep, and that there won't be a bill coming their way if they agree to talk to you.*
>
> *I listened to a trainee who was getting nowhere on a ring-round of village post offices and discovered his opening gambit was: 'I'm from the Visitor and wonder if I could interest you in a feature we're doing...'*
>
> *They all thought it was a sales pitch and gave him an abrupt: 'No thanks'.*
>
> **GLEN COOPER**
> Editor
> The Visitor, Morecambe

> *The secret of investigative journalism: a good filing system.*
>
> **DOROTHY BYRNE**
> Head of News
> Channel Four Television

Battery pack

The life of a video camera's power source can be unpredictable. Cold weather can kill an otherwise healthy battery in a matter of minutes. Preserve your power by always switching off the camera between takes, and carry a fully-charged spare.

EDITING

Modern editing software allows journalists to do remarkable things with video. Resist the temptation to get stuck into the filters menu and concentrate on getting the basics right.

A simple transition between takes is probably all you require, along with start and end titles. If you are using a professional-level software package the interface will look daunting to start with, so stick to assembling your clips and overlaying a commentary track. Mistakes are easy to rectify in software because such editing normally leaves your original clips untouched.

A journalist shooting footage out of the office can often get away with a basic edit, using the software that came free with their computer. Windows Movie Maker and Apple's iMovie HD are perfectly good editors for news clips. If you are a long way from home you can edit your clips on a laptop and email a video report directly to the newsdesk.

However you edit, remember to make a back-up and put it in a safe place. Digital video is notoriously space inefficient: a blank DVD may be okay for no more than half-an-hour or so. High-definition disc formats and portable hard disks are other methods of creating back-ups.

BROADCASTING

IN the world of print, *space* rules. News and pictures compete for column inches, headlines put the squeeze on stories, big brash adverts muscle in anywhere they choose. Happily, if the accountants allow, you can always increase the number of pages.

But when the message moves to the medium of radio or television, *time* is king. You can't put an extra hour into a day, or an extra minute into an hour in this real-time, linear environment. You can't alter a type size to make room for extra information. The broadcast world is ruled by the unerring sweep of the second hand. To get a sense of just how demanding this time regime can be, try reading a newspaper story and see how far down a column you get in a precious 60 seconds. Not very far. Broadcasters reckon that a minute of air time is a platform for about 180 words only – roughly three words per second. Turned into speech, your daily newspaper would occupy many hours of airtime.

So broadcasting must necessarily offer a different experience for those who watch or listen. The sheer volume of information carried in a newspaper can never be matched or replicated over the airwaves. Up against the clock, broadcasters work in a fundamentally different way. Where the news reporter measures a story in word length, a radio or TV reporter will measure it in minutes and seconds.

This impacts fundamentally on how people write for broadcast. If good newspaper writing has to be tight, then the best broadcast writing has to be tighter still. Time is at a premium, and much of the available time may, as you will read later, isn't used on the delivery of news stories. While many of the golden rules of print journalism – clarity, concision, accuracy, simplicity – can and should be applied to TV or radio writing, there are other considerations and demands for those who aspire to a name-check rather than a byline.

Much of what follows in the section on writing for television can equally be applied to radio. Your common sense will tell you what is relevant. But just to complicate matters, it's important to recognise that there are differences between radio and television writing too. And beyond broadcast, there are new styles and demands now emerging on the narrowcast platforms of Internet IPTV stations and web channels, mobile phones and personal digital assistants (PDAs).

TELEVISION

Be a storyteller, not a writer. It may seem glaringly obvious, but TV is a visual medium. It's picture-led. It pays homage to the maxim that a picture is worth a thousand words. It understands that no amount of brilliantly-crafted words can ever eclipse the moving image of a plane crashing into the World Trade Center. It's safe in the knowledge that, from the memory bank of the modern human mind, it's always the powerful image which emerges first.

So for every television news channel, two daily demands go hand in hand. One: get the story first. Two: get the best pictures first as well. The two are inseparable. This focussed approach to news gathering has an enormous bearing on television's news sense. The basic instinct is to say: 'If there aren't any pictures, it isn't a story.' The complex facts-and-figures investigation which makes a front page splash for a Sunday newspaper just won't translate easily into television viewing. It's not a *visual* experience. Neither are the local council meeting or the magistrates court story. Good television 'news sense' is greatly conditioned by understanding the power of pictures.

Television doesn't, of course, ignore everything which has no obvious visual appeal. Some news is so compelling that it must be covered. News in the political arena still finds its way regularly onto the TV screen, for example, even though it is still not easily illustrated. With cameras now covering parliamentary debates, things are a little easier.

You can find stories just about anywhere. I was lying in the bath idly reading the shampoo bottle, the way you do.

London, Paris, New York, Rome, Tokyo, said the label.

Closer inspection revealed a Darlington postcode.

The stuff was actually made in scrubby little premises beside a scrapyard near the town's railway station and had no connection with any of the capitals. The nearest it got was an agent in Middlesbrough.

It made a nice little story.

MIKE AMOS
Columnist
The Northern Echo

It's always worth a call – you never know what you might get.

LYNN ASHWELL
Assistant editor
Bolton News

But outside the Commons and the Lords, there are only so many times you can show minister walking though the front door of 10 Downing Street, of door-knockers on the election trail. Thus, increasingly in our visual world, we see the political story illustrated by complex state-of-the art animated graphics to help bring it alive. The thought that goes into the visualisation is just as important as the care which goes into gathering the story and verifying the facts. So, while the carefully written script is important, the newswriter has to face up to the facts: telly is about pictures that tell stories.

THE SHAPE OF TV NEWS

The standard newspaper story, as we know, carries the most important information at the top, the first paragraph communicating the most salient information. If the sub wants to cut it, the final and penultimate paragraphs can be sacrificed without greatly affecting the integrity of the information. The smaller detail may be lost.

This shape doesn't transfer comfortably to television. A single TV story is usually made up of several disparate elements, which break up the chronology. The most important information doesn't necessarily come first. Instead we get some or all of the following:

An initial link (sometimes called a cue) which starts a story, probably read live in studio by the news presenter or anchor. It may start with a bald statement: *Paramedics say it's a miracle he survived.* This direct verbal style carries far too little information about person, place and context to be acceptable as a newspaper intro. But with an **Underlay**, moving pictures of the survivor screened behind the newsreader as he or she reads the opening script, this statement works well to hook in the viewer. It establishes that there is a story to tell. You want to know more. Watch the average link on a TV story and it will very rarely be over 30 seconds. It's more likely to be a brief, bouncy 15-second taster of what is to come.

Upsound: A brief interview clip or comment which heightens the impact of the story about to be told: *When I first saw the bus down the bank, I thought there wasn't a cat in hell's chance that anyone was alive in there.*

A pre-edited package follows, put together and voiced by a reporter who has been out and about on the story. It will tell the story in greater depth, using the best of the pictures to illustrate what happened. It is likely to feature interview and may well be held together by a PTC (a Piece To Camera) in which the reporter talks directly to the audience, filling in details which are not easily illustrated.

A live two-way may follow, in which the studio-based presenter effectively interviews the on-location reporter about the very latest developments in the story. This 'live' is made possible by the on-location presence of a satellite truck, which beams the camera signal back to studio. The 'live' can also feature a live interview on location, perhaps with a fire chief or senior police officer.

A back reference to the studio rounds it off, when the presenter tidies up the loose ends before moving to a new link: *Well, police have now issued an emergency telephone number which you can ring for more information...*

LINEAR RESTRAINTS

Newspaper readers can rove round the page, re-read a story, turn the page, hunt for the headline which grabs them, hop from a half-read story to a new one. They can pick and choose. Every story is conveniently compartmentalised for them. Television news is very different.

The linear, scheduled nature of broadcasting means that viewers are locked into an order of presentation dictated by someone else. They need to be encouraged to stay the journey – constantly teased and stimulated by the promise of what they may see later.

Commercial success for a newspaper company is, in part, about selling their product. Even if the buyer reads only ten per cent of it, the cover price has already been paid. TV companies measure success not just by the number of people tuning in a programme, but also by how long they stay with it. Every programme team hopes to 'inherit' a large number of viewers who were watching whatever was on before, and hopes to deliver a large inheritance to whatever programme follows their own. For the independent TV companies, which rely on advertising, viewer loyalty throughout a programme is crucial. The trick for telly is to stop the viewer turning over, or turning off.

For the news writer, this means that a story cannot be seen in isolation. How does it fit in with what else is in the programme? What comes before or after it, which may offer the chance to create linkage? Can a story be briefly teased with good pictures before the commercial break – *He planned to climb Glasgow's tallest building, but it didn't go according to plan. To see what happened next, join us after the break...* – and then shown in full later?

Analyse a TV news programme from start to finish and you will find that a significant amount of time is devoted not to news reporting, but

> *Monitor sites like YouTube. We got a great tale about a lad working at a local supermarket who got a friend to video him as he switched on the company microphone and broadcast to everyone: 'This is a management announcement. You are all sacked. Thank you.'*
>
> **BILL BROWNE**
> Editor
> Salisbury Journal

> *Always accept the offer of a cup of tea. If you're in someone's house, it means they'll be in the kitchen while you can have a surreptitious look around; if you're in a formal interview setting, fiddling with the sugar, milk, teabag and spillages always buys you valuable thinking time.*
>
> **CHRIS LLOYD**
> Deputy editor
> The Northern Echo

TESTING, TESTING...

It wasn't always so personal. When the BBC first started broadcasting to the nation through the crystal set in 1922, it was very much a speech rather than a conversation: *This is the BBC calling...* The BBC called and the public listened in awe.

But as broadcasting matured, the tone became more conversational, more relaxed, more homely, more egalitarian even. The penny dropped that scripts worked much better when they were written to be read.

Walk into any broadcast newsroom and you will hear the proof of that – journalists testing their stories by reading them out loud to make sure that they sound right

👍 *The equipment needed for filming video and recording audio is fragile and expensive.*

Always pack it away the moment you have finished.

Don't abuse it because, if you do, you will find it lets you down at the worst possible moment.

to creating a seamless experience. The words and devices which stitch together story after story aren't there by accident. They're part of a carefully-crafted mix which hopes to keep bums on seats and eyes on screens.

You will find spoken headlines: *Bong...Thousands stranded as blizzards hit Scotland ....bong.... Police swoop on Britain's largest ever haul of heroin ...Bong... And the Ashes arrive back in Australia on a seat all of their own.*

You will hear teasers which reference stories that you cannot see yet: *Later in the programme, why the prime minister's been back to school for a history lesson... Coming up after the break, we report exclusively from inside the Vatican where a new pope prays for world peace ... In a moment, from fags to riches ... how giving up earned one woman a fortune... But first...*

There may be links to other programmes: *And you can see more about that story in Jane Smith's disturbing special report from Ethiopia tonight at ten thirty...*

There may be non-verbal devices like stings – animated graphics with music which last just a few seconds and which ease the transition from one story to another. And of course there are opening titles and end credits which top and tail a programme, making it instantly identifiable.

A ONE-SIDED CONVERSATION

One of the fundamental differences between print and broadcasting is the relationship between the originator of the news and the recipient.

In general, newspaper readers are not interested in who has written the story. It is an impersonal medium, in which very few readers will even look at a byline. But in broadcasting, there is a very strong sense of *me* and *you* – *me* the newsreader, *you* the viewer. There seems to be a one-to-one relationship, even if in reality there is only a one-sided dialogue. It's okay – encouraged – for the news presenter to direct comments directly to the viewer. For example: *Now, if you've never thought about a holiday in Siberia, perhaps this will change your mind.*

WRITING TO BE READ

The tone of TV news is friendly, often chatty and designed to be easy on the ear. And the starting point for that is the *me/you* or *us/you* relationship built into script writing which we have refered to. But there are other tricks too.

If you're observant, you may have noticed that this chapter is littered with contractions. *You are* becomes *you're... It is* becomes *it's... A man has pleaded guilty* becomes *A man's pleaded guilty*. This is the way in which we learn to write for broadcasting. But these short forms aren't anything to do with concision. They're all about relaxed readability.

👍 *Warn people you are interviewing on camera that they need to be brief and get their point across without rambling.*

There's nothing wrong with asking an interviewee to do it again if he or she has made a mess of it.

By doing so, you have made your package better and helped the interviewee get their message across.

The construction of scripts follows several rules which are irrelevant to a newspaper story, but which greatly improve verbal communication.

In the newspaper story, unless you are a headline writer, you learn to always write in sentences. Not so when writing for TV. People don't always speak in sentences, and the desire to sound conversational often means that sentence structure is overridden. Here's a studio presenter linking to a reporter who is live on location: *Jim. I gather there've been two arrests in connection with this crash. Any more word on the police investigation?* The script is written here deliberately as one side of a conversation. It's like a friendly phone call.

It's perfectly acceptable to include superfluous words to make a script sound more natural. *Well, for the thousands of fans who queued here outside Wembley Stadium last night, it's come as welcome news.* The word *well* adds nothing to the sense of the sentence, but makes it easier to read.

Sometimes the script may prompt the news magazine presenter how to react: *Hmmm...Not sure that I'd like to do that* or *Ouch. That looked like it really hurt!*

Wherever possible, words or phrases which are difficult to pronounce should be avoided. If the football result happens to be *Forfar 4 East Fife 5*, the sports reporter will just have to be nimble-tongued – the words can't be changed. But that little tongue twister is a perfect example of what the newsreader – live on air – does not want to stumble across when live on air.

In a TV or radio script, it's perfectly acceptable to start with a question: *So, you've bought your ticket, you've paid a fortune for it, but how do you know it's genuine?*

WRITING FOR AUTOCUE

A script must be as readable as possible. The way in which it appears – either on autocue or on a printed back-up script – is designed to make the TV newsreader's job more easy.

Autocue is a system which allows the script to appear on a screen just below the lens of a studio camera. The newsreader seems to be looking straight into the camera, establishing eye contact with the viewer. In fact, his eyeline is very slightly down, allowing him to read the script. As it scrolls through, the speed is controlled by an autocue operator to make sure that it matches the pace of the newsreading. Autocue displays very few words at once, with very short lines of text so that the newsreader's eyes are not seen to constantly track from left to right. This would destroy the illusion that the newsreader is actually looking at you the viewer rather than reading.

Again, this technological part of the news delivery has an effect on the way news is written. Words which need to be stressed by the newsreader may appear in CAPITALS, or in **bold**, or be underlined. Numbers are often spelt out – *10,017* becomes *ten thousand and seventeen*.

👍 On average, a news story in a regional television bulletin will run about one and a half minutes.

At the standard reading speed of three words a second, that's about 220 words – not much for a newspaper story, but usually quite enough for television because the pictures should have helped to tell the story.

Similarly, times of the day will not appear in a script in numeric form: *Join us for the national news at six thirty*. Web addresses may appear in a script like this – *www dot itv dot com* – to improve readability.

Anything which could surprise the newsreader and cause a stumble is simplified – or avoided. This includes both homophones – words which sound the same but have different spellings and meanings (is it the baker's favourite *flour* or favourite *flower?*) and homographs, word spelt the same but with different meanings (is it the ship's *bow* or the archer's *bow?*).

A FEW CHOICE WORDS

The power of pictures has a big impact on the way in which people write for television.

Go back to the images of the bombings of the World Trade Centre and you realise not just that words fail to convey the horror of what you see, but that words may actually be intrusive. Watch the hundreds of thousands of people celebrating the release of Nelson Mandela in South Africa, and you need no words to describe the scale of public joy and celebration. See the tearful gold medallist on the podium at the Olympics listening to her national anthem, and words about pride or achievement become redundant.

Television constantly reinforces our understanding through our eyes as well as our ears. And so we often 'let the pictures breathe' – with a minimum of commentary. The pictures can speak for themselves.

One advantage of being able to show moving images, of course, is that additional information can be given at the same time. While time seems to restrict TV news, in reality there are at least three information streams simultaneously available at any time to inform the viewer – pictures, voice and text. Have a look at a 24-hour news channel to see how this layered communication succeeds in greatly increasing the amount of detail.

Sometimes no words are needed over pictures. But sensitive commentary which interprets what the viewer is seeing can enhance our understanding. When a British Midlands plane crashed near Kegworth, in Leicestershire, in 1989, killing 46 people, television cameras recorded the emergency services as they battled to rescue passengers from the wrecked fuselage. The then ITV reporter Jon Snow described the *'massive gentle effort'* as a survivor was lifted from the plane, three choice words which spoke volumes about the drama unfolding on the screen.

ASKING THE RIGHT QUESTIONS

Producers and journalists who write for TV don't just write scripts. They may also write the questions which they suggest news presenters

👍 Don't be afraid to repeat good news pictures.

If you have a story about an eyesore chimney being demolished, start with shots of it crashing down.

That should grab the viewer's attention, and you can show the pictures again as you tell the full story. Take a look at any news bulletin: it won't be long before you see it happening.

use for live interviews. And they often write down the questions which they are going to ask when out with a camera crew.

Assuming that questions are relevant, there are still good and bad ways of asking them. You need to ask a question which elicits more than a Yes/No response. Don't fall into the trap of making statements and trying to turn them into questions, something which afflicts too many sports reporters: *That was probably the best you've played all season and the three goals were all superb, weren't they?* Answer: *Yes.* Much better is something like this: *What did you think of your team's performance this afternoon?* with a follow-up: *Tell me about the goals.* That last 'question' isn't even a question, of course. It's an instruction, part of the armoury of getting people to talk about what *you* want them to talk about.

The questions which work best are those which create a platform for interviewees, a stage on which they can outline their opinions and make their points. The brief *What's your reaction?* rarely fails. The follow-up *Could you tell me why?* does its job.

WRITING TO THE PICTURES

As is often done in television, we have held back some of the most important information to the end. Ask any trainer about how to approach writing for TV, and they will hammer home this advice: *Write to the pictures!* So what does it mean?

We've already established that it's primarily the power of pictures which drives television – be it news, features, current affairs or whatever. In the 21st Century TV operation, it's now highly likely that reporters coming back from a story will also edit the pictures which have been gathered on location, usually by a single camera operator. Very occasionally the journalist will operate the camera – a video journalist or VJ. The TV wordsmith needs to be a picturesmith too.

How the story is to be covered is discussed by the camera-reporter team before filming begins. Television is a partnership industry, where the skills of several individuals may be called upon before the story is delivered to the viewer. The editor or programme producer may already have briefed the reporter about what the story is, and what he/she wants from it. There may already have been liaison about additional graphics which need to go into the story – these produced by another member of the team. But central to all the discussions will be how to get the best pictures. Watch any morning newsroom conference, when a programme team gathers to discuss what may make the evening news, and you will see stories dropped because they lack picture potential, or talked up because they offer interesting visuals.

With good planning, and a deal of luck sometimes, the good reporter/camera team will get all the pictures needed to tell the story. Your job as reporter is to make sure that the words you write supplement and enhance the pictures.

One of the best ways to become familiar with how news is covered by radio and television is to listen and watch as much as possible and to analyse what you heard and saw.

If it feels comfortable to watch it or listen to it, and if you have been informed by it, then it works.

ARTHUR PICKERING
Former news editor
Tyne Tees Television

When doing a difficult death knock, plan your escape if needed.

Size up the fence you may need to vault, check for Beware of the Dog signs, and don't be afraid to make your apologies and run!

NEAL BUTTERWORTH
Editor
Bournemouth Daily News

There are two ways of editing a television package once the pictures have been recorded and the interviews completed.

In both cases, the reporter will first log the pictures and interview by going through them on a computer back in the office, identifying what will be used.

Some reporters then cut the pictures and interview clips and write the words so they fit. Others write their voice-over script and record it before adding the pictures later.

Which method is used can depend on the broadcast organisation, the time available, or the strength of the pictures and/or interview clips.

Choose the best pictures for telling the story, and then work out how much time you have to write the words. This is instinctively better than writing the story, and then trying to find the pictures which fit to your script – although in the hurly-burly of a busy news operation the latter system is often used for late stories which must be edited at speed.

The greatest mistake made by the rookie writer is that the words used fight against the pictures being shown. On screen we see a montage of wide shots and close-ups of protesters, carrying placards and chanting slogans. In the commentary we hear *There was a massive police presence as the march moved towards Downing Street.* A massive presence there may have been, but we can't see it. The pictures are showing us one thing, the words telling us something else. A better commentary may have been: *The protesters were in high spirits as they marched through central London towards Downing Street.*

When the shot changes to lines of police with arms linked outside the Downing Street security gates, we can continue: *With both the Prime Minister and Chancellor of the Exchequer in residence, there was a massive police presence to hold back a crowd of about 50,000.* Here the commentary – also known as voice-over (V/O) – is rightly being used to add detail to the story, introducing facts and information which cannot be verified by the camera.

Later in this same protest report, we may see footage of a protester being marched away by the police. This symbolic shot allows the reporter to deal with more facts: *Through the evening, over 70 people were arrested.* The good reporting team will have known they may need the shot. And the good writer is writing to the pictures, not writing about them. It's not about describing what we see. It's about using the images as a platform to increase the level of communication.

RADIO

MUCH of the guidance for television serves as good advice for radio too: the conversational delivery, the relationship with the audience, the

---

THREE TO THE BEAT

When the written word is intended to be read out loud – as the best of poetry testifies – pace and rhythm are important elements of successful communication.

One of the most common techniques used in spoken news is the 'rule of three', something often used by politicians in speech. The alliterative *It's bigger and it's better* is perfectly adequate as a piece of writing – but *It's bigger, it's better, and it's going down a bomb* extends the alliteration, adding a third phrase which creates an easy-to-read beat to the words.

Don't think *cool and calm.* Think *cool, calm and collected.*

economy of writing, the continual trailing of upcoming stories, the avoidance of words which are easily confused, writing to be read out loud, the understanding that your story is part of a much larger and longer flow of information which must keep the listener's attention.

What we try to do here is draw out some of the key differences between radio and television writing, and between radio and newspapers. No rules for writing are absolute, but what follows should help your grasp of the need for a different approach to news writing if you are appealing to ears rather than eyes.

DIFFERENT STREAMS

We've described how TV can take advantage of three simultaneous sources of information – pictures on screen, sound and on-screen graphics/text.

Radio's armoury looks more limited. It has voice, but no pictures and no screen on which to display any other information. It doesn't have a visual identity, which is why every radio station constantly tells us *You are listening to…* Some independent channels may reference themselves up to 40 times in a one-hour segment using a not very subtle mixture of music stings and verbal references. *The Radio Stoke weather now… Coming up, the Radio Cleveland traffic news…*

With media convergence, this is changing. Many digital radios now offer an LED displaying text detail of headlines, or the titles and artists of featured music. And where listeners source radio broadcasts through the internet, there are new opportunities to make additional visual detail available.

Concentrate for a moment, though, on more traditional radio broadcasting. The reality is that we don't just listen to voices. We hear sound effects, music… and silence. Alongside the words which are turned into voice, there is a stream of communication stimulating our imagination. The good radio writer understands how to ensure that this stream flows constantly, marrying tight verbal exposition of ideas to the unique strengths of the medium. One of its greatest appeals is immediacy.

FAST CHANGING AGENDA

Unless it's a 24-hour news channel, TV news is confined to certain parts of the day. It isn't every hour, on the hour. In the immediacy stakes, radio news should triumph, because stories can be updated 24/7. This means that the 1100 bulletin shouldn't sound like the 1200 bulletin. There should be new stories, and if the stories are the same ones, they should sound different, and hopefully carry new information.

Radio offers more fluidity and choice of story, partly because any information can be turned quickly into a news script, and partly because

> *Good journalism and programme making depends on new ideas.*
>
> *Free up your mind every now and again and think laterally, think originally and (a cliché, but relevant in broadcasting) think outside the box.*
>
> *Write ideas down, even if it's the middle of the night or after eight pints, you'll forget them otherwise.*
>
> *If they don't make it, don't be dispirited.*
>
> *As Greg Dyke said when he was a humble researcher: 'The great thing about working in TV is having ideas. It's the plumbing that f***s you up.'*
>
> *Don't let the mundane plumbing turn off your creativity.*
>
> **JEFF WRIGHT**
> Producer
> Topical TV

👍 *Not all 'live'
interviews on
television are as live as they
seem.*

*They may be pre-recorded,
perhaps because a satellite van
is needed elsewhere or the
interviewee isn't available at a
time suitable for a live
interview.*

*These pre-recorded reports are
called 'as-lives'.*

*Only rarely is it admitted that
they were recorded earlier, but
you can tell by the absence of
the word 'live' being flashed
on-screen.*

*Obviously care needs to be
taken with as-lives: you can't
broadcast one shot in broad
daylight on the late-night news,
for instance.*

the programming which follows a news bulletin is often live and can therefore be truncated to allow the news more time.

Conversely, TV's reliance on pictures mean that it more of a slave to technology – those pictures need to find their way back from location to studio, may need to be edited and voiced, need to go into a tightly timed running order which only very rarely can spill over from its allotted slot.

The constantly updated immediacy of radio offers opportunities. While one bulletin may lead a breaking political story with the government's line – *The Chancellor of the Exchequer has announced a 2p cut in the basic rate of income tax*, in an hour's time this story may be presented from a different angle – *The Opposition has attacked the Chancellor's 2p cut in income tax as a confidence trick.*

Immediacy has a bearing on the choice of words, too. *In the last few minutes... We go live now to... Within the next hour... This morning...* all find their way daily into radio and TV news. You do not expect to see them in newsprint. Time references in broadcasting can – and therefore should be – much more precise.

USING DESCRIPTION

Pictures tell stories, but words alone can tell stories too. Where often television lets the pictures do the talking, the radio writer must be a good describer of what he or she sees. This demands not verbosity, but a good command of the richness of language, and probably a love of words.

Radio reportage often starts with the identifying of place: *I'm standing at the gates of Buckingham Palace, and if I turn and look back down the Mall, there is just a vast, flag-waving sea of humanity stretching away as far as the eye can see.* That sense of place is vital to make a scene come alive for the listener.

Listen to a lot of radio reporting and you will find evidence of a technique called telescoping, a tried and tested way of guiding the mind's eye of the listener from the bigger picture down to the detail: *To my left I can see the Queen Victoria Memorial, and in front, toddlers on parents' shoulders, mums and dads and excited young children, all craning to get a glimpse of Her Majesty Queen Elizabeth the Second as she leaves her London home on this historic day. At the gates themselves, which are decked in bunting and strewn with summer flowers, a very solid line of uniformed Metropolitan police is keeping a welcoming but watchful eye on the proceedings. And with me, watching over them, the woman responsible for security today...* There is far too much detail here for TV, and the order is information is wrong for a newspaper story.

With radio, going from the macro to the micro takes the listener to the heart of what is happening. But remember, radio is still a time-limited medium. Be selective about what you describe.

USING ACTUALITY

The picture painted by the broadcaster's words is enhanced in radio by the deliberate use of actuality – natural sound recorded on location which helps the scene setting. *The slamming of doors, a train whistle, a rush of steam, and the pumping of wheels on rail* are the best way of telling us we are at a steam railway station.

If you haven't captured the right sound sequences, you can always go to your radio station's sound library for a bit of audio support. *The crackle of small arms fire, the distant thud of explosions, the scream of fighter planes overhead* quickly summon up a sound picture of a war zone.

Sound is the supportive sister of voice – and a good way of taking us away from the studio into the real world. For the radio writer, the lesson is that words aren't always best, however beautiful they may be.

CHOICE OF STORIES

Just as the television new editor may rate a story highly because it comes with great pictures, a radio producer may not cover it because it is too visual.

There is no hard and fast rule about what can and cannot be covered by the spoken word, and there is ample evidence that the pictures created by great writing can be just as telling as those captured on videotape or film. Indeed, some radio purists would and will argue that there is nothing which cannot be adequately – even well – described on radio.

Nevertheless, some subject matter is more than challenging. Easy to do a TV news magazine piece about a teenager who's just been accepted into the Magic Circle...let's see some of the tricks before (and after) we talk to her. It's much more difficult, though, to describe the magic of magic on radio. So expect television to favour – and radio to ignore – certain types of story: the auction of famous works of art, the opening of a photography exhibition or the arrival in the region of the tumbling, high-wire Chinese State Circus, for example. Conversely, stories which have a strong audio appeal may not make good telly.

THE PEOPLE'S VOICE

In television, the camera/sound/reporter operation is required to get interviews on location. It's possible to bring guests to a TV studio, but TV channels tend to cover very large areas and many participants are unwilling to travel. But the mobile telephone, the radio car and the ISDN line mean that a radio studio is always well connected both to its reporters in the field and to its audience – it can feature a large range of 'ordinary' and expert voices without too much difficulty.

> *The whole of journalism comes down to two questions: Am I telling the truth? And am I being told the truth?*
>
> **JEREMY VINE**
> Presenter
> BBC TV and Radio

Contact suggestion: Pest controllers. Wasps nests in back bedrooms, rats in back alleys, cockroaches closing cafes: you want to know about them. Bee-keepers will tell you about swarms out of control.

Where the newspaper reporter includes the written quotes from interviews, and the TV reporter brings back clips of a restricted number of people talking in front of the camera, radio benefits from hearing myriad different voices. The more voices, the fewer scripted words.

On radio 'to job' is to set up the story as simply as possible – *one thought, one link* is the mantra – and then allow it to be told by others. The script is the glue which holds the piece together, and the polish which adds detail that has otherwise been missed.

The radio phone-in is the perfect example of the love affair with the voices of the people. It doesn't work particularly well on TV because we expect a visual medium to show us pictures of who is talking. And it creates a platform for potentially 'exclusive' stories, although the term is greatly overused. Listen how often something said live on a phone-in show – usually from a named guest – becomes part of the next hourly news bulletin. *The Prime Minister's told Capital Radio that...*

Furthermore, most radio stations now encourage text input from their audience through emails or text messaging. This instant and constant litmus testing of public opinion is a developing feature of broadcasting, and another one which is squeezing down the contribution made by the radio writer.

With the democratisation of news – the featuring of more and more *public* opinion – news writing and presentation will inevitably have to become even more spartan and effective than it has been.

Fourteen

COURT REPORTING

THE media report court cases because, as the ears and eyes of the public, they have a duty to ensure that justice is not only done, but seen to be done.

That is the theory, and there are still a few newspapers that try to cover every case that comes up in the local magistrates' courts. Overall, however, only a tiny fraction of the thousands of cases that come to court each day are reported. The notion that the media should report every case as a public service has long gone, and the relatively few court stories that do get published or broadcast are chosen for their newsworthiness alone.

The reasons are simple. Newsrooms have not the time, the money or the staff to put people in every court day after day on the off-chance something worth publishing turns up. If they do send a reporter, who may be someone specialising in courts or one of several general reporters covering them on a rota basis, they will be expected to cover a number of courts sitting simultaneously, picking up the best stories and ignoring the rest.

Many newspapers cover courts only when they know there are particularly good cases coming up. Some follow the example of local radio stations, farming the job out to court reporting agencies that are paid a retainer or a fee based on the number of stories published.

Some make do with simple lists of decisions supplied by the court clerks, perhaps picking up extra details afterwards from solicitors or other parties involved – a potentially dangerous practice, because there is little legal protection if they get anything wrong. Some have given up and abandoned court coverage altogether.

Many regret the media's declining interest in day-to-day court cases. They can be the source of excellent stories.

It's a lottery

Whether a case gets reported is clearly very much a matter of chance. It depends, among other things, on whether there is a reporter in court at all, whether they are in the right court when the case comes up, whether they think it is interesting and relevant to their audience, whether there are better cases around competing for their attention, and, after all that, whether once it is written it gets past the news selection process back in the office. It may strike you as unfair that someone's court appearance gets publicity just because a reporter happened to be around on a thin news day, but that is the reality.

The reduction in court cover and the increasing reliance on outside sources may mean that the only time you go to court in your early days

- Courts
- Inquests
- Tribunals
- Inquiries

Never guess if you can't read your notes.

I said a defendant was supplying cocaine instead of cannabis because I'd abbreviated my shorthand outline, and got into enormous trouble.

KATE BARNEY
Reporter
Lincolnshire Free Press

Put lists of lawyers and magistrates in your contacts book, with first names, to save you asking for them each time.

Give each entry a brief description ('fat, glasses') to remind you who is who.

Find out which law firm each solicitor works for, and put its phone number in the book too in case you have queries about a case after it has finished.

Some court reporters build up a picture library of lawyers and magistrates in their contacts book to make identification easier.

as a reporter is to get a couple of stories for your training logbook. Nevertheless, day after day hundreds of journalists report on the human dramas that unfold in our courtrooms, and newsdesks expect you to be able to cover courts, if only in an emergency.

This chapter will guide you through the mechanics of doing so. It is not a legal guide: it assumes that you have studied media law and know about the different courts, what happens as a case unfolds, what privilege and contempt mean, and what you can and cannot report.

What follows is written specifically for reporters covering courts in England and Wales, but much will be applicable to those in Scotland and Northern Ireland with different legal systems.

MAGISTRATES & CROWN COURTS

COVERING court is basically the same as reporting any other event: your job is to record what is done and said, select what is important, and write it up in an interesting way. But going to court the first time can be an unnerving experience. The place is full of people you don't know, doing things you don't instantly understand, some of it in a language all their own. You are sitting towards the back of a room with poor acoustics, can't make out everything that is being said, and don't know who you would ask for help even if you dared.

The good news is that you are unlikely to be alone at first. You will probably be given the chance to shadow an experienced reporter, who will show you the ropes, introduce you to useful people, and generally keep an eye on you. Watch how they operate and learn fast: it won't be long before you are on your own.

PREPARATION

If you find you are in the diary to do court duty, make sure you know where the court is, when it starts, how to get there, how long it is going to take you and, if you are driving, where you can park.

Ask the newsdesk what it wants. There is no point in covering every tiny motoring conviction if your newspaper is only going to use one or

Contact suggestion: local historians. Good for background information and ideas for anniversary stories. They are probably researching something which, dusted off, might make a feature.

WHEN AND WHERE

Magistrates courts operate on fixed days throughout the year.

In small areas there may be only one court sitting two or three times a week, whereas in large urban centres a dozen courts might sit simultaneously every weekday.

Occasionally extra courts are added at short notice – on a Saturday morning, for instance, to remand people arrested the night before.

Crown courts sit every day, and again there may be several operating in the same place at once.

Most courts start around 10am and run until about 4pm with a break for lunch.

two newsy stories. There may be specific cases to look out for: someone arrested and coming up for remand, perhaps, the continuation of a case adjourned the week before or a new one the newsdesk has been tipped off about. You may be asked to check with the magistrates' clerks that these are on the list of scheduled cases.

If there is an on-going case, check the archives for earlier reports and speak to the reporter who covered the case previously. Make sure his or her story was accurate: you don't want to repeat errors.

TAKE:

Notebook: Keep separate notebooks for court. It stops other stories getting mixed up with them and makes it a lot easier if, weeks later, you have search through all your stored notebooks for a particular case (perhaps because a committal you have covered finally ends up in crown court, or, worse, there is a complaint about your story).

Media law book: *McNae* is bulky, heavy and a pain to carry around, but it is very useful for looking things up on the spot instead of floundering around with half-remembered memories of what is legal.

Some form of ID: Carry a press card recognised by the police or at least a letter from your employer identifying you as a bona fide reporter.

A local street map: Handy for checking the spelling and location of defendants' addresses.

EQUIPMENT

Many courts forbid you to record proceedings. Others may allow you to use them so long as you are discreet, don't use recordings for broadcast, and hand them over at the end of the day. Tape recorders are more useful after the case, for interviews outside the courtroom. There is no legal reason why these should not take place in the courthouse corridors or canteen, but some courts are unhappy about reporters doing this and you may have to settle for speaking to people outside.

Carry a camera, though you are forbidden to use one in court and even just looking as if you might can land you in trouble. Bury it deep in your pocket or bag where it can't be seen. If that is not possible, leave it in at reception for collection later.

The law bans photography anywhere within the ill-defined precincts of the court, and that can mean on the steps outside or indeed anywhere that shows the court building in the background. Making drawings is forbidden, too, but artists are allowed to make sketches from memory away from the court.

Switch your mobile phone off or put it in silent mode before you go into court. If it has a built-in camera, don't use it or look as if you might.

Get to know the court ushers and tell them which cases you are interested in. They can let you know if a case changes court rooms so you don't miss out on it.

There is nothing worse than sitting through a dull case to realise the one you wanted has been done next door.

ANDREA HYAM
Reporter
Rutland Times

I learnt never to smile in court, however amusing the case, after being thrown out by a magistrate who told me: 'This isn't a variety performance.'

I still don't know exactly what offence I'd committed, but I left in a very sheepish manner as the rest of the press, the solicitors and the court clerk watched in shock.

RICHARD THOMAS
Presenter
BBC Television

👍 *Magistrates court lists are liable to change throughout the day as cases are delayed, adjourned or moved from one court to another.*

Keeping track of what is on where can be a nightmare.

If you cover a court regularly and build up contact with lawyers and court officials, they can prove very helpful by explaining what is going on.

👍 *There is nothing illegal about hanging round the corridors of the court, eavesdropping on conversations between solicitors and clients.*

It might give you a hint of what to expect when a case comes up – or warn you that one might be adjourned.

Don't get too close, or you could end up being invited to step outside by an irascible local villain.

FIRST VISIT

Arrive early, giving yourself plenty of time to check the geography of the place. If you are planning to take pictures, identify the court entrance used by prison vans containing defendants held in custody: their arrival or departure may be the only photo opportunity you get. Identify yourself to reception (you may as well start getting your face known right away) and go through any security check. Then have a look round.

Court buildings very enormously. Some are small Victorian structures full of wood panelling, obscure offices, courtrooms just big enough to swing a couple of cats in and press benches holding three slender reporters at best. Others are vast modern edifices, designed to accommodate multiple courts and trials attracting large numbers of media people. There may be overflow rooms where the press can watch proceedings by video-link. If there is more than one courtroom, each will be numbered. Cases will be split among them, with perhaps one handling all the minor motoring offences, a second committals, a third adjournments, others full trials (these are the ones you are most likely to be interested in). One courtroom may be reserved as a youth court, another for family proceedings.

Find the press room if there is one, check if there is a phone and (if you have time) whether there is anywhere to get a cup of coffee. Most importantly, visit the clerks' office and find out what is going on.

COURT LISTS

Magistrates' clerks compile a daily list of cases scheduled for hearing. It should be posted outside the court and a copy made available to you as soon as it is ready, but this may not be until just before the courts begin business. Some courts are more helpful than others. If you are lucky there will be free copies for everyone who wants one; if not, you may have to pay for a copy, or share one with other reporters. Probation officers always have a copy, and friendly ones may share theirs with you.

Crown courts compile lists days or weeks ahead, and post these up outside the court on the day. Up-to-date details of all cases listed nationally are available on-line.

The case list will tell you the name and age of the defendant, what he or she is charged with, the Act under which the offence falls, and who brought the prosecution. Some courts also give defendants' addresses, details of where and when offences are alleged to have taken place, and an indication of maximum penalties that can be imposed. If you are covering magistrates courts, there may be some suggestion of which court will handle which cases and whether they are scheduled for the morning or afternoon session.

Don't assume the order that names appear on the lists is the order in which defendants will appear in court. That will depend on when they and any witnesses turn up (many arrive late) and when prosecuting and defence solicitors are available (many are involved in several cases in different rooms, and getting the right ones in the right place at the same time is a problem).

Crown courts tend to be more disciplined, with cases clearly scheduled and running to timetable. Judges take a very dim view of their time being wasted.

Armed with the lists, go through them to see which cases look particularly interesting. Ask the clerks which court these cases are likely to be in and when, and make sure you are there when the first one starts.

If no cases stand out, it is a question of checking what is on in each court, and you may spend the day hopping from one to the next in search of the best stories.

Don't be afraid to ask clerks and lawyers if cases are likely to go ahead: you don't want to spend ages waiting for one that is adjourned after only a few minutes.

WHO'S WHO

The foyer and corridors will be alive with people. The ones in a hurry are court officials, lawyers, police, probation officers. Those hanging around are defendants, witnesses and members of the public, some waiting to see specific cases involving friends and relatives, some just dropping by for a morning's entertainment.

Inside a magistrates' courtroom, you will find:

The magistrates: A bench of at least two (unless there is a salaried district judge, who sits alone) and there can be up to seven. One will be the chair for the day. They sit at a raised desk at the front. Nearby is a room to which they can retire to discuss cases in private or relax out of the public eye.

The magistrates' clerks: One or more, in charge of the court operation and offering legal advice to the magistrates. They sit at a desk in front of the bench, surrounded by files and legal tomes. Beside them will be a stenographer who records everything that goes on.

Lawyers: They sit (or stand, when addressing the court) facing the clerks and the bench, prosecution on one side, defence on the other. Some will be involved in the current case, others may be waiting their turn. Most will be solicitors, but you may see the occasional barrister.

Defendants: If they have been held in custody, they will be brought from the cells to stand in the dock, an enclosed area somewhere near the centre of the court behind the lawyers. Otherwise they will join their defence solicitor at the front. If the case is fairly trivial – a minor motoring offence, perhaps – they may not appear at all, merely sending a letter to the court admitting their guilt and explaining any mitigating circumstances. This should be read out by the clerk.

Talking to criminals while covering court led to my only instance of chequebook journalism.

A villain called McVicar claimed in his autobiography to be the first man to escape from Durham Jail.

I knew he wasn't: that honour belonged to a lad called Ronnie Heslop, known for ever after as Rubberbones because he had slipped through a painstakingly-excavated grill in his cell floor into the room below.

Ronnie, proud of his feat and furious at McVicar's claim, willingly talked to me, posed by the river he'd swum to escape the police, but refused to wear his trademark rag-and-bone man's hat – until I offered him a fiver.

It took some getting back on exes.

MIKE AMOS
Columnist
The Northern Echo

👍 *The office junior, fresh from a training course, is almost invariably more up-to-date on media law than the rest of the staff, many of whom studied it when the 1981 Contempt Act was still a gleam in Sir Michael Havers' eye.*

Don't be afraid to speak up if you think they are about to do something illegal.

Far better to be thought a bit pushy than to confess later, when the libel writ has arrived, that you knew all along it was a mistake but were too frightened to say so.

It works both ways: there are some ultra-cautious editors out there who aren't aware of just how much protection is available to them.

Urge them gently to be a bit bolder.

Very gently.

Witnesses: When called to appear, they give their evidence from the witness box, usually placed towards the front of the room on one side where they can be seen by everyone else. Don't talk to witnesses waiting outside the court-room: they are not supposed to know what has been said inside, and you could be suspected of telling them. In addition, what they have said to you might influence their subsequent evidence.

Ushers: Responsible for shepherding defendants and witnesses into court, fetching and carrying and generally keeping order. They are the ones in the long black flowing gowns (which some magistrates' clerks and solicitors wear, too). They know what's going on and can be very helpful.

Probation officers: Probably sitting on a bench on one side.

The public: Seated in the public gallery at the back, usually near the entrance so that people can come and go with the minimum interruption to proceedings.

The press: You have no right to special treatment, but most courts provide a bench on one side for the media, often shared with the probation service. If there are other reporters around, make the most of them. Pick their brains. They will be willing to tell you who is who, where the loos are and which is the best nearby pub. Don't expect them to tell you which cases are worth covering or how to write your story, though if you meet regularly you may well develop some system of sharing information that benefits you both.

The set-up at a crown court is very similar, except that here you will find:

The judge: Seated on the bench, probably be-wigged and gowned, possibly accompanied by one or more magistrates observing what goes on and sharing some of the decision-making.

YOU DON'T HAVE TO BOW

Courts take the administration of justice seriously, and expect you to do the same:

Dress appropriately. They won't actually throw you out if you turn up in jeans and a fcuk tee-shirt, but you will find them less than co-operative. Jacket and tie for men, smart outfit for women. No hats or bare shoulders.

Keep your voice down. If you must talk, whisper. Don't hold long conversations with your mate beside you. Don't eat or drink. Don't yawn openly, however tedious it is.

Stand up when the judge or magistrates enter and leave (it is customary for solicitors and court officials to bow, but you don't have to).

Come and go as quietly as you can, preferably when there is a lull in proceedings. Don't leave your place while the oath is being taken.

Don't sneak a look at probation officers' files when they are not around, however tempting it may be. Information in them is confidential and certainly not reportable as part of the proceedings.

It is a time-honoured tradition for reporters to carve their initials on the press bench. Don't get caught doing it.

The jury: Present only in some serious contested cases, the jurors sit on one side or in the centre where they can see what is going on.

Barristers: They present the prosecution and defence in most crown court cases, although some solicitors are allowed to appear. Barristers are the ones in wigs and gowns.

REPORTING THE PROCEEDINGS

Accuracy is vital, shorthand is invaluable, and you have got to know the law. That goes for every case you cover, whether it is a simple two-minute remand or a complex trial lasting weeks.

Being organised helps, too. Start each case on a new page of your notebook, dated and clearly identified by the defendant's name. Make it clear who has said what by putting each speaker's name or initials in the margin beside their words. Leave space at the end for additional material to be added afterwards. If you are challenged later about the accuracy of your report, a tidy, well-annotated notebook looks a lot better than a battered court list covered in scribbles.

Be patient. Justice moves slowly and there are occasions when it seems to be at a standstill or going backwards. A lot of your time will be spent waiting while cases are organised, solicitors are found, adjournments are negotiated and magistrates deliberate.

Use your time to write up cases that have already taken place, or to chat with other people in the same boat. Everyone at court – ushers, police, the canteen assistant, the villains waiting outside – is a potentially useful contact.

THE ESSENTIALS

Whatever kind of case you are covering, some basic details are essential for your story. You need to include:

The name of the court.

The defendant's name: First name (or the one they are known by) and surname. Ignore middle names, though they may be given in full on the court list.

The defendant's age: This should be on the court list (you may have to work it out from the date of birth). It is important that you know whether a teenage defendant is legally a young person or an adult. It is news if someone committed an offence or is appearing in court on their birthday.

The defendant's address: It will be on the court list, but check this against the address given in court, because the defendant may have moved. Giving the address is vital to avoid confusion with other people of the same name who could sue you if people think they are the guilty party. Most newspapers omit house numbers (easily misprinted, and they

> *As a young and inexperienced reporter, I left a courtroom halfway through a trial and was approached outside by a girl who asked me what was going on.*
>
> *I told her. Then an usher came by and asked why I was talking to a witness. I had to give evidence of my misdemeanour on oath before the magistrates (a truly terrifying experience), the trial was abandoned, and I was lucky not to be done for contempt.*
>
> **SKIP WALKER**
> Editor
> Wiltshire &
> Gloucestershire Standard

> *The policeman taking details of a woman involved in a road accident said:*
> *'You won't want to be bothered by the press, will you?'*
>
> *She was one of my reporters.*
>
> **JOHN MURPHY**
> Editor
> Evesham Journal

spotlight homes that might be targeted by thieves or people intent on revenge) but will insist on street names unless the defendant lives outside the circulation area, in which case a village name or locality will do. You may come across people referred to in court as *of no fixed abode* (which you should translate into *of no fixed address* or, better still, *homeless*).

The charge or charges: Check that what is read out in court is the same as on the court list. Charges get amended or dropped altogether. New ones gets added at the last minute. It is up to you to make sure the facts in your story are accurate. Note when and where offences took place.

The plea: The defendant will be asked whether they admit or deny the charge when it is first read out. A not-guilty plea must be reported, but you can sometimes leave a guilty plea out if it is implicit in the way you have written your story.

The verdict, if a not-guilty plea: announced by the chair of the bench after hearing the evidence.

The sentence, if guilty: If sent to crown court for sentence, say where; if jailed, say how long for and whether multiple sentences are concurrent or consecutive. Give details if all or part of a sentence is suspended. If the defendant is fined, say how much and mention any orders for costs, compensation or restitution.

Adjournment, if any, why, and how long for. Say whether the defendant is remanded in custody or on bail, and if bailed, on what conditions.

Those are the minimum details you will need to write even the simplest story. If you haven't got them all, ask. Wait until the case is over or the magistrates have retired to consider things, and approach the clerk for names, addresses, and anything else you don't know. Solicitors will probably be helpful too. There is no reason why you should not question defendants once they have left the courtroom, but be prepared for them to start arguing whether their story should be reported at all, which could turn nasty

There is much more information available, of course, and how much you use depends on what the story is worth. You may not be able to judge that until well into the case, when something is said or done to turn what looked like being a routine one-paragraph short into a potential front-page lead. If that happens, you look silly with only the bare essentials in your notebook.

THE DETAILS

Record as much as you can about:

The case: Who did what, where, when, why and how. Note the prosecution claims, the defence's response, the defendant's explanation, any witness statements and comments from magistrates as the case unfolds. Get accurate quotes from all of them if possible.

REMEMBER THE RESTRICTIONS

Court orders: There may be orders banning or restricting your report.

Don't assume, for example, that a Section 39 order forbidding the identification of a young person has not been made just because you did not hear it or were not around at the time.

Some courts make such orders automatically or with little more than a nod. If in doubt, ask the clerk whether any orders have been made and, if so, exactly what is covered and why. Ignorance is no defence.

Contempt is a danger if you report things said outside open court or in the absence of the jury – guilty pleas to other charges, plea bargains, arguments about the admissibility of evidence, details of previous convictions.

Absolute privilege covers only what is said during the proceedings. Libellous accusations made outside carry no protection.

Remember that your stories have absolute privilege so long as they are fair, accurate and contemporaneous.

That means publishing them at the first available opportunity. Don't leave stories lying in your notebook for days.

Qualified privilege covers non-contemporaneous court stories.

This means that as well as being fair and accurate, their publication must be in the public interest, without malice and subject upon request to 'a reasonable letter or statement of explanation or contradiction'.

This has implications for newspaper websites, where reports may remain accessible long after the public interest has evaporated. Stories left on the web might also be seen to be in contempt if a case goes to re-trial and new jurors could access them.

Reports of preliminary hearings of cases which could end up in the crown court are severely restricted by the Magistrates Courts Act.

The defendant: Occupation, marital status, children – anything that might add colour to your story or give you a different angle. Are they on legal aid? What are they wearing? How do they behave? Are they distraught, hostile, indifferent to their fate? Do they respond to questioning readily or in a whisper? How do they react to the court's decision – do they give the magistrates a V-sign or break down in tears?

Magistrates or judge: Their names (they are not allowed to remain anonymous) and any comments when delivering a verdict or passing sentence.

Lawyers: Their names and, in the case of the prosecution, who they represent. By no means all cases are handled by the Crown Prosecution Service. Trading standards, health officers, transport police, the NSPCC and RSPCA are among other bodies who regularly prosecute.

Witnesses: Names, plus ages and addresses if known.

The jury, if one is present. You are not allowed to identify or question members of the jury about how decisions are reached, though it may be permissible to ask general questions about, for example, the wisdom of a prosecution being brought. You should note jurors' general behaviour (*the jury was visibly shocked at the photos...*) and whether they convict on a unanimous or majority verdict (though the fact that someone is acquitted by a majority is normally not reported for legal reasons).

I was set upon in a department store by a furious old lady who announced venemously: 'I hate and despise you, you vindictive, horrible little man.'

My sin? Working for the local paper, which years earlier had reported that a member of her family had been sent to jail.

I had nothing to do with the story, but it made no difference. She hated me.

BRIAN TILLEY
Deputy editor
Hexham Courant

If you don't understand, ask. Too many people think it is a sign of weakness. It isn't.

The real sign of weakness is being too feeble to ask.

PAT STANNARD
Editor
Waltham Forest Guardian

👍 *Don't mix up fines, costs, compensation and restitution. By all means say someone 'was ordered to pay a total of £500' but break it down later to explain how much was the fine, how much costs, and so on.*

Previous convictions: Read out after someone pleads or is found guilty.

Offences taken into consideration (TICs) when sentence is decided. If the charge was a specimen, one of many others not being dealt with, say so.

Any mitigating circumstances raised by the defence when arguing for leniency, such as the defendant's state of health, domestic responsibilities, employment circumstances or financial status.

The sentence: Is a jail term the maximum possible? How long is the defendant given to pay a fine?

The public gallery: Is it crowded? Are there outbursts of protest or approval when the verdict is reached?

Anything else, from a power failure that disrupts proceedings to the accused knifing his solicitor, that might enhance or even make your story.

FOLLOW-UPS

After the case, it may be worth talking to the various parties involved for their reaction. You may get comments from defendants (*I was a complete idiot, This will cost me my job*), victims (*She ruined my life, He should be strung up*) and solicitors (*We are considering an appeal*). Beware of libel (and contempt if there are other cases pending).

If the case has attracted a lot of interest, there may be an angry crowd outside jeering as the defendant is driven off to jail (or cheering as he walks free).

There may be comment from elsewhere – from MPs on the wider implications of the case, from the defendant's employer saying there will now be internal disciplinary proceedings, or from third parties mentioned in the case.

👍 *Keep up-to-date with the law: it changes all the time.*

Look for items in the nationals' law pages and log on regularly to websites that carry news of legal matters affecting journalists: HoldTheFrontPage, for example, and the NUJ and Society of Editors websites.

There is a site carrying updates for McNae, and PA has an excellent online service offering regular media law updates, available for a modest fee: persuade your editor to subscribe.

It could save your newspaper a fortune.

DO YOU GIVE MISS A MISS?

Know your house style for names and titles.

Until recently the media mostly denied defendants their titles (*Mr, Mrs, Miss*) from the moment they were involved in a case, referring to them by their first name and surname at first reference and by their surname only thereafter – even if they were denying everything or had been acquitted.

It was a curious discourtesy, given our supposed belief that everyone is innocent until proved otherwise. Today many newspapers have recognised this and give defendants their titles until they plead or are found guilty.

Know your house style, too, for addresses (do you include house numbers?) and abbreviations (is it *Detective Constable Jones, Det Con Jones,* or *DC Jones*?).

Check your newspaper's policy on identifying young people: some keep victims' and witnesses' names secret, even when legally allowed to publish them.

This is the time when the media get sound and pictures, still or moving, to back up their reports. There may be other illustrative material available. The police may provide headshots of convicted defendants, maps of crime scenes, CCTV footage, or pictures of unclaimed stolen goods. The story may lend itself to graphics created in-house: how thieves broke into the bank, perhaps, or a chart showing the extent of benefit fraud.

WRITING IT UP

Some stories can be written in court while waiting for the next case to start or during long unreportable legal wrangles. Write the rest as soon as possible afterwards, while they are still fresh in your mind and notebook. Remember to take the court list back to the office so that you can check details from it.

THE INTRO

Treat court stories like any other: they just happen to come to light in a courtroom. One of the biggest problems with some inexperienced court reporters is that they always treat what happened in court as the most important thing.

Sometimes this is indeed the case *(Driver banned for speeding, Pensioner jailed for shoplifting)* but often the court appearance is secondary and the best story is actually about events that happened long before but have only now become known *(Wife went berserk with chainsaw, Banker put client's money on 1000-1 horse)*. It is possible to write some court stories without mentioning the court at all until the end.

Look for a non-court angle before you leap in with a boring intro about *Magistrates were told yesterday* or *A man appeared in court today*. Ask yourself:

Who was involved? Is the defendant (or anyone else in the case) famous, important or unusual in any way? It may be their sex, age, occupation, disability, hobbies, religion, or anything else that makes them different *(Film star drunk on bus, One-legged fishmonger held up bank, Vicar stole to support crack habit)*.

What did they do? Was the crime unusual, horrific, ridiculous, out of character, a record of some kind? *(Teacher stole deadly snakes, Hold-up man fell off getaway bike, Shopgirl hid 2,000 manhole covers in bedroom, Publican first to flout new law)*. Does the defendant have a long string of previous convictions or ask for multiple other cases to be taken into consideration? *(Teenager's two-year reign of terror)*.

Where and when was it? Did it involve somewhere unusual or take place at a special time? *(Robber broke into zoo on Christmas Eve, Bridegroom arrested on stag night)*.

Why did they do it? What were the reasons for the crime? What was the defendant's explanation and were there mitigating circumstances? *(Jilted lover burned house down, Father-to-be in 140mph hospital dash)*.

Always be wary of working in a pack. Other reporters can be unreliable.

At a police press conference following a murder near Ripon, we noticed the man from the local weekly was missing.

He was in the cells.

Not only had he written the first reports of the murder, he was the killer.

As the man from the Yorkshire Post said: 'He didn't even have the decency to give us the full story first...'

SHARON GRIFFITHS
Feature writer
The Northern Echo

If you're not highly inquisitive – or downright nosey – don't be a journalist.

SIMON O'NEILL
Editor
Oxford Mail

👍 *Make sure you get titles correct. High Court judges get very twitchy if they are referred to as Judge instead of Mr Justice.*

Queen's Counsel expect you to tell readers they are a QC.

How were they caught? Was the defendant unlucky, was it by chance, who caught him or her? *(Midnight swoop netted drugs gang, All-in wrestler trapped thief when his trousers fell down).*

Sometimes you can hang a story on reaction to the result. Defendants may break down in tears, whoop with joy, or threaten revenge on the judge. The response of other people – victims, witnesses, the crowd outside the court – may be worth highlighting.

There may be long-term implications for those involved *(Bus driver sacked after late-night brawl, I'll never be the same, says victim)* or the public at large *(Thousands may get speeding bans overturned, Court decides smoking at home is illegal).* There may be more prosecutions to come.

Solicitors may announce plans to appeal or issue statements saying their client's reputation has been restored. Employers may announce

👍 *Ask if you can have a trip round the cells. It's an eye-opener.*

GET RID OF THE JARGON

Police and court officials have a language all their own. Turn it into plain English whenever you can. Common examples include:

Alleged
= *Said* or *Claimed*

Appearing for the defence
= *Defending*

Attempted to apprehend him
= *Tried to catch him*

Disqualified
= *Banned*

Entered a plea of guilty
= *Admitted*

Expressed regret
= *Said he was sorry* or *apologised*

Found liable
= *Convicted* or *Found guilty*

Had occasion to question
= *Questioned*

Imposed a fine
= *Fined*

In control of a moving vehicle
= *Driving* (or trying to)

Knowingly and with intent
= *Deliberately* or *Intentionally*

Motor vehicle
= Usually a *car*

Observed
= *Saw*

Occasioned
= *Caused*

Pending
= *Awaiting* or *until*

Pleaded not guilty
= *Denied*

Proceeding
= *Going*

Refuted
= *Disproved* (<u>not</u> *Rejected* or *Denied*)

Stated
= *Said*

The accused
= *The defendant* or, better, his or her name

The property of
= *Belonging to* or *owned by*

Was found to be
= *Was*

Was in possession of
= *Had*

Was the property of
= *Belonged to*

Witnessed
= *Saw* or *Watched*

👍 *If you ever get a story about a doctor falling foul of the General Medical Council, the body that hears accusations of GPs' professional misconduct or incompetence, don't say he or she has been struck off the register: there's a right of appeal. Say the doctor 'was ordered to be struck off'.*

internal inquiries or changes to procedures *(Police probe after detective jailed, Death-trap firm promises safety drive)*.

And, yes, sometimes the result of the case does provide the strongest intro:

The sentence may be particularly tough *(Ten years for litterbug)* or lenient *(Serial killer walks free)*, the most or least that could be imposed *(Judge throws book at librarian)*.

The judge or magistrates may say something outstanding *(Man jailed for 'totally unprovoked' attack)* or make recommendations *('Life will mean life')*.

Whatever angle you choose, however long or short your story, make sure you include all the bare essentials mentioned earlier in this chapter.

QUOTES

If there has been a guilty plea or a conviction, you can make statements as fact *(Gardener mowed down pedestrians)* but until someone has admitted or been found guilty of an offence, make it clear claims made in court are just that, not established truth.

Attribute them to the speaker *(Gardener killed seven, says prosecution)* or turn them round *(Gardener ran amok, court told)*. Headline writers may get away with using quote marks *(Gardener 'ran amok')* but your story has to make it clear who said so.

BALANCE

Your story should be balanced. That means including the plea and a summary of the defence in any case where the defendant has denied the offence, and even guilty-plea stories longer than just a couple of paragraphs should mention mitigating circumstances (if there were any, of course).

If a case is adjourned, you should write a balanced report of the proceedings that have taken place so far. It may be that only the prosecution case has been heard by the time you go to print, but that is not a problem so long as you mention any not-guilty plea and make it clear the case is continuing: say so at the end of your story.

Translate charges couched in legal jargon (see the panel opposite) into normal language but beware of getting it wrong (there is a serious difference between *actual* and *grievous* bodily harm).

Don't call someone just over the breath-test limit a drunk. Don't mix up car theft with taking a vehicle without consent (known as TWOC).

Be careful with phrases like *escaped jail* or *got off scot-free* that suggest you think the defendant deserved a tougher sentence than the one that has been imposed.

Watch your pronouns. *Brown's solicitor, Mr Algernon McFuddle, said he drank like a fish* is not going to please teetotal Mr McFuddle.

If your shorthand is rusty, there is no point thinking you can cover it up.

After Tony Blair visited my patch, I was granted an interview with him on the train back to London.

Without time to borrow a dictaphone and tape his words of wisdom, I had to take down what he said in longhand while sitting opposite him in the carriage.

After the first paragraph he knew and I knew that his words weren't making it onto the page.

It was a nightmare.

MATT JACKSON
Reporter
Swindon Advertiser

Read your story through TWICE for the mistake before you send it to newsdesk. You know there's one in there...

GRAEME HUSTON
Editor in chief
South Yorkshire
Newspapers

👍 *Some court reporters have ready-made speeches to hand, prepared by themselves or their newsroom's lawyers, laying out detailed, coherent and persuasive arguments why the most common orders should be overturned.*

It works a lot better than trying to cite the law off the top of your head and looking foolish when you can't remember it or, worse, get it wrong.

Watch your phrasing. *A driver was fined for doing 135mph at Midthorpe magistrates court yesterday* is silly. He was fined by Midthorpe magistrates yesterday for speeding somewhere else weeks ago.

AFTERWARDS

If the case is continuing the next day, advise the newsdesk. It makes sense for you to cover it again, but if this is not possible you will need to brief whichever reporter is taking over.

If worthwhile cases are adjourned or sent to crown court, put them in the diary. If your newspaper has carried a paragraph saying someone has been committed for trial, it should at the very least carry the result when the case comes up.

Store your notebook somewhere safe.

BACKGROUNDERS

If the case is a big enough story and you have known about it in advance, you may be asked to work ahead on background features to appear once it is over: a profile of the defendant, an analysis of the crime, an article on how it has affected the victims' lives.

Make sure the information you get is not later discredited in court.

Be wary of contempt if you are interviewing witnesses who may appear in court later. Their evidence could be swayed by what they have told you (or you have told them).

Don't offer payment to witnesses without the prior agreement of your editor. Such payments are banned by the Press Complaints Commission's code of conduct once a case becomes active (unless it is clearly in the public interest and the only way to get vital information) and must never be made on condition that there is a conviction. Payments to convicted criminals for stories that might glamorise their activities are banned at all times, unless there is a demonstrable public interest.

👍 *When covering youth courts, remember that some of the terminology is different.*

Young people don't plead guilty or not guilty, they admit or deny offences; they have findings of guilt, not convictions; they are not sentenced, they are made the subject of a court order.

PROBLEMS

If you make a mistake, own up. A rapid correction is better than a long drawn-out legal battle. Make sure any correction is archived with the original story so the error is not repeated in the future. If the story went on the website, amend or delete it.

Defendants may contact you before or after your story is published to complain that what was said in court was not correct or the whole truth, and demanding you print their version of the facts.

If they are on the phone, re-direct them to the newsdesk straight away. If you are confronted outside the court, be courteous, but tell them this is not possible: your story was an accurate report of the proceedings, and you would have no legal protection for claims made out of court. Suggest they ask their solicitor to make a statement in open court that you might then be able to report. It is highly unlikely the court will go along with this, but it should get the complainant off your back. Inform your newsdesk about the request.

More often you will be approached after a court case by someone asking you to keep it out of the newspaper (*I'll lose my job if the boss finds out* or *It'll kill my sick mum if she reads it*). You may feel sympathy but never give in. Your reputation, in and out of the office, is at stake.

Explain that it is your job to report cases and it is not your decision what gets published; say you will pass the request on to your editor, who they should contact if they want to take it further. Then write the story, making absolutely sure every word is accurate (you can bet the defendant will go through it with a fine-tooth comb looking for reasons to complain). Tell the newsdesk what happened. It may want to make sure the story is printed just to prove the newspaper can't be bought or bullied.

Requests for cases to be overlooked may come from people you know, which puts a strain on friendship and can mean the end of a useful contact, but it is vital that you don't put personal relationships before your duty to report cases fairly and honestly.

In rare cases you may be offered a bribe, or threatened. Again, tell your newsdesk (or the police). If someone close to you is due to appear in court, ask the newsdesk if another reporter can cover the case.

CHALLENGING THE COURTS

If you cover courts regularly, it won't be long before one imposes an order you think should be challenged. It may be lawful but unjustified: a ban on naming a persistent young offender, perhaps. It may be downright illegal: a ban, for example, on identifying an adult defendant simply because they would be embarrassed by publicity. Lay magistrates are not legally trained and rely for advice from their clerks, who, although trained in the law, are not always well up on media rights and restrictions. Even judges can be hazy about their powers.

Challenging a court, especially a crown court, takes some courage. The secret is to be well prepared. If you have advance notice that an

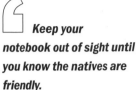

Keep your notebook out of sight until you know the natives are friendly.

MARK DICKINSON
Editorial director
Trinity Mirror Midlands

Don't be afraid of making mistakes – just try not to make them in the first place.

MARK JONES
Editor
Basingstoke Gazette

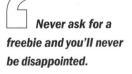

Never ask for a freebie and you'll never be disappointed.

GRAHAM PRATT
Deputy editor
The Journal, Newcastle

IF THE VICAR GOES ASTRAY...

He could end up being de-frocked by a Consistory Court, run by the Church of England to handle cases of alleged misconduct by church officers.

They can be the source of good stories: *Deacon runs off with organist's wife* is a perennial favourite.

The courts also deal with matters affecting changes to churches and church-yards, which sometimes make the news when, for example, there are disputes about boundary walls or graveyards being moved.

They are presided over by a lawyer known as the chancellor, with a 'jury' made up of church members. Appeals go to the Court of Arches.

You are entitled to attend and report.

👍 **Don't pre-judge the verdict of an inquest unless the cause of death is unarguable.**

Coroners dislike you telling the public someone commited suicide before the inquest has been held.

Not everyone found dead in a river has drowned themselves, or indeed died of drowning.

Not everyone found dead beside a shotgun meant it to blow their head off.

👍 **Contact suggestion: the coroner. Formidable figures, some of them, but most are human and will be happy to explain inquest procedures and discuss the ethics of media coverage.**

Make yourself known to pathologists, who will translate medical descriptions and might even offer you a tour of the morgue. Don't accept unless you've got a strong stomach.

order might be made (there is nothing to stop you asking defence lawyers if they plan to ask for one) you can marshall your case beforehand, gathering evidence of past rulings and appropriate quotes from your copy of *McNae*.

Often, though, orders come out of the blue and you have to act swiftly. Pass a note to the clerk explaining that you want to do so and requesting permission to address the court: as an interested party in the case you are entitled to ask for that. The chances are that they will agree and you will be invited to speak at the next appropriate break in the proceedings.

Take a deep breath and do your best. If it works, you will get a better story and a pat on the back at work. If you fail to convince the bench that their order, while legal, is not in the best interests of justice you will probably have to put up with it, though you might highlight their refusal to agree with you in your story (*JPs refuse to name and shame public menace*).

If you are convinced they are acting illegally, take it further. Tell the newsdesk, and if they agree with you they can pursue the matter at a higher level. *McNae* has an excellent chapter on challenging the courts which (like many others) is worth looking at before you embark on court reporting. It also contains the Code of Conduct, pocket-sized versions of which are available free from the Society of Editors which helped to create it.

The society was also instrumental in persuading the Home Office to issue clear and explicit guidelines about media rights and restrictions to judges and magistrates, and having a copy of these (available on the society's website) could greatly add to your credibility when challenging a court.

OTHER COURTS

MUCH of what has been said above about covering magistrates and crown courts applies to other legal proceedings you may occasionally be asked to report.

YOUTH COURTS

These are less formal than adult courts, with special panels of magistrates. Parents are usually present. The press are allowed to attend but not the public. Remember that there is an automatic ban on identifying any young person involved in the proceedings. This includes witnesses and victims as well as the accused.

FAMILY PROCEEDINGS

These are civil, not criminal courts, dealing with family matters, and empowered to make a wide range of orders, such as maintenance, care, supervision, affiliation and access. The press may attend but can be excluded if children are involved. You need to be aware of the extensive restrictions on what you are allowed to report.

COUNTY COURTS

These decide relatively small civil disputes (major cases end up in the High Court). They are rarely covered as a matter of course, but it is worth keeping an eye on forthcoming cases. Some of them make good copy: feuds between neighbours, customers disputing bills, tradesmen trying to recover debts, landlords battling with tenants. They also handle divorce and bankruptcies.

You have the right to attend and report, whether they are held in open court or in the district judge's chambers. Remember that these courts deal with civil cases and nobody is accused, charged or sentenced: claimants sue defendants and the courts make orders.

COURT MARTIALS

These are a military version of crown courts, dealing with serious service offences such as desertion or dereliction of duty (servicemen or women accused of criminal offences face civilian courts like anyone else). They are presided over by a president, sometimes aided by a legally-trained judge-advocate. Officers act for the prosecution and defence.

The press is allowed to attend and newsrooms should have a system for being informed of impending cases, though details are posted publicly at the army, navy or airforce based involved.

Court martials (or courts-martial: check your house style for the plural) are covered by absolute privilege and are subject to the same contempt laws as any other court. The findings and sentences of army and airforce court martials are subject to confirmation, and your story should say so.

INQUESTS

CORONER'S courts are a rich source of news stories and open to the press and public unless national security is involved. They are run by coroners, usually sitting alone, though a jury (of between 7 and 11 members) can be summoned if public health or safety may be involved.

I covered an inquest of a man who died after a night spent taking drugs with his girlfriend. I didn't take notes about her involvement, but included it in my story.

When she complained, I had to admit to my editor that I had no proof it was said at the inquest, though I was certain it had been.

He made me go to her house with a bunch of flowers and apologise. I was mortified.

CLARE BOURKE
Former editor
West London Times

👍 **If you cover inquests, it won't be long before you listen to some fairly graphic descriptions of how people met their deaths. Most news organisations avoid giving the most gruesome and intimate details of people's illnesses and injuries unless there is good reason for doing so.**

The law bans the publication of what it describes as indecent medical, surgical or physiological details calculated to injure public morals, but what these details might be has yet to be tested.

In large towns inquests may be held on a regular basis, perhaps once a week or more; elsewhere they may be called only when needed. Coroner's officers (sometimes police officers) know when inquests are taking place and newsrooms include them in their regular calls. Details may be given on police voicebanks.

The Home Office has repeatedly urged coroners to ensure that the media are given adequate notice of inquests, but not all are as keen on inquests being covered as we would like them to be.

PROCEDURE

Unlike criminal courts, the procedure at inquests is inquisitorial, with the coroner leading witnesses through their evidence and allowing interested parties such as relatives of the dead person to ask questions.

Some evidence may be given in written statements which the coroner should read out to the court, though they have discretion on this and the detailed content of suicide notes, for example, is rarely disclosed.

Most inquests are opened for evidence of identification and then adjourned to a later date for a full hearing. If you cover the opening, put the date of the full hearing, if known, in the diary.

Inquests hear reports from pathologists who carry out post-mortem examinations (also know as autopsies) to determine the cause of death. Their evidence will be couched in medical language that you may need to translate. *Haemorrhaging*, for example, is *bleeding; carcinomas* are *cancers; lacerations and contusions* are *cuts and bruises*, a *fractured femur* is a *broken leg*. If you have any doubt, ask for an explanation or look it up: a good newsroom will have a medical dictionary among its reference books.

VERDICTS

Verdicts may be simple – *accidental death* or *misadventure*, for example, or an *open verdict* if the cause of death cannot be decided – but narrative verdicts, giving a short summary of the cause of death, are increasingly common. Don't say the cause of death was suicide if the coroner says someone hanged themselves while suffering from depression.

The verdict may be the obvious intro to your story (*Poisoned painter killed himself, Husband was stabbed by accident*) but often the story is more about why rather than how somebody died, which has already been reported (*Bridge leap man was due in court, Faulty kettle blamed for tragedy*). Comments by the coroner or jury may be the strongest angle, or it may be the response of relatives to the verdict.

Make sure you include all the basic details in your story – name, age, address and other details of the deceased, the time and place of death, and the verdict. Remember that coroners *record* verdicts, juries *return* them.

If there is any suggestion that criminal proceedings may follow, check with the police if any prosecution is planned and put it in the diary.

TRIBUNALS

THERE are many different kinds of tribunal, some exercising powers not dissimilar to the courts, some purely adminstrative. They are not criminal courts, though they do make legally-binding decisions. A chairman or chairwoman, sitting with two or more other people, hears evidence from the parties involved. Procedures vary, but most are less formal than courts.

Reporters are allowed in unless their presence threatens national security or confidentiality. Reports are covered by absolute privilege if a tribunal exercises judicial powers, qualified privilege if not. Some may be subject to the laws of contempt, though this is a hazy area.

The ones you are most likely to cover are employment tribunals dealing with such matters as unfair dismissal, redundancy claims and allegations of discrimination or harassment. You may also come across tribunals making decisions about rents, valuations and benefits. Lists of forthcoming cases are available in advance from tribunal offices. Names of the parties involved, the date and place the tribunal will be held, and a case summary will be posted outside. Tribunal clerks will help you sort out details.

Tribunals may reserve their decisions, and their reports may not be available until weeks later. You can arrange for copies to be sent to you. Adjournments are common. Be careful if reporting only one side of a case and make sure the rest is covered later.

McNae lists a selection of other tribunals whose proceedings might attract media attention.

> **Be tactful. I arrived on the doorstep to interview a woman whose husband had been blown to smithereens in an industrial accident. A reporter from the rival paper was there too and met every quote with 'Great!' 'Good!' or Excellent!'**
>
> **ANTHONY LONGDEN**
> Managing editor
> Newsquest,
> Herts, Bucks & Middlesex

WATCH OUT FOR ID BANS

In cases of alleged sexual harassment, either side can ask the tribunal to ban you from reporting their identity until the final report is published.

If such an order is made, take care that your story does not identify someone who, though un-named, is readily recognisable by some readers.

Naming a firm whose sales manager is alleged to have assaulted a secretary, for example, would be dangerous if it employs only one sales manager and few secretaries. Even giving the name of the firm might be a problem.

Orders can be challenged by the press.

If you cover a planning inquiry, there may be plenty of references to the council's local plan. There should be a copy of it in your library.

Take it with you to help unravel what they are talking about when they say a proposal contravenes section 97, sub-section B, clause 19(b).

INQUIRIES

LOCAL inquiries, held into matters such as planning applications, are similar in many ways to administrative tribunals. They are conducted by an inspector appointed by the relevant government minister, are open to the press and carry qualified privilege.

Decisions are made public later and usually issued to the media.

Fifteen
LOCAL POLITICS

EVERY day of our lives we use services provided directly by our local authority or subsidised by money collected from us in council tax. They are there because councillors elected to serve our interests make decisions on our behalf, decisions ranging from whether we use plastic sacks or wheelie bins for our rubbish to whether the town centre should be flattened, rebuilt and made traffic-free.

They wield power over planning applications for tiny bathroom extensions and mammoth supermarket developments, vote the budgets for our schools, set rents, determine how much we should pay for our leisure services, and make a host of other judgements affecting the everyday life of the public.

In return for giving them this power, the electorate expects them to get it right, and councillors and local authority officers are accountable to us for their decisions.

WE ARE THE WATCHDOGS

The media have a vital role to play in this accountability, keeping the public informed of not only what decisions are being taken in the town hall corridors of power, but by whom and why – and, sometimes more importantly, flagging up issues before those decisions are made.

To fulfil this role, reporters cover council meetings and report those decisions, the part played by our councillors, when the things they decide upon are likely to happen and what impact they will have on readers' lives. Without us, democracy suffers. Consistently empty seats on the press bench encourage a culture of secrecy which some councillors and officers have been only too willing to embrace. We are, in the words of Thomas Macauley a century and a half ago, the fourth estate of the realm.

Covering the meetings of councils and their committees is not always the most exhilarating part of a reporter's life. They can be long, boring and frustrating, particularly when you have a million and one other jobs to do. But they produce plenty of stories. Some of them are routine, some make first-class front-page splashes.

Meetings are also an excellent way of establishing and maintaining contacts, even if there is only the opportunity to smile at them across the council chamber. It helps to build relationships with councillors, imperative if you are to keep your finger on the pulse of local government.

This chapter assumes that you have studied the workings of local and central government, know how the various different kinds of council are structured and organised, and are aware of your rights to attend their meetings.

- Contacts
- Council meetings
- Town hall sources
- Parish councils
- Parties and MPs
- Elections

A reporter is only as good as his or her contacts. This is never more true than in coverage of councils.

OLWEN VASEY
Former municipal reporter on the Telegraph & Argus, Bradford, who contributed much of this chapter

👍 *Councils are required to publicise agendas and certain papers and reports before their meetings are held.*

This often means that news editors and reporters are drowned in mountains of information, but if your contacts are good you will be aware of major or controversial items and be ready to home in on them.

If you are on deadline – and in these days of the 24-hour website that will be all the time – this knowledge will enable you be first with the news and ahead of your rivals.

👍 *Contact suggestion: rest homes. They are full of people hoping to reach their centenary. Make sure you get tipped off about milestone birthdays and people who don't quite make them.*

The descriptions that follow are based on a typical English district council. The way your local authority works will differ in some respects but most of what follows should be relevant wherever you are.

CODDLE YOUR CONTACTS

They should be established, cultivated, nurtured and, above all, protected to the hilt. They must trust you, because they could be putting their jobs or positions in jeopardy by giving you stories. They may well, of course, have their own political or personal agenda in providing you with information and you should not take everything you are told at face value. Be aware of these hidden motives and research information carefully to ensure that your reports are fair and impartial.

Among the contacts you need to make are:

Party group leaders

These are the people who guide policy and set agendas. If the parties have whips to ensure councillors toe the party line, make contact with them. Leaders of major councils have their own political researchers, paid by the council, who are useful contacts when dealing with complex political issues.

Individual councillors

Get to know all of them, from all parties and of all persuasions. Every one should be aware of who you are and when, where and how to contact you.

You will find some who regard the media with deep suspicion. They may speak to you only if they absolutely have to and are convinced it is in their interest (which will be when they are up for re-election). Most, however, will be friendly and forthcoming. They want publicity, and you are the person to provide it.

Some, in love with political intrigue and back-biting, will actively seek the company of the media to swap gossip, peddle minor items of news, and perhaps slip you the occasional confidential document. Keep them happy: they are the ones who may talk when the big news breaks. Don't expect too much of them, though. Those who belong to a political party will keep a careful watch over their shoulders for the whips, knowing that if they embarrass their leaders too often by giving you confidential information they may be ousted from the group – the kiss of death in many places where party labels over-ride the merits of individuals at election time.

Independent councillors have no such qualms about talking to you, and are often good for quotes. Sadly, however, they rarely have much idea of what is going on behind the closed doors of group meetings

---

FIRST, THE BAD NEWS...

A common council ploy is for a statement to be leaked to the media, predicting a huge rise in council tax weeks before the actual decision is due to be announced.

Later a much lower increase is announced, enabling the leading group on the council to claim credit for being prudent in the hope that people will say: 'Well, it's not as bad as we thought.'

Your readers are unlikely to be taken in by this – and neither should you. Do not allow yourself or your newspaper to be used in this way. Always consider why you are being given information.

---

when the ruling party makes its decisions. You don't get into these either, of course, but leaks are not unknown.

Council press officers

Many of these are former journalists and know all about your job. They may well once have sat at the same press bench before being lured into the press office by the offer of more money and a less disruptive life. They will be helpful, but their first role is to promote the council in the best possible light.

They know how to slant press releases in the hope that journalists will simply lift their contents and use them as they are. Don't let them succeed. There has not been a press release yet written, to quote former *Times* editor Harold Evans, that does not need at least one phone call and a question.

Take, for instance, press releases announcing council tax rises. They may well be heralded as good news, but when you delve deeper you discover the reason given is that the rise is lower than that being imposed by some other authorities. It's bad news, just not as bad as it might have been. Say so. Your readers will not be fooled if you repeat the council line, because they know their pockets are being hit. Simply repeating the press officers' spin will antagonise your readers and put the newspaper in a bad light.

Press releases issued by councils about reports, such as those from the Audit Commission, should also be handled with care. They could show a council near the bottom of performance league tables, but become 'good news' in a press release because the council isn't rated the worst. It is a good idea to get hold of a copy of the actual report for yourself. It often gives a different picture and leads to a much better story.

Council officers

Don't rely solely on councillors as contacts. Seasoned senior council officers, who have seen scores of politicians come and go, are often

I covered a parish council outside my patch because the regular reporter was away, and a colleague gave me councillors' names and a plan of where they all sat.

I came back with a good tale which I wrote up, including emotive quotes from a lady I identified according to the seating plan.

After the paper came out I was dragged into the editor's office to be told the lady I quoted had been dead for six months and the one speaking was her replacement.

To make things worse, the story was about a lack of burial plots. It took an apology and a promise never to cover that meeting again to end the matter.

'Check, check and check again' is much heard in journalism, and for good reason.

ROB JERRAM
Deputy news editor
Lincolnshire Free Press

very useful. They explain issues well, give correct information and may be willing to give you a personal briefing on important issues. The chief executive and director of finance can be particularly good contacts, and their mobile phone numbers are beyond price when you are struggling with figures on the night of the annual Local Government Finance Settlement. Remember that officers do not have the power to make political decisions: they make recommendations which councillors decide whether or not to accept.

Their subordinates are worth cultivating, too: meet a friendly planning officer for a pint and you could glean all sorts of information about what people are applying to do, well before it appears as an official press release.

Trade unions

These are another important target when making local authority contacts. As they represent people employed by councils, they will be able to provide a different viewpoint.

AGENDAS, MINUTES AND RECORDS

Council agendas and papers arrive ahead of meetings and contain a wealth of stories. You may have to search for them, though. Some pre-meeting reports are extremely long, and you should never assume that the best line for your story is waiting for you at the beginning. Council officers are not journalists and their news sense can be poor or non-existent. Each report will have a summary of its contents at the start and you will find any recommendations listed at the end. An initial top-and-tail glance at these should suggest whether the report might make a story, either now as a prelim (written in advance) or after the meeting. But it is wise to read the entire document and any accompanying background papers, however long, to assess whether or not there are other, potentially better, stories buried within it that your readers should know about and will want to read.

Each report will carry the name of the officer who wrote it, and you can contact them for more information.

PLANNING APPLICATIONS

Many of the best stories appear on the weekly lists of planning applications. They usually arrive before the agendas and reports are prepared for planning committees, which means you can get well ahead of the game.

They are brief, containing reference numbers and perhaps a one-line description of the application. Many newspapers publish the lists in full, but any unusual items should be followed up. They can produce first-class human interest stories which can be prelimmed.

CONFIDENTIAL INFORMATION

Sometimes agendas recommend that the media should be excluded from discussion about certain items.

Confidential items are ones which central government or a court has said should not be disclosed. *Exempt* items are those which the council has decided to keep away from the media because they involve personal matters, such as employees' contracts or material that is commercially sensitive.

Don't ignore them. You can ask the council's legal department what the item is about and why it should not be reported. Ask for a copy of the item. If the request is refused, try to get hold of a copy from a contact: every councillor will have one.

If you decide its contents should be made public, tell your newsdesk. It can take legal advice on whether it is in the public interest to publish.

When the item arises at the meeting, you can ask the chairman if you can stay while it is discussed.

If you are excluded, you should request a statement on the decision and the reasons for it. Councillors should pass a formal resolution to exclude you: don't leave until they do.

Tempting though it may be, don't go along with any suggestion that you stay in the meeting while confidential or exempt matters are discussed, on the understanding that nothing you hear will be reported.

If the confidential item is something sensational, you are going to have great difficulty not breaking your word. And even if you do keep quiet, you may learn about it from some other source and, when you publish it, be accused of breaching the council's trust.

Better to leave and hope one of your councillor contacts inside will tell you all about it later.

The best way to a town clerk's heart is through his or her stomach.

When you take on a new patch and arrange to meet them for the first time, take buns, biscuits or cakes – and some for the rest of the staff you meet, too.

They will then always be pleased to see you, and feel obliged to tell you everything in return for being fed.

There's no such thing as a free bun.

SKIP WALKER
Editor
Wiltshire & Gloucestershire Standard

You are entitled to ask the council for details of such applications, as a member of the public as well as in your role as a reporter. If possible, visit the planning department: it can take days to get information by phone. Ask for the file and any correspondence, and request to see the duty planning officer for details. Then contact the applicant for more.

PREPARING FOR MEETINGS

If you are covering a council or committee for the first time, check the minutes of previous meetings. Copies arrive with the agendas, and they are available on council websites. See what the long-running issues are, and go through the archives to see what has already been written about them.

Ask your newsdesk how much you are expected to produce and check your deadline. Take agendas, clearly marked with items already prelimmed in your paper and others that might make good stories. Carry your mobile phone. Telephones in public buildings are usually pay phones which do not allow transfer charge calls enabling you to send copy without spending a fortune. You cannot receive calls on them, either.

Be persistent and always check every fact and quote.

ANNE HAYES
Former editor
Wiltshire & Gloucestershire Standard

Get to the meeting in good time. There will be somewhere allocated for the media: the council has to provide you with the facilities to take notes of its meetings. Get any documents issued at the last minute (there may be emergency items being slipped in that the council didn't want advance publicity about). Chat with anyone you know. Make contact with those you don't, or at least find out their names. Switch off your mobile.

WHO'S WHO IN THE COUNCIL CHAMBER

Full council meetings are attended by the chief executive, senior officers (directors of legal services, housing, education and so on), and press officers. The leaders of political groups and their councillors will be there, occupying different sections of the council chamber.

Chairing the meeting, depending on the type of council you are covering, will be the council chairman or mayor. Some places have elected mayors with executive powers, but on most councils the title-holders are councillors chosen by their colleagues to hold the position for a year. They play a largely ceremonial role – representing the town, greeting visiting dignatories and so on. While in office they are expected to be non-political, and should not be questioned about policy issues.

There are other people in the chamber, too. Clerks, secretaries and junior officers will be there to assist the proceedings. Union officials may be present when staff matters are discussed. Members of the public may attend and sit in the public galleries. The public can present petitions at a full council meeting, in which case you may have to follow the petitioners out of the room to do a quick interview and take pictures, or, if you haven't time for this, to arrange to contact them later.

Note who is and isn't at the meeting. Find out why important councillors and officials are absent: nine times out of ten there will be a simple explanation, but you don't want to miss the story if senior councillors are away visiting the site of a proposed and yet-unpublicised

---

PUBLIC DEMONSTRATIONS

These take place occasionally, both inside and outside the council chamber. They should be covered thoroughly.

Sometimes you will be given notice of them in advance of the meeting, in which case you should make sure you get pictures of demonstrators arriving. If the demonstration is impromptu, take photos if you can; though most councils will not allow pictures to be taken during meetings without prior permission, in the chaos of a noisy protest nobody is likely to notice until it is too late.

Talk to those involved and arrange to contact them later if you can't leave the meeting straight away. Get reaction from councillors and officials.

major development, or the director of environmental services has just dropped dead.

Many large authorities occupy ornate listed buildings and retain a certain amount of pomp and ceremony at full council meetings. If you attend the annual meeting and mayor making, you might well walk into a room resembling Ladies' Day at Ascot, with female councillors wearing large hats and the latest fashions while the new civic head looks faintly embarrassed in traditional robes and chain of office.

Stand when the mayor arrives to take his seat as chairman. He is there to keep control, clamp down on unruly behaviour, admonish members for outbursts, and make his own announcements before the agenda starts.

The meeting usually starts with question time, worth listening to because it can provide unexpected jewels that did not appear on the agendas. Then it is into the cut and thrust of the main business as reports are dealt with one by one (see the guide to how meetings work on page 66). At a full council meeting progress may be straightforward, with much of the business little more than rubber-stamping recommendations made at earlier cabinet or committee meetings, but be prepared for anything to happen.

WHAT TO COVER

If you have studied the agendas properly, marked the stories which have been prelimmed and others in which you are interested, much of what you cover will be pre-ordained. However, meetings can be stormy, with lots of political flak flying. Councillors play to the media, particularly when elections are near. Slanging matches are staged to grab the headlines.

They can make good copy, if the combatants have a neat turn of phrase and their words expose revealing sides of their character and political convictions. The public love colourful characters having a good argument. But be careful not to lose sight of the issues involved, because it will be these that affect your audience more than colourful quotes. The arguments may be dramatic or amusing, but the issues could involve serious matters such as changes in school admission policies or closure of old people's homes.

Be selective. Don't try to take down everything that is said: you haven't got enough notebooks or shorthand-writing stamina for that. Note the main points and pick up the occasional good quote. Keep an ear open for any hint of scandal. Record the votes and note the name of anyone who has voted against the party line: you might want to talk to them afterwards.

Look and listen for anything that might be worth pursuing later. If someone says that the housing books are in the red, it is obviously worth taking time later to go to the director of housing, the chairman and your own contacts to find out how much is involved, why there is

There are 18 councillors called Jones in the area I cover, some of them with the same first name.

I still don't know which is which, and reporting meetings when several speak – and do they speak! – is a nightmare.

NAME WITHHELD
Reporter
Somewhere in Wales

The same names crop up time after time in council stories: those of the party leaders and the vociferous publicity-seekers always ready with a quick sound-bite.

Don't totally ignore the rest, the backbenchers whose voices are heard less often.

They deserve the occasional mention and will be grateful for it.

Some, of course, are rarely or never heard.

Nobody keeps an accurate check of who speaks or how often (unlike in Parliament).

If you cover the same committee month after month, you might like to keep a running total of members' contributions to debates.

It will make a good little story after a year, when you announce which councillors take part the most, and which ones seem to be there just for the travel allowance.

a deficit, and what effect it might have on council rents, council tax or planned maintenance programmes.

Don't leave the meeting till the end of the open business, even if the last items on the agenda look dull. Anything might spark a controversy and provide copy. If you are excluded, wait outside until the meeting ends, and then ask the council clerk or press officer about anything you don't understand. Check any uncertain names. Remember to take the agenda and any other paperwork away with you.

WRITING IT UP

Your story is rarely about the council meeting as such: it is about the decisions made and, most importantly, the effect they will have on your public. Write with them in mind. Remember that most of them find councils so boring and distant that they can't even be bothered to vote once every few years. It's your job to make what their local authority does seem interesting and its decisions relevant to their lives.

Humanise your story. Keep the words *council* and *committee* out of your intro if you can. *Thousands of Midthorpe householders face bills for new wheelie-bins* is infinitely better than *Midthorpe District Council's Environmental Health Committee decided at a meeting last night to introduce revised refuse collection procedures.*

Get rid of all the jargon. Council reports are always littered with officialese. Houses are *dwellings*, paths are *footways* and public seats are *street furniture*. Turn these words back into easy, everyday language your audience can understand.

Your story should be a balanced report of the proceedings, giving both sides of the debate. Try to include comments from all parties taking part. This can be difficult when faced by space limitations and you might often have to summarise rather than give full quotes. If you are doing a story based on a press release and someone refuses to comment, say so.

Put to one side anything that is unbalanced and clearly needs investigation: further inquiries often lead to a much better story.

Remember when you are covering committees that, unless they have been given delegated powers, many of their resolutions are only recommendations, subject to approval by the full council. Make this clear in your story.

Use the correct house style when referring to councillors. Some newspapers give party affiliation after names at first reference – *Coun John Parrott (Con)* – to help the public work out what is going on.

SCRUTINY COMMITTEES

Scrutiny committees, surprisingly given their role, are generally regarded as rather toothless set-ups, and covering them can be the first diary jobs to be axed by a busy newsdesk with too many jobs to cover and not enough staff.

However, this doesn't mean they should be ignored. Their role is to make sure the council is doing things in the correct manner, and make recommendations for improvements. Members set their own agenda and can decide what to look into. It could be a controversial issue, such as plans to open new facilities for drug addicts close to houses whose owners object. This is when scrutiny committees can be at their best, digging out information that otherwise might not come to light and inviting the public to attend and express their views.

Members can look beyond local issues. They can examine national matters such as the siting of mobile phone masts, and hold inquiries during which they call evidence. Even though they cannot make binding decisions, their presence cannot be ignored and they often provide good copy.

NEIGHBOURHOOD FORUMS

These are the grass roots arm of the council. They operate in different communities, chaired by local people, and are attended by councillors, council officers and members of the public. While they often struggle to fill seats, when feelings are running high on a strong local issue they are packed and well worth reporting. They make excellent copy and you make contacts who will stay in touch when events have moved on.

IT'S NOT JUST MEETINGS

There are many other sources of potentially good stories from the council. They include:

Council accounts: You have the right to inspect the council's books, and make copies of anything you find in them, in a period of 20 working days before a date set by its auditor. This date, around the time the annual audit takes place, should be announced at least a fortnight beforehand.

The moment you see your story in the paper, if not before, you should be thinking of follow-ups.

A splash should always be followed by a page lead next day.

Take ownership of your story and don't rely on the newsdesk to think of all the follow-ups.

They are key sources of stories and can be as good or better than the original tale.

You could find somebody else gets the glory if you don't grab it for yourself.

NICK NUNN
Assistant editor
Lancashire
Evening Telegraph

DON'T BE SEEN TO TAKE SIDES

It is generally accepted that reporters, especially those covering local government, should not to be members of any political party.

It is all too easy for politicians to seek favours because they know you as a party member. Members of other parties will find out and accuse you of bias, even when you believe your coverage is entirely fair. They will not believe it, and neither will readers who become aware of your political allegiance.

Harold Evans, the former editor of The Times, took this to extremes, refusing to join any organisation because it just became another pressure group. There are editors around today who will not even join their local Rotary Club.

Never under-estimate the vanity of MPs and health authority chairmen.

HELEN STANLEY
Sub-editor
Daily Echo, Bournemouth

Many councillors and MPs hold regular surgeries, a good opportunity to meet them and hear their constituents' tales of woe, which are often the start of good stories.

People with problems also write to their elected representatives for help.

Encourage MPs and councillors to tell you about them.

They may be happy to do so, especially if they have found solutions and can make political capital out of it by claiming credit for themselves and their party – and blame their rivals for causing the problem in the first place.

Councillors' expenses: Details of these have to be made available to electors at any time, and an annual statement showing all claims has to be issued to the media. It always makes good copy, arousing public outrage and defensive responses from councillors pleading that, even with the expenses, they are well out of pocket.

Register of gifts and hospitality: Although this is not usually on display, it is a public document and anyone can ask to see it. Some councillors follow the requirement to register gifts to the letter: one Green Party councillor declared receiving a dozen free-range eggs. If you see a pattern of wining and dining between a councillor and a property developer, alarm bells should start ringing. Following up such stories is fraught with traps, and inquiries should be very discreet. When asking questions, don't suggest that the councillor has done anything wrong or you could be accused of slander.

Standards Committee: This oversees ethical issues and investigations allegations that councillors have broken the local government code of conduct, which requires them to behave with integrity and not bring their office into disrepute. Serious cases can be referred to the National Standards Board for England. Cases they have dealt with include failing to declare an interest, having pornographic material on a council laptop, and yelling abuse at a councillor colleague. Once a complaint is made, you will need to check the board's website and with your contacts for a decision, as it is not announced in a press release and the board does not contact journalists to give its decision. It can take a long time.

Ombudsmen: Properly called Commissioners for Local Administration, these investigate allegations that a council has been biased, followed the wrong procedures, or failed to tell someone of their rights. Complaints should be made first to the council, though the public can approach the commission directly. The ombudsmen will issue a report and, if the complaint is upheld, recommendations for action: an apology, perhaps, or payment of compensation. These findings are not binding on the council, but they make excellent stories.

Freedom of Information Act: If the council fails to answer your questions properly, you can use the Act to get information. It can be effective: one weekly newspaper, fobbed off for three years when it tried to find out whether a director of education received a pay-off when she left her council's employ in unusual circumstances, used the Act to discover that she had been given £250,000. Making applications for information, however, takes time and costs money (for councils as well as the media), and many local authorities have been less enthusiastic about responding to them than we would like.

Staff magazines: Local authorities are major employers. Thousands of people work for them and human interest stories abound. Some appear in the staff magazine that circulates around the town hall: ask for a regular copy. Chasing up such stories helps you to meet employees and make non-political contacts.

DISPUTES

Councils regularly restructure departments and their methods of providing services, usually to save money, and your internal contacts can be a valuable source of information about the effect this has on council employees and the public at large.

These changes can be hugely unpopular among the workforce and can lead to unofficial or official industrial action, which affect thousands of council taxpayers. Good contacts with the town hall unions are a must.

Don't take anything you are told by either side in a dispute at face value. Check the facts with the other side, particularly when it comes to figures. Different interpretations will be put on them and the figures themselves may be challenged.

Unofficial work-to-rule action is the hardest to handle because often neither council nor union will admit it is happening. However, any kind of action will inevitably have some effect on the public. If refuse collectors are taking action, people's rubbish soon piles up and readers get in touch with their local newspaper. Interviews with the public and pictures of rotting garbage will be enough for it to run the story, even if there is no official admission that anything is wrong.

PARISH COUNCILS

THESE are a constant source of stories for local newspapers. Some are tiny, representing perhaps a single village and its surrounding area; others cover quite large populations and often call themselves town councils.

Parish councillors levy a precept on the ratepayers and are responsible for how this is spent. While they do not have the final say on major issues and merely make recommendations to higher authorities on planning applications and many other matters (make this clear in your copy), they can have considerable influence.

Most parish councils meet monthly. There is also an annual parish meeting at which officers are elected, including a chair, a clerk and a treasurer. This is open to all electors, who can raise issues and take votes, though these are not binding on the council.

Generally speaking, there is less formality at parish councils than at higher-tier councils and councillors tend to be more approachable. Politics usually takes a back seat and members give personal opinions rather than follow a party line. The main council and major committees (finance and general purposes, for example) are worth attending.

Parish councils are often the starting point for issues which later become major stories. Contact with them is as important as with the larger authorities. If you can't cover all their meetings, make sure the clerk sends you agendas and minutes. They may be happy to send

Problems getting your shorthand speed up to cope with meetings?

Try taking down news-readers on the telly, as they speak at about 110 wpm.

If you're not up to that, try Coronation Street or Eastenders.

KATE HELYER
Community editor
North Devon Journal

👍 *Refer to would-be MPs as prospective parliamentary candidates until they are officially adopted by their party, when the 'prospective' can be dropped.*

Failure to do so can cause them problems over what they are allowed to claim as election expenses.

It's worth checking on these when the voting is over.

Expenses claims have to be submitted within a few weeks after an election and there are stringent rules on how much candidates are allowed to claim.

It's a good story if they break them: they can be disqualified.

reports of what goes on, which you can use, although they might need extensive re-writing. Check anything controversial and watch out for libel.

Very small communities may do without a formally-elected council, settling instead for just a parish meeting which may meet only a few times a year. Again, everyone on the electoral role for the area is a member and can take part in debates, with decisions taken on a vote of all attending. It would be local democracy at its best, but for the fact that their powers are even more limited than those of parish councils. They do, however, have the same right to raise money by a precept on their members.

PARTIES, AGENTS AND MPS

LOCAL politics isn't just about what goes on at the town hall. In the background are local political parties, each with its members, activists, officials, and an MP or someone who wants to be. Larger parties have an agent, probably full-time, perhaps shared with neighbouring constituencies, who may act as the election agent when voting comes round.

Parties have branches representing wards within the constituency, each with their officials. Most parties hold social and fund-raising events, worth attending for the chance to cement contacts, initiate new ones, and find fresh stories.

Make good friends with MPs, prospective candidates and agents, whatever their political persuasion. They are obviously very good contacts, whether in or out of office. It should not be difficult, as they are anxious to court the favour of their local media. Without a good press, their chances of election or re-election are much reduced. They are always ready to give their opinion on any subject that might enhance their electability, and some are so willing to speak out that they earn a reputation as instant rent-a quotes.

Your newsdesk may have an arrangement with a Commons-based political correspondent or news agency to supply stories about speeches made and questions asked in the House by your local MPs, but the politicians will be happy to supply you with copies and further details.

You can find out how often they attend parliamentary debates, and there are annual stories about which MPs are most often on the benches and which ones are never seen. Remember, before you leap on the he's-never-there bandwagon, that some are very active away from the green-benched showcase we see on television, and absence from the debating chamber does not necessarily mean they are lazy or ineffective. But if they really don't appear to be doing much apart from claiming their expenses, it's a story.

👍 *Contact suggestion: window cleaners. They see a lot from up there.*

When you meet MPs, ask about their current engagements, plans for the future and personal life – a legitimate subject of public interest. Their holiday plans, for example, arouse public interest and sometimes envy and disapproval.

Make sure they tell you about any activities outside parliament, such as political rallies, and arrange for their speeches to be covered. Once you have got to know them, they may invite you to tour the Commons with them and sit in on a debate.

Don't forget members of the House of Lords living in your area. Remember MEPs, some of whom have such large constituencies that the media tend to forget that they, too, need regular contact and a close eye kept on their activities. They will welcome attention and might even invite you to Brussels, though your newsdesk isn't likely to pay for it.

ELECTIONS

ELECTIONS, even local ones in which only a few hundred people bother to vote and the result is often a foregone conclusion, can be fun and give you good stories.

Broadcasters covering elections operate under a strict code of conduct which imposes an obligation to give balanced coverage of all candidates. The press have no such restrictions, and there is no reason why a newspaper should not totally ignore one or more parties if it wishes, or carry only bad news about politicians and policies they dislike.

Most, however, feel it their public duty to give at least some space to all involved, apportioning it according to parties' significance and past success. No candidate ever believes that he or she has been treated by the media as well as they would like, which is probably how it should be. They will battle for publicity, putting themselves in the public eye as much as possible and coming up with an abundance of stories and picture requests. Take advantage of this, but don't be used. If candidates give views on contentious issues, ask their rivals to comment. They will happy to do so.

Remember, as you write stories in the run-up to an election, that candidates' literature has no legal protection, that factual errors about candidates' personal character or conduct can land you in court if they could influence the result, and that not everything said at heated election meetings may be of public concern and protected by qualified privilege. Avoid non-party and potentially libellous descriptions of candidates and their supporters as *fascists, neo-nazis, marxists* and the like.

When nominations close, check whose names have been put forward: there may be surprise last-minute candidates. Your contact for this is the acting returning officer, probably the town clerk or an equivalent officer. He can arrange for you to take photos of candidates handing in deposits. Keep an eye on the progress of postal voting: it has been used by unscrupulous candidates to rig results.

There are few good reasons for smoking, but making contacts is one of them. There is a guilty camaraderie among nicotine addicts, never greater than since the ban came in.

Outside every meeting venue there are small huddles of smokers eager to share their problems with fellow sinners. Join them. If you don't smoke, say you've given up: how you managed it is a source of great fascination to those who haven't.

I make a point during council meetings, when non-newsworthy items are being laboriously debated, of having a quick drag outside with councillors and officers in need of a fix. They can be quite indiscreet as you share the indignity of it all, especially if it's raining.

Please don't print my name: the wife thinks I've given up.

NAME WITHHELD
Among the fag-ends, somewhere in Scotland

The media usually avoid giving publicity to new claims and arguments in the 24 hours before the polls close, on the basis that rivals have no opportunity to reply.

Polling day can have its own incidents and it has been known for violence to occur at polling stations. In some cities there have been allegations of electors being accosted or attacked on their way to vote. Police usually maintain a high presence on the day, but reporters should also drive around, checking on the situation.

THE COUNT

Attending an election count is quite an experience. Admission is usually granted to the media, but it is at the discretion of local returning officers. You will need to obtain a pass in advance and sign a declaration of secrecy, and once inside will have to wait there until the result is announced. It can be a long night. You can spend the time talking to candidates and their agents about what has been happening during the day.

When the result comes through, note the number of votes gained by each candidate, do a quick mathematical calculation of the majority, record the speeches made by winners and losers, do quick interviews with them – and then get the whole thing quickly over to your newsdesk. Don't forget to mention whether the seat is a loss or gain for a party, the overall swing, and what the turnout was. Any recounts or rows over spoiled papers should obviously be included in your story.

Other reporters will be at other counts sending results and stories for the newsdesk to collate, and the team effort involving the whole newsroom will produce coverage that will not only impress your public but give you great satisfaction.

Sixteen

SPECIALIST AREAS

ONE of the stock questions that editors ask would-be reporters applying for their first job is: *'So where do you see yourself in five years' time?'*

The bravest applicants are honest, and say: *'Doing your job'*, which demonstrates commendable ambition but worries editors slightly that within the next 60 months they might be stabbed in the back by the new recruit.

Some have a clear idea where they want to be: the sports desk (realistic), investigating for the *Guardian* (idealistic), roaming the world on BBC expenses (fantastic). Others mutter vaguely about maybe getting into features because they have always liked writing, not always the best response: editors are wary of those with literary pretensions who may jib at being asked to sit through five-hour meetings of the local policy and resources committee.

Very few say they want to become specialist reporters. But that is what many of them will end up doing, covering areas such as crime, education or health. Many of the larger newspapers have such specialists, some employed full-time, others doing the job in addition to general reporting duties (full-timers tend to be awarded the title *correspondent;* the rest tag their speciality on to their job title, as in *crime reporter*).

Being offered a specialist area can be a hit-and-miss affair. The current title-holder gets a new job, and a replacement is needed. If the newspaper is big enough and the specialism high-profile, editors may seek to poach an established journalist from elsewhere. Often, however, they decide that advertising the position and interviewing applicants is too expensive and time-consuming, and look round the newsroom for a likely candidate. Their eye lights upon you and you're asked if you fancy giving it a try. Ten years later, if you're very lucky, it helps you to get that job on the *Guardian*.

This chapter looks at some of these specialist areas, starting with the one that many newcomers nominate as their target and which most reporters will end up covering, at least part-time, somewhere along the line: sport. Later there is a brief introduction to the worlds of crime, education, environment, health and industry/business reporting, and the section rounds off with a look at life as a district reporter.

SPORTS REPORTING

SPORT plays a major role in the media, and a place on the sports desk is the aim of many young entrants into journalism.

- Sport
- Crime
- Education
- Environment
- Health
- Industry
- District reporting
- Churches

> *Don't specialise too soon. Do the whole range of journalism – hard news, politics, business, show biz, sport – before settling on the one you do best and like best.*
>
> *Work very, very hard. And be honest with your readers and yourself.*
>
> **TOM CLARKE**
> Former editor
> The Sporting Life

For a sports fan, it sounds almost too good to be true: free seats at top games, face-to-face chats with the stars, insider knowledge of what is really going on, and tens of thousands of sports fans eager to read your opinions.

It isn't always that glamorous, any more than news reporting is a constant round of chasing fires and exposing corruption. Would-be sports reporters lucky enough to realise their ambition soon discover they spend long hours researching background material, attending obscure events, hanging around to interview people with little to say, and typing up long lists of results.

Before they get their own premiership team to cover they will spend many Saturdays at windswept non-league grounds and Sundays in the office subbing other people's copy for the next day's edition. Nevertheless, reporters in love with sport readily accept that all this is worthwhile in return for the joys of covering tense cup matches and winning exclusive interviews.

News experience helps

Getting a job on a sports desk is not always easy. Some sections of the media will recruit trainees straight from accredited courses or university, especially if they have specialised in sports journalism, but others prefer their sports reporters to have had some news-gathering experience first because it gives them a good general introduction to such skills as researching, interviewing and writing. Many reporters start off in the newsroom and do some part-time sports reporting to prove their potential before switching over to sport full-time.

Not everyone, of course, is passionate about sport, but it plays so great a part in many people's lives that every reporter needs a working knowledge of the sporting world, just as they need to know about shopping, food, drink, health, television, pop stars, pets and all the other everyday things that occupy the public's time, attention and enthusiasm.

This section is not a guide to being a full-time sports reporter. It is intended for news reporters who are routinely required to handle sport as part of their weekly duties or are expected to step in to cover sport if and when the need arises.

The thought of doing this daunts many journalists, who fear they know nothing of the sport they are being asked to cover and will make fools of themselves if they try writing about it. The good news is that much of what has already been said in this book about news reporting applies equally well to sport.

There is the same need for efficient preparation, good contacts, interviewing skills, time management and accuracy. Sport stories, like those on the news pages, should be about people, well-constructed, well-written, informative and entertaining. There are, however, some major differences, as we shall see.

It's not just watching football

Larger news-gathering organisations have fulltime sports desks, run by a sports editor. Some of their reporters may concentrate exclusively on one sport, or even one team; others will be expected to switch from football and rugby to cricket and tennis as the seasons change, and to turn their hand to a wide range of other sports as well.

On newspapers, they may well be required to spend part of their time subbing, helping the fulltime sports subs to re-write contributed reports, format results and lay out pages.

On smaller newspapers, especially weeklies, much of the sports pages' content may come from club secretaries, press officers and other correspondents. Their contributions will be knocked into shape by the sports editor, if there is one, or by news reporters who may be expected to cover additional sports stories when necessary.

Sports page content divides broadly into diary stories relating to specific events and matches – previews, reports of the actual event and follow-ups – and off-diary stories, ranging from hard news about the activities of sports organisations to softer profiles of individual players.

On daily newspapers, the emphasis at the start of the week is mostly on what happened the previous weekend. Midweek editions have more space for other items and features, before attention turns towards the next weekend's events.

Weekly newspapers, most of which publish towards the end of the week, know that by the time they appear their readers will probably have seen details of the previous weekend's major events elsewhere, and may give them only a brief summary. They will concentrate instead on what lies ahead, restricting detailed coverage to lesser events which have not already been reported.

You've got a captive audience

Whereas news reporters must battle to capture their public's attention, sports reporters have a captive audience eager to read about their subject. Players, managers, their families and friends want to see their names and exploits in print; fans want to read about what they are going to see, have seen or have missed. However minor the sport, someone out there is interested and every word will be read.

This means every mistake will be noticed, too. Accuracy is vital. Mis-spell the name of a goalscorer or report that someone was bowled out when they were caught, and everyone who was there will know you got it wrong – and say so.

Reporters covering news stories usually have to work on the assumption that readers need an explanation or at least a reminder of what has happened before. Sports writers can often take it for granted that their readers know much of the background to an on-going story, and just a brief reference to a club in crisis or an injury-hit player may be enough.

Similarly, they can assume a certain amount of reader knowledge of sport, and don't have to explain technical terms each time they crop up: rugby fans know what is meant by a drop goal, racing fans know the difference between a nose and a short head.

Reporting local sport can be as difficult as reviewing amateur dramatics – nothing but unadulterated praise will do.

When I covered a semi-professional football team, I rode my motorbike to the ground and then caught the team coach.

One week, after suggesting in print that the centre-half had lost a bit of pace as he turned 40, he handed me my crash helmet as I got off the coach.

It was full of beer – pints of it, all strained through his kidneys during the trip.

BRIAN TILLEY
Deputy editor
Hexham Courant

Most players and managers will accept constructive criticism, but don't bank on it.

There are some sensitive souls out there, however tough and thick-skinned they seem on the surface.

There have been cases of clubs banning the media from their grounds for what they regarded as excessively negative reporting.

Fanzines and unofficial club websites can be a useful source of stories, quick to instigate controversy and say things the club doesn't want to hear.

Some of them are embarrassingly good at beating the 'official' media to the latest news. Keep an eye on them.

You've got plenty of space

It is usually a struggle to get all the facts and quotes into a news story. Copy has to be written as tightly as possible to maximise the amount of material that can be fitted in. This is by no means always the case with sport.

On daily newspapers particularly, sports reporters often have large spaces to fill day after day. They can write at length without worrying about being selective. This makes the job easier in some ways, but it can be a challenge when there is very little fresh information around.

Good sports reporters will phone round their contacts, dig into the statistics and come up with something interesting; others take the lazy way out: sentences ramble on, repetition abounds, quotes are used in full regardless of their worth, the slightest hint of disagreement turns into a major confrontation and every groin strain is milked for all it is worth.

You can say what you think

News reporters are expected to produce objective reports based on facts and the opinions of others. Sports reporters, on the other hand, are often encouraged to say what they think about the performance of a team or individual player, and comment, analysis and speculation are welcome.

It is a freedom sports writers exercise with enthusiasm, knowing that the public want to compare their own opinions with those of the supposed expert in the local media. They may or may not agree, but will respect them if they recognise that they are, in the words of the Defamation Act, honestly-held and based on fact.

However, a sports reporter who constantly damns a team will soon exhaust readers' patience, as will one who takes blinkered partisanship to the extreme and refuses to write anything critical regardless of reality.

You can be colourful

Sports reporting has a language all of its own. Readers who would be aghast to read that a defence solicitor *crumbled pathetically before a wave of blistering prosecution attacks* will relish being told of their football team's prowess in such a fashion.

Colourful descriptions, adverbs and adjectives can be used more readily than in news reports. They still need to be handled carefully, though, and sports writers have to resist the temptation to over-indulge in flowery and extravagant language.

REPORTING EVENTS

You cannot be expected to know everything: many seasoned sports reporters confess uncertainty about the finer details of, for example, the rules of

THE FIRST TIME SINCE WHEN?

Arm yourself with statistics. Sports fans love them: facts and figures about the highest attendance, the 70th time teams have met, the record run of 18 games since a score draw at home on a Tuesday night in January.

Find out, too, about players' personal details and home lives, so that you can blame a poor performance on their birthday celebrations the night before or a good one on their partner having just given birth to twins.

cricket and rugby. But you should arm yourself with some basic facts about the way the game is played, the terminology and the people taking part.

Preparation

As with any other kind of reporting, the better you are prepared, the better you will perform. Find out something about the sport you are covering.

Get a reference book or search the internet; ask colleagues for explanations. Look up teams and players in your archives. Log on to clubs' websites, official and unofficial, to discover the latest talking points. Don't try to disguise your ignorance: sharp-eyed readers will spot your mistakes immediately.

Find out what is expected of you. Read previous reports and ask the sports desk for guidance. If, for example, you are covering a football match, you need to know about:

Access: Do you need a press pass to get in and where do you base yourself? Are you going to be exposed to the weather and, if so, have you appropriate clothing?

Length and timing: How many words do you write? Are you writing a detailed account or just a summary of the game?

Details: What must be included? Team names, substitutes, scorers, bookings, injuries, referee, man of the match, attendance figures?

Post-match: Is there a press conference to be covered? Are you likely to get a chance to interview the manager, talk to players in the dressingroom or be invited into the boardroom?

Transmission: When is your deadline? If you are working to a tight deadline, are you producing one report or sending it in sections, with an intro added when the final whistle blows? Does the sports desk want goal flashes for the website? Are you expected to phone copy (from an evening event or a distant venue, for example), and if so, how do you go about it?

Pictures: Are you expected to provide them for the newspaper and/or the website? What about audio and video?

At the game

Get a programme as far in advance as possible. It may contain comments from the manager or other club officials which are worth including in

---

A lot of managers are grumpy and cantankerous, so do it the old-fashioned way: go to training, get your face seen, put in the hours.

They'll respect you for it.

MARK WOOD
Sports editor
Bedford Times & Citizen

One of our reporters arrived at Newcastle's central metro station to discover they were holding a press conference there to announce a clampdown on fare dodgers.

The gathered scrum of hacks watched as she was led away and fined £20 for not having a ticket.

GRAHAM PRATT
Deputy editor
The Journal, Newcastle

your story. There may be other useful information, such as statistics about previous encounters between the two teams suggesting this is a lucky ground for the visiting side or that they view their opponents as a bogey team.

Check for team changes: there are few things worse than getting a goalscorer's name wrong because he was brought into the team at the last minute and you didn't know.

Once the game has kicked off:

Don't try to record every move. Make notes about those that lead to something: a goal, a near-miss, a free kick, an injury. Note the timing: when goals are scored, players sent off, how much extra time is played.

Watch individual players: are they having a good game or playing badly? How are they reacting to each other? Are they combining well or angry at their team-mates' mistakes?

Keep an eye on the referee (is he doing a good job?), the weather (does it affect the game?) and the crowd (how do they react?)

Get quotes afterwards, if you can, from the manager, players and supporters. How do they think it went? Was it a fair result? What decided the game?

Work out what effect, if any, the result has had upon the teams' league table positions.

Writing it up

If your report is the first your readers will see, you will probably intro on the result and the nature of the game. If you are writing a story that comes out after readers have seen or heard about the game elsewhere, on radio or television or in the Sunday newspapers, you may want to look beyond the scoreline and focus on the manager's reaction, on the implications for the next match, or on one memorable element of the game. Ask yourself what made this game different to all the rest: one brilliant strike, a disputed penalty, a late substitution?

Either way, you still need to record what went on in the game. Few newspapers these days publish minute-by-minute accounts of matches, which are space-consuming and, frankly, boring to all but the most dedicated fans. Unless you are asked to produce a full chronology of events, concentrate on the highlights, the moves that proved to be turning-points in the game.

Use crisp, direct, active and colourful language. Good match reports will reflect the passion and excitement of the event. Imagine how it felt for the spectators, the players, the manager.

Bring the players to life: say how they behaved, what they were thinking, why they did what they did. Why write *Jones lost the ball to Brown* when you could say *Jones dithered nervously once too often and Brown saw his chance*?

Avoid clichés. The days of goalkeepers being described as *custodians of the net* are thankfully dead and buried, but sports-writing is still littered with others: *cliff-hanger games, nail-biting finishes, balls clutched from thin air* after *hitting the woodwork* and, of course, the managers' favourites, *sick as a parrot* but *looking at one game at a time*.

Remember it is, after all, only a game. Going down six-nil at home is not a *tragedy* or a *disaster*, and however much tempers may flare on the pitch, it isn't *all-out war*.

Don't forget that sport can become news. If the ref drops dead halfway through the match, phone the newsdesk.

OFF-DIARY STORIES

TREAT sport just as you would education, health, business, the environment, or any other area of life you cover as part of your everyday reporting life. Look for sports stories, whatever you are doing. Many of the people you deal with will follow some sport or other; many will be players or the family and friends of players.

Contacts are crucial

Build up contacts: athletes, team members, managers, coaches, trainers, physiotherapists, press officers.

Go along to larger clubs, make yourself known, find out how managers spend their working day, when training sessions are held and so on. Find out if and when they hold regular press conferences and attend. Contact the secretaries of smaller clubs and encourage them to send you information. Persuade them to think of photo-opportunities. Get in touch with local education authorities, schools and colleges, sports councils, bodies running training courses. Google-search for local people doing weird sports. Remember young people, old people, the handicapped and the disabled, the women's football teams and the men playing netball. All of them are potential sources of stories and all of them are seeking publicity.

Look beyond the game

You want more than just details and results of events. Look for news about moves, transfers, signings, illnesses and injuries, youth teams, friendly matches, new facilities, fund-raising, sponsors and commercial activities, fan clubs, management crises and players' personal lives. If the club's oldest fan dies at the age of 99 or the goalkeeper's wife runs off with the physio, you want to know about it first. Don't ignore the reserves and youngsters coming through training academies.

I take a briefcase, not for carrying things but as a journalistic aide.

If you are doing shorthand you have to be comfortable. Everyone tells you to have spare pens and paper; no one tells you to carry a table.

Sitting with a notepad waving away as you scribble is no way to do a job. A briefcase on the knees does the trick.

It can buy you time, too. I was interviewing a leading Tory peer, and tried in vain to get some personal colour.

Out of desperation, I unflipped the briefcase and everything came pouring out. As I scrabbled about on my knees, I saw a drumkit in the room next-door.

Yes, he said, he played in a little jazz group in the Lords. His last public performance was at John Cleese's first wedding...

CHRIS LLOYD
Deputy editor
The Northern Echo

Interview people for profile features. Find out about them as people, rather than just churning out a list of their achievements. What do they do apart from sport? How else could (or do) they earn a living? What do they think of their team-mates and sporting rivals? What are their favourite foods, bands, nightclubs and holiday resorts?

Look at the issues: there are stories to be written about racism, doping, ticket touts, expensive replica strips and a host of other controversial matters affecting sport.

Final warning:

Good relationships with clubs and their managers are important, but don't let them compromise you with drinks in the boardroom and offers of a place on the team coach.

Accept both by all means – good for building contacts and finding stories – but remember that your job is to report and to criticise if it is justified. Clubs need publicity just as much as you need news. If they try to blackmail you or threaten you with a ban because they don't like what you have written, remember that managers come and go (some very quickly), but your newspaper will still be around long after they have been forgotten. Tell your editor, and stand firm.

CRIME REPORTING

THE job of the crime reporter is often the most coveted of specialisations, an opportunity to go behind the scenes, cover dramatic events and write front-page exclusives.

It can be exciting, but to be successful at the role takes a lot of hard work. Apart from covering courts (which we have dealt with earlier), crime reporters are expected to bring in a wealth of other stories, and that means having excellent sources of information. Good crime reporting, like every other job in journalism, is all about contacts.

POLICE REPRESENTATIVES

Police officers below the rank of superintendent are members of the Police Federation, a national body that looks after welfare, financial and disciplinary matters.

Within it are groups representing, among others, women, black, disabled, gay and Jewish officers.

It has local branches whose officials should be among your contacts; its website is worth a visit to identify current issues and problems.

The federation rigorously defends its members, will help to fund libel actions if you defame one, and carries a lot of clout with government.

Senior officers belong to the Association of Chief Police Officers, which has a central press office.

Police press officers

Based in area control rooms, they are usually the first port of call for information about major incidents, crimes and forthcoming court cases. Police press officers usually have a media background, understand what news is all about, and know what questions you want answered, unlike many police officers who don't always recognise what is important to the media or why. They also know the value of keeping the media satisfied: reporters can be very helpful to the police, by publicising appeals for witnesses, warnings of traffic problems, and so on.

The best press officers will provide background material about crimes and court cases in advance, once they trust you not to print confidential material. They can supply photo-fits of wanted people and pictures of defendants, murder victims, crime scenes and courtroom exhibits. They may be able to provide interviews with victims' families, official police statements on the progress and result of prosecutions, and interviews with the police officers involved. They can arrange for reporters to join the police on drugs raids and other activities.

Away from the business of current crime, they can provide information about forthcoming inquests, escaped prisoners, deaths in custody, complaints, missing people, crime prevention initiatives, personnel changes, bravery awards, and officers' activities outside work. They will be happy to arrange for features about different aspects of police work: the motorcycle unit, the underwater divers, the wildlife protection officers, the air support crews, the men and women who train and look after police dogs and horses.

Police forces produce newsletters that can be a fund of stories: ask the press office to provide you with copies.

If press officers fail to supply the information you need within a reasonable time, phone the control room. The duty inspector may not speak to you, but he or she will soon get sufficiently irritated by your calls to speed things up. If you are regularly frustrated in your quest for information, bring it to your news editor's attention. He or she will take it up at a higher level.

Individual police officers

Many crime reporters by-pass the press office on occasion and try to speak to the senior officer in the police control room first. Some duty inspectors will talk to the media once they are confident that reporters are responsible and trustworthy. Lower ranks are not usually authorised to make official statements, and there is nothing to be gained from hassling officers whose jobs may be on the line if they are seen openly talking to you at the scene of a crime.

That doesn't mean, of course, that these don't make good contacts: they can be among the best. Meet and talk to as many as you can, in court, in public, on and off duty. It takes time and effort to build up

I once was told it was all quiet by an army unit press officer only to then be told casually in passing that the regiment had now got the country's biggest drum horse, used to carry the dual bass drums on ceremonial duties.

It transpired that the huge black beast was so strong they were unable to keep it within the stable as it kept bending the metal restraining bars at the front of its stall and walking out.

A great little human interest piece that the young officer completely failed to appreciate.

JOE SCICLUNA
Editor
Andover Advertiser

If you are given information off the record, whether from a press office or a police officer, make sure it stays that way.

Be clear about what must not be published under any account, and what you can use so long as its source is not disclosed.

One mistake, and your career as a crime reporter will probably be over.

IT'S A CRIME... OR IS IT?

Be careful when handling crime figures.

Differentiate between all crime (which nobody can measure), reported crime (the proportion of crime the police are told about), recorded crime (the proportion of reported crime the police put on record, rejecting the rest as unreliable), and, of course, the number of crimes actually solved (a much smaller propor-tion still). The police will, naturally, prefer to highlight their successes.

Be sure about the reasons for changes in these figures. What appears to be a rise in one kind of offence may in fact simply reflect an increased public willingness to report them; an increase in the number of crimes solved may be the result of changes in prosecution policy.

---

their trust, but once you have gained it you will get valuable background, information and tip-offs.

Police authorities

These are independent bodies made up of local people (councillors, magistrates and members of the public) with the job of monitoring the efficiency and effectiveness of the police.

They control general strategy, appoint chief constables and other senior officers, control the police budget, decide the amount of council tax raised for policing, and ensure the police give value for money. They are expected to consult with the public, and respond to complaints.

Police authorities have their own press officers, but individual members can be approached and some (particularly councillors) may be eager for publicity.

Other policing bodies

These include the transport police, river police, harbourmasters, customs and immigration authorities, military police, the RSPCA and the NSPCC. Fire services can initiate prosecutions, as can trading standards and council health departments.

Lawyers

There is a reason why so many pubs are called *The Wig and Pen*. Solicitors and barristers are as keen to gossip about what is going on as you are, though they will not, of course, reveal confidential information about their clients or discuss forthcoming cases in detail.

Make yourself known to them in court; find out where they go for a drink afterwards. They have lives outside the office which could provide human interest stories. Judges are less approachable, but, like all of us,

Don't get so close to police contacts that you forget your duty as a reporter and are tempted to ignore stories reflecting adversely upon the force.

And don't think for a minute, however matey you get with them, that they will get you off a parking ticket.

they are susceptible to flattery: ask them politely in the pub for advice on a tricky point of law and you will be surprised to discover just how human they can be.

The Crown Prosecution Service can be contacted for information and official comment: it has area press offices.

Villains

Cover crime for a while and you will soon get to know the local under-world. Its members can be useful contacts (they are sometimes the first to tip you off about crimes) but they are well aware that you have close relations with the police and will not be pleased if they believe you are passing on information. Be wary of becoming too close or accepting what they tell you without checking it carefully.

Check with your newsdesk before embarking on any investigation into serious crime that might involve personal danger. No story, however exclusive, is worth a posthumous byline.

News blackouts

There are times when the police approach the media asking for a news blackout about matters they are pursuing: kidnaps, hostage-takings, sieges, blackmail threats, imminent arrests.

Refer these requests to your newsdesk. Most will accede to them if there are good reasons for suppressing material, such as protecting the life of innocent people. The fact that there has been a blackout is usually included in stories once it has been lifted.

YOUR OWN PAGE

AS we said in the introduction to this chapter, some daily newspapers have specialist journalists covering areas such as health and education full-time. Small weeklies can rarely afford this luxury and instead expect each reporter to be able to handle all aspects of everyday life. In between are publications that give the title of specialist reporter to an experienced journalist, who will oversee the specialist topic in addition to other duties, deal with major stories in the field, and perhaps be allocated a regular page devoted to their speciality. Whether full-time or not, these specialists cannot handle everything and there are times when general reporters have to stand in for them.

If you aspire to becoming a specialist reporter, you should start building up contacts and extending your knowledge of your chosen area from the moment you join a newspaper. This section offers tips on where to begin.

Plough through the small print – many of the biggest stories affecting people are hidden in big reports, appendices, statistics, graphs.

Tease out what they mean and then seek the real life human stories that illustrate that real meaning.

OLWYN HOCKING
Multi-media producer

Contacts equal stories. Make 52 contacts and if each one gives you one first-class story a year, you'll have a good story every week.

ALAN KIRBY
Editor
Coventry Telegraph

EDUCATION

Education reporters cover everything from retiring village school teachers to national debates on the future of A-levels. In between come Ofsted reports, league tables, exam results, sports and open days, fund-raising events and a host of other everyday activities.

Contacts

Educational establishments: Identify all those in your area. Start by trawling the Yellow Pages and internet, move on to educational handbooks, check the archives. Build up a contacts list for all of them, with the names of head teachers, staff, governors, union officials, parent-teacher representatives and officials of former pupils' associations. Large establishments will have public relations officers. Your list will include schools (nursery, infants, junior, secondary, public and private), technology colleges, further and higher education colleges, and universities. Remember faith schools and those catering for people with special needs (the disabled, deaf, blind).

Unions: There will be local branches of the main teachers' unions, which include the NUT (National Union of Teachers), NUSUWT (National Union of Schoolmasters Union of Women Teachers), PAT (Professional Association of Teachers), ATL (Association of Teachers and Lecturers), NAHT (National Association of Head Teachers) and UCU (University and College Union). The NUS (National Union of Students) will have representatives in colleges and universities. List the head office numbers for all these.

Councils: Local education authority officers, councillors chairing education committees, and other councillors (in power and in opposition) with educational responsibilities. Find out who deals with problems such as truancy.

Government: List education department press office numbers and the names of MPs with educational responsibilities. Find out who to contact about school league tables and Ofsted reports.

Also: There may be organisations running evening classes, Workers' Educational Association groups, ballet schools, agricultural courses, adult literacy programmes, foreign language schools, business courses, Open University support groups and private teachers offering home tuition. Local MPs and other political figureheads will always comment on educational matters.

Contact as many of these people as you can, meet them, and let them know how to contact you. Arrange regular calls. Talk to teachers, governors and teachers about how schools are run, budgets managed and problems challenged.

Welcome suggestions for stories, including picture opportunities: foreign trips, sports days, students winning awards, caretakers retiring, nativity plays, pupils digging ponds, octogenarians doing GCSE computer studies. Attend meetings if you can: PTAs, school prize-givings, education committees.

Background

Obtain council minutes and agendas and go through them thoroughly.

Read copies of school and college prospectuses, reports and magazines; year-books and directories; union handbooks, journals and newsletters; guidelines for school governors.

Study your subject: teachers' magazines, education supplements in the national press, education-based websites. Follow debates on education in parliament, at union conferences, and elsewhere. Learn what the big issues are so that you aren't left open-mouthed when someone talks to you about discretionary SATS or HEFC funding strategies.

Know your newspaper's style for handling league tables and examination results. Come up with ideas for stories and features to accompany them.

Your page

Aim for a wide variety of stories and pictures sampling the whole range of education issues: it is not just about teachers in front of classes. Look beyond the learning environment for human interest stories: retirements, fund-raising projects, pupils overcoming obstacles, sporting events, outside-school activities.

Be sensitive to schools' problems. Teaching is not always easy, teachers are defensive about their role and their school, and a negative story may have repercussions well beyond the school walls. If there are complaints, get both sides.

Welcome contributions from readers, especially teachers, parents and pupils. Start debates, conduct polls, run competitions.

Plan well in advance. Work out how you are going to fill your pages in August when educational institutions are closed down.

ENVIRONMENT

Environment specialists handle stories ranging from local recycling initiatives and minor pollution scares to the problems of global warming.

Contacts

Go through the archives, internet and Yellow Pages to find potential sources of information, stories and comment. Remember there are two sides to most environment stories, those who cause problems and those who complain. Identify:

Industry: Everyone from major state employers to back-street craft shops. Your list will include private and public utilities (gas, electricity, water, telephones), agriculture (farmers, landowners, fisheries, organic growers, forestry, fish farms, wildlife centres), transport (road, rail, bus,

> *When figures about the increase in heart attacks are released, we're all running around, chasing the game, looking for consultants, researchers and heart patients to interview.*
>
> *Why wait for some dull report to set your agenda? On a quiet day, arrange to spend it with a heart consultant. Keep your ears open for anything that sounds interesting and keep asking. Then when the news peg arrives you'll already have plenty of great material.*
>
> *In short, turn your job on its head. Instead of looking for a story, then chasing the best guests, organise yourself some good guests and see what stories you can find.*
>
> *Political reporters do it all the time. It can work even better for general news.*
>
> **MARTIN FORSTER**
> Reporter
> BBC Radio Cleveland

air, water, council, cycle clubs, motoring associations, passengers' and transport users' groups) and schools.

Retailers: Supermarkets, food shops, health stores, cosmetic shops, co-operatives, re-cycling companies, charities.

Government: Defra (the Department of the Environment Food and Rural Affairs), National Parks, Countryside Commission, government and opposition MPs with responsibility for environmental issues.

Councils: Environmental health officials and councillors, re-cycling officers, planners, tourism officers, museums.

Pressure groups: The CBI, other employers' groups, industrial and commercial workers' unions, National Farmers' Union, chambers of trade and commerce, Greenpeace, Friends of the Earth, Green Party, Transport 2000, National Trust, English Heritage, CPRE (Council for the Preservation of Rural England), other eco-political groups, high-profile individuals, wildlife groups (RSPCA, RSPB).

Also: Meteorologists (Met Office, local weather monitors, amateur weather forecasters) and scientific experts (biologists, zoologists, ecologists: there may be experts at your local university). Don't forget the public (ramblers' associations, angling clubs, cycling enthusiasts). Contact as many of these people as you can, meet them, and let them know how to contact you. Arrange regular calls and invite suggestions for stories, including picture opportunities.

Ask them to tell you about environmental hazards, clean-up campaigns, school projects, new products and services. Attend meetings of environment committees and pressure groups.

Background

Obtain council minutes, agendas and reports, and go through them thoroughly.

Study your subject: the national media, specialist magazines, pressure group newsletters, environment-based websites. Follow environmental debates in parliament, at conferences, and elsewhere. Become knowledgeable about the issues so that you can talk confidently about such subjects as non-sustainable energy sources and European directives on toxic emissions.

Look for potential stories wherever you go: smoke from factories, exhaust fumes from buses, shops selling environmentally-unfriendly goods, noise and light pollution.

Your page

Aim for a wide variety of stories and pictures covering the whole range of environmental issues. Many of your stories will be about environmental problems, but look for the good news, too. Strike a balance and cover both sides. Page after page of pro-green propaganda will destroy your credibility.

Welcome contributions from readers as producers, workers, retailers and consumers. Start debates, conduct polls, run competitions.

HEALTH

Health reporters cover stories ranging from hospital fund-raising bazaars to outbreaks of avian flu, taking in a host of topics from the world of medicine and its periphery.

Contacts

Go through the archives, internet and Yellow Pages for potential sources of information, stories and comment:

Health providers: Department of Health, hospitals (NHS and private), ambulance services, clinics, hospices, care homes, organisations and schools providing specialist care (for children, the blind, deaf, disabled, mentally ill), social services (home care, meal on wheels).

Practitioners: Those in mainstream medicine (doctors, dentists, chiropodists, opticians, physiotherapists) and the alternatives (osteopaths, aromatherapists, acupuncture clinics, hypnotists, yoga and meditation groups).

Managers and supervisors: Council health committees, health authorities, hospital trusts, primary care trusts, medical officers, the British Medical Association and the British Dental Society.

General health: Gyms, health clubs, leisure centres, swimming pools, slimming clubs, sports clubs, health food shops.

Pressure groups: Unions representing medical and non-medical staff, patients' associations, carers, support groups, friends of hospitals, charities dealing with drug abuse, alcoholism, smoking, cancer relief, heart disease and a host of other illnesses.

Also: Pharmacists, fitness and nutritional experts (find them at your local college or university), vegetarian groups, drug manufacturers, private health insurance companies, the Samaritans.

Build up a contacts list for as many of the above as you can. Let them know how to contact you, arrange regular calls, and encourage suggestions for stories and pictures: patients triumphing over illness, fund-raising activities, hospital pantomimes, slimmers of the year, new products for vegans.

Background

Get minutes, agendas and reports and attend meetings open to the media. Scrutinise the activities of health providers, especially trusts that operate behind closed doors.

Never apologise for what you do because nobody will believe you anyway.

Just be honest with people. Be confident, tell them you are writing a story and need to get your facts straight.

If you apologise for being there they will see right through you and slam the door in your face.

SIMON REYNOLDS
Editorial director
Lancashire Evening Post

Never apologise for ringing someone. It gets you off on the back foot immediately, and why would you want to apologise for doing your job?

If must have an opening gambit, try: 'Hi, it's Fred Bloggs from the Gazette, could you spare me a couple of minutes?'

MICHAELA ROBINSON-TATE
Deputy head of content
Westmorland Gazette

👍 *You may come people taking various types of industrial action.*

The most common are <u>strikes</u> *(withdrawal of labour, officially backed by a union or unofficial, sometimes called* <u>wildcat strikes</u> *when called at short notice);* <u>lock-outs</u> *(where an employer closes a workplace in retaliation);* <u>work-to-rules</u> *(where employees strictly enforce workplace rules to do the minimum work allowable);* <u>disruptive action</u> *(any action designed to interfere with production); and* <u>overtime bans</u> *(refusal to work outside normal hours).*

Disputes may be referred to the Advisory Conciliation and Arbitration Service (ACAS), run by the Department of Industry.

Study your subject. Read the national media (for medical and political news affecting health provision), medical press, specialist health magazines, pressure group newsletters, health-based websites. Follow current debate in parliament, at medical conferences, and elsewhere. Become knowledgeable so that you can discuss issues such as hospital funding and the latest flu outbreak with confidence.

Your page

Aim for a wide variety of stories and pictures covering a range of health and fitness issues. Keep a balance: look for good news as well as gloomy warnings. Do local follow-ups on national stories.

Welcome contributions from readers as practitioners and patients. Start debates. Offer advice on common complaints (hay fever, holiday ailments) and topical issues (healthy cooking, slimming). Invite experts to write on specialist topics.

INDUSTRY & BUSINESS

This is another wide-ranging area, covering manufacturing, services, commerce and industrial relations among many other aspects of the business and industrial world. It produces stories about everything from new product launches to company closures that devastate communities.

Contacts

Go through the archives, internet and Yellow Pages for potential sources of information, stories and comment:

Industry: Public and private companies, employers large and small, including manufacturers, utilities, service industries, agriculture, transport, leisure and (if there are not other specialists for these) education and health. Major organisations will have press officers or employ public relations companies to handle the media.

Business: Retailers, the CBI, chambers of trade and commerce, professional firms, business clubs, public and private development agencies.

Unions: Officers at national, regional, branch and shopfloor levels. There may be individual officers responsible for certain industries, and shop stewards and works committees in the workplace.

Government: Central and local government, involved in stimulating business activity, financing initiatives, trading standards, advice and training. Make contact with councillors and MPs.

Trade associations: Almost every manufacturer or service company has a national body representing its interests; many have local representatives.

Also: ACAS (the Advisory Conciliation and Arbitration Service), customer protection agencies, consumer organisations.

Build up a contacts list for as many of the above as you can. Talk to local people, and let them know how to contact you. Arrange regular calls. Welcome suggestions for stories, including picture opportunities, product launches, promotions, employee activities, human interest stories about members of staff.

Background

Obtain company reports and analyse them. Monitor local companies' share prices. Cover meetings of bodies such as chambers of trade that are open to the media. You may be able to attend company meetings (and will have the right to do so if you buy just one share). Keep an eye open for industrial tribunals.

Study your subject. Follow the national media, read the financial press, specialist business magazines, trade and technical journals and business-based websites. Ask for company newsletters. Follow current debate in parliament and elsewhere. Read the job ads in local newspapers and websites to spot companies that are expanding.

Get a working knowledge of how businesses work and how to read a company report. Find out how unions are structured and what kinds of industrial action are possible. Become knowledgeable about issues so that you understand talk of corporation tax levels and industrial relations legislation.

Your page

Aim for a wide variety of stories and pictures covering a range of business, industrial and commercial topics. Balance bad news about bankruptcies with good news of job opportunities. Do local follow-ups on national stories. Focus on people rather than cold company facts. Give both sides when reporting industrial disputes.

Avoid business jargon (*adverse cash-flow, down-sizing*) and explain financial news in language readers can understand. Don't use figures and statistics for the sake of them: put them in context, compare them with others, and explain what they mean in human terms.

Welcome contributions from readers as employers and employees, shop-owners and customers. Offer advice on family finance. Invite experts to write on specialist topics.

YOUR OWN PATCH

IF you are working on a newspaper with more than one office, there may come a time, once you have gained some experience and proved you can be trusted, when you are given the chance to cover one of the outlying areas on your own.

> *District reporting is all about good-humoured persistence.*
>
> *The first time you knock on someone's door or call at their business, you get nothing.*
>
> *The second time you might get acknowledgement.*
>
> *The third time a smile.*
>
> *The fourth time, a smile, perhaps a cup of tea, and, maybe, a story.*
>
> **MALCOLM WARNE**
> Editor
> Darlington & Stockton Times

> *Ask very awkward and difficult questions of those in authority.*
>
> *It's not desirable, it's compulsory.*
>
> **SIMON O'NEILL**
> Editor
> Oxford Mail

👍 *You can find out who owns property through the Land Registry. Details may be available, too, of lease-holders, mortgage holders and prices paid.*

The registry has regional offices which you can visit to search records, and an online service is available.

👍 *If you are expected to fill a regular page in your newspaper or on its website with stories from your patch, aim for a variety of serious and light material, backed up by pictures.*

Make sure it carries full details of how to contact you. Encourage readers to write or email or text. Run a mini-noticeboard of forthcoming events.

Distribute posters outside newsagents saying there is a page devoted to the place each week.

Being offered your own district (often called your 'patch') is flattering, exciting and faintly terrifying. How are you going to make sure you report everything that is going on?

You have most of the answers already from what you have read earlier in this book: know the area you are working in, make plenty of contacts, and keep your ears and eyes wide open.

First...

Start off by talking to your predecessor, if he or she is still around. Find out about the area, major issues, newsworthy people and, of course, the best pubs. Ask if they will share their contacts. Ask other colleagues what they know of your new patch.

Follow this up with a trawl through the archives. Look for previous stories about the area. Identify on-going problems and photocopy pictures of prominent people for your contacts book.

Consult the internet, reference books and local guides for more information about the area. Learn about its history, environment, population, industry, tourist attractions, sports teams and anything else you can discover.

Explore the area

Get a street map and do a thorough tour. Track down the council offices, police station, fire service headquarters, hospitals, ambulance stations, schools, post offices, newsagents, chemists, garages, theatres, cinemas, meeting halls, churches, cemeteries, parks, public gardens, allotments, libraries, museums, art galleries, tourist information centres, leisure centres, sports clubs, swimming pools, night clubs, social clubs, bus and rail stations and taxi ranks.

Find out where the major industries and businesses are based. Walk the main streets. Note the name and place of every major store, every unusual shop, every pub, cafe and restaurant. Drive round housing estates and nearby villages to get a feel for the way the inhabitants live, what they do, what they are proud of and what problems they face.

Make contacts

Make yourself known to as many people as possible, from council executives to chip-shop owners. Call on the vicars and teachers and publicans. Contact officials of interest groups. Lists will be available from the town hall or tourist information office, and there will be details on noticeboards all over the place.

Look for the Chamber of Commerce (representing business and industry), Chamber of Trade (traders and retailers), Rotary Club (business people, traders and professionals), Inner Wheel (Rotarians' wives), Round Table ('junior' version of Rotary: members must be under 40), Ladies' Circle (Tablers' wives), Business and Professional Women's Club, Soroptimists (women), Townswomen's Guild (urban), Women's Institute (rural), Scouts and Guides. There are support groups,

A STORY EVERY TEN YARDS

One editor, notorious for boasting that he could find stories just by walking down the high street, was challenged to prove it by a sceptical trainee.

In the 250 yards from office to pub, he came up with the following questions, any of which could have led to a story:

? Why is that shop for sale? Is the owner retiring? Has he gone bust? Does nobody want what it sold any more? Why not? And who's taking over?

? Why has that one got a new security grill on the window? A break-in? Vandals? Insurance companies getting tough because our crime rate is up?

? What's being advertised on that noticeboard?

? There's rubbish all round that takeaway – are the neighbours complaining?

? Not a parking space in sight – are the residents angry? Do the shops have delivery problems?

? Dog muck – has anyone ever been prosecuted for letting their animal foul the pavement? Why not? Who's supposed to take action?

? That tattoo shop – how's it doing? What's the most popular tattoo?

? Ten weeks to Christmas – is that toy shop geared up for it already? *(The same question could be asked in the run-up to Easter, Halloween or Bonfire Night)* What's its best-seller going to be? Has it run out of anything yet?

? Didn't the council promise to get rid of all these pigeons?

? Why is this newsagent stocking eight copies of *Self Defence Practitioners' Monthly*?

? Why haven't we got cycle lanes like other town centres?

? This must be the third time this month they've dug up this bit of pavement – why?

? We did a story last year when that butcher introduced ostrich steaks – did anyone buy them? What's his latest gimmick?

? Why are kids playing down that alley? Where's the nearest safe place for them? What do their parents think?

? Who are the band named in this fly-poster?

? Another sandwich bar – what's special about this one?

? What's the oddest thing for sale in that junk shop?

? How many shops in town are illegal because they still haven't got proper access for the disabled?

? Thousands of people pass this statue every day – how many have a clue who it is?

? There's a date on the top of this pub – built nearly a century ago. Are they going to celebrate? Let's find out.

Before going in, the editor stopped five passers-by and asked what they were most ashamed of about their town. He got five more story ideas.

Then he made the trainee, now thoroughly demoralised, pay for the beer.

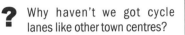

Launching into a new area? No contacts? The best place is your opposition paper.

Read some back copies and it will be fairly obvious who the stories are emanating from.

Ring them up and ask what's new. It's an instant contacts book.

STEWART GILBERT
Former editor
Worcester News

GO LOOKING FOR PROBLEMS

Identify the potential problems of every community in your patch – public transport, housing, vandalism, crime, pollution, bored teenagers, untidy village greens, dying shops, rights of way disputes, late-night disturbances – and see if they exist.

If they do, you have a story. If they don't, get residents to say what a model community it is and why.

---

charities, show organisers, allotment holders, ramblers, model railway clubs and many more – Google the name of your patch and see what comes up. There will be enough to keep you busy for a long while and yield regular stories. Tell them all who you are, where you are, and how to contact you.

It's all out there

Get out of the office (but make sure the answerphone is on while you are away). Chat to people in the street, in shops and cafes and pubs. Make regular calls on your best contacts.

Attend as many meetings as you can, to make fresh contacts and find stories. As well as the obvious council gatherings, drop in on chambers of trade, church meetings, drama clubs, scout groups, parish assemblies, the lot.

Leave business cards wherever you go – in pubs and shops, in phone kiosks, on village noticeboards – and make sure your contact details are in your newspaper and on its website.

There are photo opportunities wherever you go. Never be without a camera.

CHURCHES

IF you are given your own patch to cover, you suddenly realise what a significant part that churches, chapels, mosques and synagogues play in many people's lives. They have a minor role in those of nearly everyone else.

Religious leaders are useful contacts. They can offer non-political comment on events and moral issues affecting their community, and some are refreshingly outspoken and provocative. Nurture them and learn how to refer to them correctly in print (see your house style book). Don't forget minority sects, the Salvation Army, the YMCA, YWCA and humanist groups.

Here is a brief alphabetical guide to the major religions you are likely to come across.

Christian

Baptist Church: Congregation-based, similar to United Reform (see below) but baptises only adults. Local areas, headed by minister called a general superintendent, are grouped into county associations which together make up the Baptist Union of Great Britain and Ireland.

Church of Jesus Christ of Latterday Saints: Popularly known as Mormons. The emphasis is on missionary work (each member must do two years of this at their own expense). Grouped in parishes, headed by bishops, which form dioceses headed by stake presidents.

Church of England: The country's established (officially recognised) Protestant church, sometimes referred to as the Anglican Church. It is divided into two provinces, Canterbury and York, each with an archbishop or primate. Senior is the Archbishop of Canterbury, Primate of All England. There are provinces divided into dioceses, each with bishop and cathedral with a dean or provost. Dioceses divided into two or more archdeaconries, each with an archdeacon. Dioceses divide into rural deaneries headed by rural dean. Finally, these divide into parishes, each with a rector, vicar or priest (all are clergy: there is little difference between them, but you should get their titles right). Curates are priests' assistants, but may have their own church. Deacons are lay officials. Parishes elect a parochial church council from members, choose churchwardens, and send representatives to the deanery synod, a meeting of local clergy. Dioceses hold diocesan synods and there is an annual general synod at national level.

Church of Ireland: Anglican-based but autonomous, operating in Eire and Northern Ireland. Two archbishops: senior is the Archbishop of Armagh (Primate of All Ireland), the other the Archbishop of Dublin (Primate of Ireland).

Church of Scotland: Established church, with Presbyterian structure and ministers. Basic court of the church is the kirk session. Churches are grouped into presbyteries, presbyteries into synods. There is an annual general assembly. All meetings are chaired by a moderator.

Church in Wales: A member of the Anglican Community, which split from the Church of England and disestablished in 1920. Six dioceses.

First Church of Christ, Scientist: Lays emphasis on mental and physical healing. Followers are known as Christian Scientists.

Jehovah's Witnesses: Organised into branch committees, and further divided into districts, circuits and local congregations meeting in Kingdom Halls. Districts and circuits have overseers; congregations have elders. Each congregation divides its area into territories to which individuals are assigned to visit all the homes therein. There are circuit assemblies. Witnesses refuse blood transfusions and military service.

Judaism: Three main forms: Orthodox (the major group in Britain), Reform and Liberal. Worship is in synagogues. Services, mostly in Hebrew, are led by ministers, some of whom are rabbis, a title indicating scholastic achievement. Jews mark the Sabbath from sunset Friday to sunset Saturday.

Methodist Church: Formed by the union of Wesleyan, Primitive and United Methodist Churches. Churches are grouped into circuits, each with a superintendent minister; circuits are grouped into districts, each with a ministerial chair. Ministers and lay representatives meet in local synods which appoint representatives to the national Methodist Conference.

Don't be afraid to say: 'Wow, fantastic tattoos, where did you get them done?'

It can quieten down an aggressive householder.

And when the family dog starts peeing down your leg (or worse), laugh it off. It WILL happen.

NEAL BUTTERWORTH
Editor
Bournemouth Daily Echo

If you are using cuttings from your archives, don't rely blindly on stories published in the past.

They may be wrong; corrections may have been published but not linked to the original; people's circumstances may well have changed.

Remember that every repetition of a libel is a fresh libel.

Be especially wary when reproducing details of old court cases.

There may have been an appeal; convictions may be spent.

Pentecostal Church: Two main groups: Assemblies of God, run on congregational lines, and Elim, more centralised.

Plymouth Brethren: A Christian sect with strict Puritan rules.

Roman Catholic Church: Headed by the Pope and College of Cardinals. England and Wales divide into four archiepiscopal and 14 episcopal sees or dioceses, Scotland into two and six. Each diocese has bishop and is divided into parishes, each with a priest properly termed a vicar-general. They may be assisted by deacons, ordained members of the church. There are many orders of monks, friars and nuns. The principal service of the church is Holy Communion, usually referred to as Mass: Low Mass is said, High Mass sung; both are *celebrated* or *offered*.

Society of Friends: Often called Quakers, but members prefer to be known as Friends. They worship in meeting houses. There are no clergy, but there are officials called clerks, elders and overseers. Renowned as pacifists.

Seventh Day Adventists: A Protestant church, observing the Sabbath from Friday to Saturday evening and practising adult baptism by total immersion.

United Reformed Church: Formed by the union of the Congregational Church in England and Wales, the Presbyterian Church of England, the Reformed Churches of Christ, and the Congregational Union of Scotland. Provinces, presided over by moderator, divide into county unions, divided again into districts made up of churches and congregations.

Non-Christian

Buddhism: A religious and philosophical system developed from Hinduism. It has no gods: its scriptures are the recorded sermons of Buddha, not books of divine revelation. Followers strive for spiritual enlightenment.

Hinduism: Made up of many sects worshipping variety of gods. It has a caste system and strict rules on food, marriage and burial. Hindus believe the soul passes on death to some other creature.

Islam: Many sects including Sunni, Shi'a and Shi'ite. Followers are Muslims (or Moslems: check your house style for spelling), their prophet Muhammad (check spelling of that, too), their sacred book Koran. They worship in mosques, where priests are called imams. There is a prohibition on alcohol and gambling, but some polygamy is permitted. The global religious centre is Mecca, to which each member must pray five times a day. Ramadan is a month-long fast.

Sikhism: Developed from Hinduism, abandoning the caste system.

Unification Church: An anti-Christian religious movement. Followers are known as Moonies, after the founder Sun Myung Moon, a Korean claiming to be messiah. The church has been the subject of allegations of brainwashing recruits.

Seventeen

FEATURES

FEATURES comprise more or less everything in a newspaper's editorial pages that is not news. They can be topical or timeless, earnest or entertaining. They range from hard news backgrounders to horoscopes, celebrity profiles to cookery columns, opinionated think-pieces to money-making advertorials. Their function is to add information and colour, to analyse and explain the world around us, to humanise events and illuminate behaviour, and, not least, to educate, entertain and assist the reader.

Some features arrive from outside the office, syndicated by agencies or submitted by regular correspondents. Some are the work of fulltime feature writers. Many are written by general reporters, working on their own initiative or on instructions from the news or features desk.

These are an opportunity for the reporter to explore new subjects, carry out in-depth investigation, and write in a more colourful way than is normally possible when handling hard news. They are not an excuse for long rambling essays in flamboyant language. There are more words to play with, but quantity does not guarantee quality and there is no place for waffle. Features, like news, require keen observation, careful research, a focus on people, meticulous accuracy, and disciplined construction.

Most newspaper features are between 600 and 1,000 words long, but you may be restricted to much fewer for a review or allowed to run well beyond for a major investigative piece. Find out what the maximum length allowed is before you start writing, and stick to it.

Features divide broadly into two: the topical and the entertaining.

NEWS FEATURES

THESE are features linked to current issues: background pieces explaining what is going on, exploring the causes and consequences, profiling the people involved. They retain the urgency of news stories, and are written to be published as soon as possible, often in time to accompany the news story which prompted their creation.

Preparation

Whether you are exploring the reasons why a major company has gone bust or profiling a talent show winner, you need to research the background and arm yourself with the facts. Readers may skip through the news, but tend to read features with more care. Errors are spotted

- News features & backgrounders
- Entertainment features
- Reviews

I learned all I know about feature writing from the late Marje Proops on the Daily Mirror.

She said: 'Write from the heart. Identify with the people you're talking to and remember every little detail about them, no matter how insignificant. That will provide the colour when you write the story.'

BEV CREAGH
Features writer
Herald & Post, Luton

more readily, and if your facts are wrong your arguments and opinions are unlikely to convince anyone.

Decide before you start exactly what your theme is going to be. Ask yourself what you have new to say, whether it will interest your readers, whether there is enough of it to retain their interest, and whether in the end it is worth saying. Your theme will give your feature unity and coherence. It should be simple, however complex the subject. You cannot write a feature on the state of the entire NHS. Narrow it down to one aspect, perhaps a day in the life of a hospital ward or a profile of one patient that illustrates the wider picture.

Your theme should run like a thread throughout the feature, connecting the intro, the body and the ending. If you are writing the NHS profile, come back to the patient from time to time, using him or her as an example and a source of quotes, and perhaps rounding off with reference to them.

The words

News features are written tightly, often following the same structure as news stories: a concise intro making the main point; background, explanation and quotes; less important detail towards the end.

They may include opinion, but much of it is likely to come from the people being quoted rather than from the writer. Specialist reporters, with a degree of knowledge in the subject, may be in a position to assess differing views, comment upon them with authority, and reach conclusions. The views of general reporters, whose expertise is usually no greater and quite possibly less than that of the audience, may be of little value or irrelevant. If so, their role is to stay in the background, presenting the arguments and leaving readers to judge for themselves.

ENTERTAINMENT FEATURES

THESE are usually less time-constrained than news backgrounders, though most still require some kind of news peg to justify their existence. They usually have a strong human interest element, dealing with people rather than faceless facts.

The language is more relaxed than that of a news story, the approach often subjective, the structure quite different. They are a complete package, with a beginning, a middle and an ending, all equally important, connected by the established theme which flows throughout. Writing to length is critical because they cannot be sliced off halfway through if space gets tight without destroying the structure and message. The writer needs to plan what will be included and the order in which it will go before making a start.

Intros

With more words at your disposal, there is a temptation to think you can afford to take your time getting to the point. This is true, but a successful feature must still grasp the readers' attention from the start. The intro must have urgency and be provocative enough to make them want to read on. It should set the mood for what follows.

That doesn't necessarily mean giving everything away immediately. You can lead up to the main point gently, arousing the readers' interest, provoking reaction and encouraging them to continue. The intro may be a scene-setter, a quotation, a question, a paradox. If stuck for the intro, ask yourself what is the most surprising, evocative, or memorable thing you have discovered about your subject.

That said, the main thrust of your feature has to be explained fairly early on. American journalists talk of placing *nut graphs* after the opening few sentences, vital paragraphs containing the main point, its significance, its news peg and a summary of the background.

Development

The body of the story should be informative and entertaining. It may include more facts, quotes, description, anecdotes and opinion. Don't give away all your best bits straight away. Spread them through the feature.

It should be arranged in sections, each dealing with a different aspect of the subject, each introduced smoothly with its own mini-intro making readers wonder what comes next. Visualise the middle of your feature as a series of waves, high points of fresh angles followed by lower-key troughs of explanation and example.

WHO CARES WHAT <u>YOU</u> THINK?

Entertainment features often include the views of the writer.

If the feature is about your personal experience, they are welcome, possibly essential.

They are valid in other features if relevant, but should not overwhelm the reader.

Unless you are an expert in the field, your opinion has little authority and is probably of not much interest to the reader.

Stop for a moment before you type the words *I, me* or *myself.*

Ask yourself whether your reader really wants to know what you think rather than read the opinions of people better placed to comment.

You will often achieve more if you make points through the mouths of people to whom you have spoken.

If you do have something to say, whether you are arguing that a law should be changed or merely opening readers' eyes to what somebody you have interviewed is really like, back it up with evidence.

Your conclusions can be stated early in the feature and then justified, or left to the end after the evidence and arguments have been presented.

Think creatively what the effects of changes around us might mean to people.

For example, when temperatures rise or fall to extreme levels, there will be huge implications for many people, from health consequences to demand for goods in shops to changes in patterns of behaviour.

Dream up what they might be and then research whether they're happening.

Don't follow the pack just because every media outlet appears to be taking the same angle – be prepared to question it.

You may be surprised at the story-lines neglected by a 'feeding frenzy' that has taken one particular direction.

OLWYN HOCKING
Multi-media producer

👍 *Tapping other people's calls is illegal. Recording your own is not, though it is courtesy to let whoever you are calling know about it.*

Some journalists routinely record their calls, as a back-up for shorthand notes, to avoid accusations of mis-reporting, or to gather evidence during investigative inquiries.

The code of conduct forbids you to use clandestine cameras or listening devices, or to intercept phone calls or other messages, unless it is in the public interest.

👍 *Think about the ending before you start writing.*

It will focus the direction of your feature and concentrate your mind on its structure.

You may even decide that your ending is better than your intro: if so, start again.

The structure should be logical and easy to follow. Link paragraphs by the use of transitional words, phrases and quotations. These move the feature smoothly from one section to the next, so that the reader is not jolted by a sudden change of direction. It can be a word or phrase at the beginning of a sentence: *but, and, now, meanwhile, therefore, however, despite all this, evidence of this can be seen in...* Quotes should add extra information, not be dropped in at random just because you have them.

The words

Because features are likely to be read at a more leisurely pace than news stories and their content considered more thoughtfully, the writing should be of a high quality. This doesn't give you a licence to over-indulge in extravagant language or intricate sentences, but it does mean you can employ vivid description to set the scene and give atmosphere, and can use metaphors, similes and other literary devices inappropriate in news stories. Don't use vague adjectives: *A beautiful garden* tells the reader very little except that you thought it attractive; a detailed description of the contents, the colours, the composition, the scents and the sounds will create a picture from which readers can judge its beauty for themselves. Vary sentence length. Establish the tone of the feature from the start – serious, concerned, outraged, light-hearted, chatty – and stick to it throughout.

Climax

News stories often trail off into minor detail and end without impact. Features need a strong climax. It can be a final twist, a reference back to the intro, a look forward to what happens next, a revealing quote, advice to the reader, a call for action, a provocative conclusion wrapping up all that has been said before.

Whatever you choose, your ending should leave your reader on a high note, feeling rewarded and satisfied that the effort put into reading your work has been worthwhile.

COLOUR PIECES

BACKGROUND features are often written to go with a news story about an event. They are softer than the main story, looking for unusual and entertaining angles: the activities of minor participants, perhaps, or the behaviour of the crowd.

Their success relies on close observation, colourful description, good quotes and lively writing. If you are asked to do one, liaise closely with the reporter doing the hard news.

UNDER THE TOWN CLOCK

Some newspapers still carry diary columns: collections of brief gossip items, usually not too serious, often anonymous and written under a general title like the one above.

They may be produced by one reporter or consist of items submitted by many.

Diary columns can be little more than dustbins for snippets that would otherwise be spiked, but good ones are readable, informative and entertaining.

They are very much about people. Look for potential items wherever you go: in court, during council meetings, at social events and so on. Note odd events, unusual behaviour, memorable quotes.

Use humour where appropriate but don't ridicule people.

Follow the column's style: it may always be written in the first person, for example, and signed off with a fictitious name (*Bystander* is an old favourite).

PROFILES

THESE are usually the result of interviews, conducted to reveal what lies behind the public face of celebrities or to tell readers about ordinary people who happen to be in the news or are in some way unusual.

You are trying to paint a picture of them in words, revealing what and why they think and feel and believe the way they do. Describe them: what they look like, what they wear, how they act. Use plenty of quotes, allowing your subject to unveil their thoughts, character and personality in their own words. Don't overload your profile with facts, which should be dropped unobtrusively into your copy or, perhaps, relegated to biographical fact boxes.

Some profiles work well when written in a question-and-answer format, which allows you to reproduce conversations verbatim (definitely a time to use a tape recorder unless your shorthand is superb) but precludes any description or analysis. Some publications carry regular features giving celebrities' answers to stock questions, often submitted to them by post or email rather than posed in a direct interview.

LIFESTYLE FEATURES

MANY newspapers offer their readers added value in the form of special lifestyle sections, pull-out weekend supplements or glossy magazines. They tap into trends and issues of the day, often with an eye on commercial spin-offs from advertising. Although these publications tend to have specialist writers, reporters may still be asked to contribute.

Content covers a wide area: it could be a key-hole piece on a celebrity's home, a fashion spread, a look at how career women cope with work and family, or a feature on travel opportunities for the newly-retired.

A few times in tricky interviews, I've desperately asked the interviewee: 'If you were interviewing yourself, what would you ask?' It often gets a good result.

But one elderly scratchy actor looked at me disdainfully and said: 'I'd ask myself what the hell I was doing talking to such a damn fool reporter...'

SHARON GRIFFITHS
Feature writer
The Northern Echo

The great Alistair Cooke once said: 'Ask the questions a child would ask.'

That way you get the basic questions answered.

TIM GOPSILL
Editor
The Journalist

You will find yourself fending off people who want to see what you have written before it is published.

Don't let them. However good it is, they will want to make changes, withdraw quotes, and generally mess you about.

By the time you have come to a compromise you will probably have missed your deadline.

Tell them gently that it is not the newspaper's policy and refuse. If they are still a problem, offer to read out their quotes, but keep the rest to yourself, especially any comments or interpretation.

The only exception to this is if your interviewee is a specialist in some field and you want to check the facts and analysis for accuracy.

Even then, let them see just the relevant section of your story, not the whole piece.

PERSONAL FEATURES

THESE are first-person pieces written about a reporter's own experience. They may be serious *(My battle with cancer)*, exciting *(My first parachute jump)* or light-hearted *(Why I'll never make pancakes again)*. They need to be written carefully to retain the readers' interest and sympathy: it is very easy to sound self-centred and self-congratulatory.

You may be offered the chance to join in other people's activities: a trip to report on local soldiers abroad, perhaps, or a place beside police on an early-morning drugs raid. Your story in such cases is not really about you, though you may include a little of your reaction, and you should focus on the soldiers' lives, the drama of the raid, or whatever.

TRAVEL FEATURES

THESE, too, are written from personal experience, and should also be less about you than the subject matter. The feature should be entertaining as well as informative, because you are writing not only for readers who want to know whether places are worth visiting, but also for all those who don't but are interested nonetheless.

Many travel features are written after reporters have taken advantage of a freebie – the universal term for a trip paid for by a travel operator or other holiday provider. If this is the case, don't be bought. The fact that you haven't had to pay for it should not be allowed to sway your judgement. Be fair but honest in your appraisal. The same applies to similar features in which you get the chance to review services and products, such as pubs, restaurants and cars. However tempting it may be to give nothing but praise in the hope of further freebies, readers will rapidly catch on if you never say anything critical, and your opinion will become valueless.

ADVERTORIALS

THESE are features written to accompany advertisements, and the space they occupy may be paid for by advertisers.

They should be honestly written, though sadly this is not always the case.

Features on *Spring Weddings* and *Christmas Shopping in the High Street* too often end up as sycophantic lists of bridal-wear suppliers and cheap gift shops.

Many journalists resent being asked to provide this kind of uncritical copy, feeling that it prostitutes their trade.

If you have to write advertorials – and you probably will, because they help to pay your wages – be as objective as you can.

By all means mention the advertisers, but stick to the facts and avoid describing them in eulogistic terms.

Before you set off on your travels, paid-for or otherwise, do some research: get travel guides and look the place up on the internet. When you write it up afterwards (or better still, while you are still there and it is fresh in your mind – the immediacy will be reflected in your story), find a fresh angle on which to peg your feature: an outstanding attraction, an unusual person, a building or event that sticks in your memory.

Don't forget to mention travel costs, accommodation, entertainment, food and drink. Remember to bring back plenty of pictures.

THINK PIECES

TRAINEE reporters are not often offered 1,000 words in which to let off steam, but there are times, because of their special expertise or experience, that their views are as relevant as those of any other member of the public.

Make absolutely sure of all your facts and be certain your arguments stand up before sticking your head above the parapet. Try them out first on your colleagues: if your opinions withstand their onslaught, go ahead.

REVIEWS

NEWSPAPERS carry reviews (often called crits) as a matter of public record, as an opportunity for readers to compare their opinions with others, and as part of the media's role in publicising and encouraging the artistic life of their community.

On some large newspapers, reviews are written by journalists employed full-time to cover the arts world. They are highly knowledgeable about their subject, and qualified to make intelligent analysis and offer expert criticism. Their views are sought and respected by readers and by those whose work they review. Elsewhere, the job falls to the general reporter. You should expect early in your reporting career to be asked to produce reviews of a wide range of productions, performances and publications.

It can be worrying if you feel you know little about the area involved, but you are not expected to write with the expertise and authority of a professional critic. You are covering a story like any other, acting as the eyes and ears of your readers, giving them factual information about the work plus, perhaps, a little of your reaction to it and some guidance as to whether it is likely to appeal to other people.

As you do more reviews, readers will come to recognise your name and, if you do them well, respect your judgement even though they may disagree with it.

I investigated an anti-epilepsy drug which, though successful with many patients, had terrible side-effects for some children. Three died in horrible circumstances.

After my story was published, hundreds of worried readers rang in and I spent two weeks explaining that the drug could be fine but people should act fast if the side-effects appeared.

One caller said her grand-daughter was displaying the danger signs. After speaking to me she took the girl to the doctor, who insisted nothing was wrong.

But she persisted, a different drug was prescribed, and the symptoms stopped.

More than 20 years later I still feel that, whatever else I've achieved, nothing could be better than believing I might have saved that little girl's life.

DAVID SEYMOUR
Former political editor
Daily Mirror

LIVE PERFORMANCES

THOSE you are likely to cover fall broadly into three categories.

Amateur and fun

Village pantomimes, nativity plays, school concerts: productions that make little or no pretence to be anything more than an evening's entertainment. They may well be one-off performances, social gatherings that bring communities together and, perhaps, raise funds for a local cause.

The participants know that they will make mistakes, and will be happy enough to get through it all without anything going seriously wrong. They, and the rest of your readers, look to you to record the event, mention who took part, publish a picture or two, and give praise if any is due.

Hard-line criticism is not appropriate. Indeed, there are many newspapers whose policy is to avoid any comment that might cause offence and urge reviewers, if they cannot say something good, to say nothing at all.

You may not be so restricted, but even so you should err on the side of generosity. You cannot avoid mentioning catastrophes such as the scenery collapsing or the lead singer's voice packing in, but base your overall judgement on whether or not the production succeeded in its aim of entertaining you and, more importantly, the rest of the audience.

Amateur and serious

Every local newspaper covers a host of amateur dramatic clubs, choral societies, musical ensembles, orchestras, bands and the like.

The difference between these and the first group is that they are attempting to present works of artistic merit, and your readers expect you to judge how well they achieve this. Those who have seen the production want to compare their opinions with yours. Those who have not want to know whether it is worth going if there are more perform-ances to come.

The performers and producers will accept and even welcome criticism so long as it is fair and constructive. Bear in mind that they are amateurs who have put a lot of their time and effort into the show, probably fitting in rehearsals around full-time jobs.

Many, nevertheless, know a great deal about what they are doing and will expect any criticism levelled at them to be just and justifiable. Your judgement should be based ultimately on whether they deliver a performance living up to their intentions.

Professional performances

You may get the opportunity to review these: repertory companies at the local theatre, national orchestras at the concert hall, big-name bands on tour. They are full-time performers who make their living from people paying to see them, and your readers deserve to know whether they are worth it.

Those involved expect to be criticised if they fail to live up to audiences' expectations. Equally, they deserve to be judged by reviewers who know what they are talking about, and unless you have expertise in their field you cannot analyse the finer points of their work. Concentrate on your reaction, and that of the audience: did they enjoy it?

Preparation

Whatever you are reviewing, know what is expected of you: a serious critique or just a record of what went on, plus your reaction as a member of the audience?

Do some research. Find out about the play or the music, so that you can write about it swiftly and with some authority; about past performances, so that you can judge whether the latest one is bigger, better, or a new departure; about the producer, the performers and any newcomers taking part.

Talk to performers and producers, beforehand if possible, during the interval or at the end if not. Find out if anything unusual has taken place, whether there have been special problems, whether there are good reasons for anything that has gone wrong.

Make notes during the performance if you can, though this is not always easy in a darkened theatre. Don't attempt to record everything: concentrate on the highlights.

Writing it up

Approach your review as you would any other story. It needs an intro. Look for one aspect of the performance that stood out: an exceptional performer, perhaps, a dramatic scene or a memorable song. There should be an early summary of the content: the plot if a play, the programme if a concert. Don't assume readers are fully acquainted with it, however well-known it may be. If it is a thriller, don't reveal whodunnit.

Go on to discuss individual performances and mention other aspects of the show. You may be able to comment on the design of the set, the use of lighting or sound, the audience reaction or the appropriateness of the production for its audience. Sum up at the end and offer an opinion on its success.

Don't be a smart-arse if you don't really know what you're talking about.

I had to review an art exhibition in my first few months as a reporter, and mentioned loftily that a lady called Carol Wright seemed to have a bit of talent. This rather amused the noted Royal Academician Carol Wright, sadly a man, who lived in the area and had provided some work for display as a favour.

JOHN FRANCIS
Group editor
Bedfordshire Newspapers

👍 *Check with the author and publishers three months after your story or review comes out to see how the book has sold.*

It might have been a runaway success (which makes a new story) or an abject failure (which doesn't, unless you want to humiliate the author).

Include the names of the work, the group performing it, the principal performers, and the venue; the dates it is running, times and admission prices. Remember that names sell newspapers. When covering a local amateur production, mention as many of the cast as possible, plus the producer and others behind stage.

Don't try to be too clever. By all means exhibit your knowledge and write entertainingly, but don't blind readers with technical terms, pompous phrases or pseudo-intellectual language.

Make your criticism constructive. Say where the performance went wrong and why, how faults could be improved, whether justice was done to the work, and whether the players lived up to their past standards. Don't be wholly negative. If a performance is dire, say so, but offer some praise too. Don't libel anyone: call a performance bad if you must, but don't call a professional actor incompetent.

Don't over-personalise it. You are expected to say what you thought, but don't overload your copy with references to yourself. Good reviews use the words *I* and *me* very sparingly.

Remember that your words will be read by many people who won't see the performance, and your story needs to be worth reading for its own sake.

Avoid time-battered clichés such as *trod the boards*, *brought the house down*, *totally believable performance* and *not a dry eye in the place*.

Much of the above applies if you are reviewing films, radio and television programmes, or recordings on CD or DVD.

BOOKS

THE heavier national dailies and Sundays carry book reviews, but very few other newspapers have the space, expertise or reader interest to justify their inclusion unless they are of local interest. Even then they are likely to be used, not as the subject of a straightforward review, but as the basis for a news story or feature.

The angle may be that the author has local connections, or that the content has local relevance – a novel set in the newspaper's area, perhaps, or a non-fiction work dealing with a topic of local interest.

The news or feature desk will hand you the book and any accompanying press release giving background material about the author and the contents. Then:

Do some research

First, obviously, read the book: in full, if possible, and certainly if it is a work of fiction. Read the blurb on the back, the author's biography inside, and the press release. Note who publishes it, how much it costs, and whether it has any illustrations that might be reproduced to go with your story.

Check the archives and the internet for information about the author, anything they have previous written, and background on the subject matter if the book is non-fiction. See if there are any previous reviews.

Contact the author

The publisher will help, though you may have to go through an agent. Ask about:

Personal details: life story, education, employment, family, other publications.

The book: How long it took to write, where the idea came from, whether characters are based on real people, how it was written and how long it took, how it was researched, writing methods, problems finding a publisher, what the author hopes to achieve, whether another book is planned, who is his or her favourite writer, and any advice they have for budding authors.

Reaction: What do the author's spouse, family, friends and work colleagues think about it all?

Illustrations: Arrange to get pictures of the author, on-site if the book has a local setting. Check any copyright issues if you plan to reproduce illustrations from the book.

Contact the agent and publisher

Find out how many copies have been produced, how sales are going, plans for reprints or other editions, foreign sales, film or television spin-offs. Ask about publicity plans and marketing ploys: there may be book signings at local shops or appearances before local literary associations.

Get reaction

Contact local people who are mentioned in the book or might have a particular interest in its content. If it is non-fiction, try to find someone local who might comment on (and even argue about) what it says. It may carry opinions or have implications for future action that deserve a response from people affected. If the reaction is hostile, go back to the author for comment. Beware libel.

Ask local bookshops how well the book is selling, and what kind of people are buying it.

> *Never be afraid to ask the senior staff a question – except at deadline, when you should be mousely-quiet.*
>
> **MARK WOOD**
> Sports editor
> Bedford Citizen & Times

Advertorials should be clearly labelled as such, with a prominent line saying 'Advertising feature' or something similar in or above the feature.

If they masquerade as genuine editorial, your newspaper is seriously misleading its readers and should be ashamed of itself.

Writing it up

Like any other review, it needs an intro. Focus on whatever you think will most interest your readers. It may be the author, the story-line, the subject matter, one small section of the book or the effect it may have on the public.

If it is fiction, say what kind of work it is, explain its underlying theme, and comment on how well the characters are developed, how well you think it is written, how it made you feel. Don't give away the ending.

If it is non-fiction, give examples of the content. Don't try to cover everything. If there are inaccuracies, say so (but be certain you are right). Use quotations from the book to make your point if necessary: brief extracts do not infringe copyright.

Conclude with your opinion of whether the book succeeds in doing what its author intended, whether it is worth the money, and whether it will appeal to your readers.

Check your newspaper style for giving basic information about the book. You will probably be expected to add a footnote containing details of its title, author, publisher, publication date and price.

Eighteen
TRAINING

MOST journalists in Britain do their training through the National Council for the Training of Journalists (NCTJ). It offers a number of alternative pathways for a trainee to choose from, depending on what they want to be: a newspaper reporter, magazine writer, sports reporter, sub-editor, online journalist, press photographer or photo-journalist.

All take preliminary examinations, which vary according to the chosen pathway. Those aiming to become newspaper reporters, sports reporters or sub-editors undertake a period of employment in the media before sitting the National Certificate Examination (NCE) to qualify as a senior journalist.

Most trainees study for their preliminary examinations on a fulltime course accredited by the NCTJ at a college, university or commercial provider. These pre-entry courses range from short (usually 20-week) fast-track programmes to longer periods of study incorporated within degrees running for three years or more.

Some entrants into journalism find a job before starting their training, and are then sent to accredited centres on day or block release. There is also an NCTJ distance learning programme available to people, whether already employed in the industry or not.

- NCTJ Training pathways
- Preliminary examinations
- The National Certificate
- Examination Grades

PRELIMINARY CERTIFICATE

TRAINEES have to pass all the relevant examinations and assessments to be awarded a preliminary certificate in Journalism. Examinations are offered at regular intervals throughout the year, with each subject area on a different day. You don't have to do all the examinations at the same time, and some exam centres put candidates in for some of them halfway through the course, the rest at the end. Journalism examinations are done on computers, others vary depending on the centre.

Below is a brief description of the examinations and assessments on the various routes available.

THE PATHWAYS

Newspaper reporters

News Writing: Candidates have to write three news stories from printed material provided: one of 275-325 words, one of 70-80 and one of 40-50. They are also required to provide five ideas for follow-ups, to a given scenario, based on the third story. The time allowed is two hours.

> *Once trainees have completed 18 months of logbook training, they can go and work at any news agency, newspaper or broadcast company and tackle whatever is thrown at them. They'll have covered everything in their logbook.*
>
> **SALLY STEVENS**
> Editor
> Slough & Windsor
> Observer

Full details of qualifications required and how to apply are available on the NCTJ website, *nctj.com*, and in the NCTJ Guide to Careers in Journalism, written by Andy Bull.

THE NCTJ TRAINING AIMS

The NCTJ's syllabus for courses training newspaper reporters aims to ensure, among other things, that trainees can:

Recognise what is news

Identify and use a range of news and information sources

Build up contacts

Record what people say and report it accurately

Conduct effective interviews

Cover courts and write stories that don't break the law

Understand and report the workings of local and national government

Write informed, accurate and well-constructed news stories and features

Use the English language correctly

Suggest follow-up ideas

Work to a story length

Produce copy to deadlines

Operate in a professional, legal and ethical manner

Public Affairs Part 1: A compulsory local government finance question and two further local government essay questions and ten key terms. Time allowed is two hours.

Public Affairs Part 2: Ten key terms and three essay questions on central government. Time allowed is two hours.

Media Law Part 1: Questions examining knowledge of court reporting and related issues in defamation (privilege) and contempt (sections 4 and 11 of the Contempt of Court Act), sources of law, crime terminology, and relevant aspects of the PCC code. Time allowed is two hours.

Media Law Part 2: Questions examining knowledge of general reporting, including defamation, contempt, copyright, confidentiality, and other parts of the PCC code. Time allowed is two hours.

Shorthand: A practical examination set at 100wpm, consisting of two passages of two minutes each with an interval of 30 seconds between them. Transcription time of 45 minutes is allowed. Examinations are also available at other speeds from 60wpm to 120wpm.

Portfolio: A record of training that provides evidence of a range of reporting and writing exercises, undertaken as part of coursework or during work experience. Candidates have to submit ten cuttings, with original copy and explanatory cover sheets, of real-world news stories, and one cutting of a feature of at least 500 words.

Depending on the centre, trainees may also complete optional certificates in **Online Journalism, Sports Reporting** and/or **Sub-editing**. Ensure the course you choose covers these additional subjects if you are interested in them. Trainees are strongly advised to complete the Online Journalism option if they wish to qualify as multi-skilled reporters as this is now becoming core in many newsrooms.

Sub-editing

This pathway includes all the above, with the exception of shorthand. In addition trainees do:

Subbing: There are two elements to this: a 90-minute examination comprising three on-screen story-subbing and headline-writing exercises (a page lead, a filler and listings) using appropriate software, plus a hard copy page-proofing exercise; and a piece of coursework involving the creation of a page of real stories for the course newspaper.

Magazine journalists

This pathway includes the **News Writing**, **Public Affairs 2** and **Media Law 2** examinations, plus:

Shorthand: A practical exam set at 80 words per minute consisting of two passages of two minutes each with an interval of 30 seconds between them. A transcription time of 35 minutes is allowed. Examinations are also available at other speeds from 60wpm to 120wpm.

Subbing: A two-hour exercise in subbing hard copy; subbing on screen; copy correction using proof correction marks; cutting copy; writing headlines, captions and pull quotes; dealing with pictures/images; and laying out and designing a two-page spread.

Portfolio: Evidence of knowledge and competence in feature writing; production and design; background to magazine industry; and work experience.

Press photographers

Four examinations:

General Photographic Knowledge: Questions examining knowledge of light; cameras; lenses and accessories (still and moving images); exposure and processing; colour (image production and output); current and new technology; health and safety. Time allowed is 90 minutes.

Photographic Practice: Questions examining the history and traditions of the press; moral and ethical issues involved in digital imagery; professional working practices. Time allowed is two hours.

Law for Photographers: Questions examining knowledge of the PCC code of conduct; knowledge of general reporting relevant to photographers, taking in contempt, copyright, confidentiality, reporting restrictions, courts and the law. Time allowed is 90 minutes.

Caption Writing: Candidates are given two photographs and associated written material and have an hour in which to write a clear, accurate and balanced news caption of 80-100 words for each. Time allowed is one hour.

Photo-journalists

Photo-journalists sit the **General Photographic Knowledge**, **Photographic Practice** and **Law for Photographers** examinations and in addition:

> *At a job interview, show enthusiasm and motivation.*
>
> *It impresses far more than academic qualifications.*
>
> **ALAN KIRBY**
> Editor
> Coventry Telegraph

> *Make your job application inventive.*
>
> *Post your CV and picture into a newspaper front-page layout.*
>
> *Make your application into a video and post it via the newspaper website. What have you got to lose?*
>
> **ANDY DOWNIE**
> Editor
> East Wales Weeklies

👍 *If you apply for a place on an NCTJ-accredited course you may be asked to sit a two-hour entry test and have an informal interview with tutors and, perhaps, a local working journalist.*

The test is fairly straightforward, asking you to write a simple news story, suggest some ideas for follow-ups, and answer a few general knowledge questions.

If you read newspapers and keep up with current affairs, you should have no difficulty passing it.

Those who interview you will hope to see evidence that you have done a little work experience, or at least applied to do some.

Take along any cuttings. Make sure you have read the day's newspapers and are abreast with the news.

News Writing for Photo-journalists: Candidates are required to write a caption of 80-100 words for a single photograph and a composite caption of 150-170 words for three photographs with a common thread. Time allowed is 90 minutes.

Sports reporters

This is a new pathway, under development at the time of going to press. It reflect the reality that reporters can now specialise in sports reporting and move straight onto the sports desk in some newsrooms rather than starting as general reporters.

Trainees are advised to complete the Sports Reporting certificate as an additional subject if they want to keep their options open to be general news reporters. Check the NCTJ website for the most up-to-date information on the requirements for this pathway which will include News Writing, Public Affairs, Media Law, Portfolio and Shorthand as well as a Sports Reporting examination.

Online Journalists

Trainees taking this pathway do the **News Writing**, **Portfolio**, **Public Affairs Parts 1** and **2** and **Media Law Parts 1** and **2** examinations, and **Shorthand** and in addition:

Online Journalism: A two-hour examination in online writing and editing requiring candidates to demonstrate their ability to re-write, merge and edit stories and features for online publication, with heads, sells and other devices, and the application of appropriate interactive elements.

Coursework: Candidates have to submit a video news package compiled during their programme of study.

NATIONAL CERTIFICATE

TRAINEES on the newspaper reporting, sports reporting and sub-editing pathways must pass all the appropriate preliminary examinations and assessments to become eligible to enter for the National Certificate.

RE-SITTING THE PRELIMS

Preliminary exam passes in Media Law and Public Affairs remain valid for up to five years.

If you fail one or more of the examinations first time, you can try again as often as you like. You can re-sit the shorthand examinations at any time the NCTJ is setting them, which may be several times a year at different centres.

Re-sit examinations for other subjects are normally available on two dates each year, specified by the NCTJ, usually in May and November.

They can be taken at any training centre which is running them: you don't have to return to the one you first attended.

The NCTJ will provide a general exam report for each group of candidates, and, for a fee, individual reports explaining reasons for failing an exam.

To be awarded this (known as the NCE), candidates must pass National Certificate Examinations and submit a logbook of achievement. Examiners' reports on each element of the NCE are produced after each examination and can be found on the NCTJ website.

PATHWAYS

Newspaper reporters

There are three examinations and a logbook, each worth a quarter of the total marks. The examinations are all held on the same day and are offered three times a year. Logbooks are submitted at the same time. All examinations are type-written.

News Report: Candidates are required to write a news story of 275-325 words based on written material and a five-minute speech. The time allowed is 75 minutes.

News Interview: Candidates are given written material, allowed up to 20 minutes to carry out a face-to-face follow-up interview, and then required to produce a story of 375-425 words or two linked stories within the same length limits. The time allowed for the whole exercise is one hour and 50 minutes.

Newspaper Practice: This is a written examination in two parts: the first, worth half the marks, requires candidates to answer a question on media law; the second requires answers to two questions about general reporting, feature writing, professional conduct or workplace problems. The time allowed is one hour.

Logbook: This is a record of trainees' training while working as a reporter and includes evidence that they have completed a number of key reporting tasks.

Sub-editors

There are two examinations and a logbook, each worth a third of the total marks. The examinations are all held on the same day and are offered twice a year. Logbooks are submitted at the same time.

Sub-editing: Candidates are required to use appropriate computer software to sub a number of stories, design a page, write headlines and incorporate pictures. The time allowed is two hours.

Newspaper Practice: An examination similar to that for the Newspaper Reporting pathway but targeted at sub-editors, with two compulsory law questions. The time allowed is one hour.

Logbook: This is a record of trainees' training while working as a sub-editor and includes evidence that they have completed a number of key sub-editing tasks.

Sports Reporters

A new qualification under development. There will be three examinations and a logbook, each worth a quarter of the total marks. The examinations will be held on the same day and offered at least

> *When you apply for a job, make sure you get the sex and name of the editor right. Check your letter and CV for spelling and grammar. Do your research.*
>
> *It is a competitive industry and that little bit of extra care could be the difference between a passport to a fantastic career or the end of your dreams.*
>
> *I once terminated an interview after less than one minute when the candidate told me the tabloid Evening Chronicle was a morning broadsheet.*
>
> **PAUL ROBERTSON**
> Editor
> Evening Chronicle, Newcastle

> *Advice I ignored: 'Get out of journalism and find a proper job' (my dad). I'm working on it.*
>
> **IAN MURRAY**
> Editor in chief
> Southern Daily Echo

RE-SITTING THE NCE

If you fail one or more of the exams, you can re-sit them on a future NCE day.

You don't have to re-take any of those you have already passed.

You can re-sit as often as you like until five years after you passed your preliminary examinations, when your eligibility expires.

The NCTJ will provide individual exam reports on why you failed for a fee.

Failed logbooks can be re-submitted at any time and will be marked on receipt and then returned.

twice a year. Logbooks will be submitted at the same time. All examinations will be type-written.

Sports Report: Candidates are required to produce a story of 275-325 words based on written material and information given at a press briefing at which a speech is delivered. The total time allowed for this is 75 minutes.

Sports Interview: Candidates are required to produce a story of 375-425, or two linked stories within the same length limits, based on written material and a face-to-face interview of up to 20 minutes. The time allowed for the whole exercise is one hour and 50 minutes.

Sports Newspaper Practice: An examination similar to that for the Newspaper Reporting pathway, but targeted at sports reporters, with questions on law, information sources and general professional behaviour. The time allowed is one hour.

Logbook: This is a record of trainees' training while working as a sports reporter and includes evidence that they have completed a number of key sports reporting tasks.

PRELIMINARY EXAMINATION GRADES

EXAMINATION results are graded to show the different levels of achievement in each examination, portfolio or coursework.

Not only does this give trainees and employers more information on the level of achievement, the grades are used to measure the performance of education and training providers delivering accredited courses.

You must achieve grades of C or above in all the preliminary examinations required, including shorthand at 100wpm, to be eligible to sit the NCE, and many employers will expect you to have achieved these grades before they offer you a job. Grades are listed on certificates.

The grades and marks are:

A	70-100 marks
B	60-69 marks
C	50-59 marks
D	40-49 marks
E	30-39 marks
F	0-29 marks

APPENDIX 1
REFERENCE SOURCES

THERE are tens of thousands of reference books and millions of websites available to you. Here are a few of the ones you might find most useful.

- Reference books
- Websites

BOOKS

MANY of those listed below have online versions, some free, some available on subscription.

Local

Phone books (BT and Thomson) and Yellow Pages

Electoral register

Local *Who's Who* (some newspapers publish these annually)

Yearbooks: local authority, chamber of trade, chamber of commerce

Local town and area guides

A-Z street maps

General

Encyclopaedia Britannica and *Pears Cyclopaedia*

Whitaker's Almanack and *Chamber's Book of Facts* are gold-mines of general information – everything from tide tables and trade unions to crime statistics, Nobel Prize winners, and how much a teaspoon measures

People

Who's Who and *Who Was Who, Dictionary of National*

Biography, Chambers Biographical Dictionary and *Hutchinson's Dictionary of Biography* for famous people, living and dead

Debrett's Peerage and *Burke's Peerage* for royalty, peerage and aristocracy (look up dead ones in old copies of *Kelly's Handbook of the Titled, Landed and Official Classes*)

Times Guide to the House of Commons, Vacher's Parliamentary Companion and *Dod's Parliamentary Companion* for MPs and Government

International Who's Who and *The Statesman's Year Book* for world figures

Civil Service Yearbook and *Diplomatic Service List*

Municipal Year Book for local council members and officials

Stock Exchange Year Book and the *Directory of Directors* for companies and people who run them

Navy List, Army List, Air Force List for serving officers

> *Knowledge is of two kinds. We know a subject ourselves, or we know where we can find information upon it.*
>
> **Dr SAMUEL JOHNSON**
> Letter, 1775

👍 **Eight non-fiction books about journalism that you should read:**

All The President's Men (Bob Woodward & Carl Bernstein)

Anyone Here Been Raped And Speaks English? (Edward Behr)

Good Times, Bad Times (Harold Evans)

Maxwell (Tom Bower)

Point Of Departure (James Cameron)

Stick It Up Your Punter! (Peter Chippendale & Chris Horrie)

Strange Places, Questionable People (John Simpson)

Tickle The Public (Matthew Engel)

👍 **Contact suggestion: fancy dress hire shops. What's their most popular costume? Who wants to be Napoleon and why?**

Crockford's Clerical Directory, *The Catholic Directory, Who's Who in the Free Churches* for churches, vicars, priests and ministers

Willings Press Guide, Benn's Media, Guardian Media Guide, Hollis Press & Public Relations Annual for media and PR people and organisations

Halliwell's Film Guide and *Who's Who in the Movies.*

Spotlight for actors and entertainers, with agents' contact details

Grove's Dictionary of Music and Musicians

Who's Who in the Theatre, Who's Who in Music, etc: (There's a *Who's Who of...* for just about every category you can think of)

Oxford Dictionary of English Literature for fictional characters

Events

Chambers Dictionary of World History

Dictionary of Dates

Chronicle of the Twentieth Century

Places

Times Atlas

Michelin Guides

Bartholomew's Gazetteer

Achievements

Guinness Book of World Records

Guinness Book of Hit Singles/ Albums

Shell Book of Firsts

Sport

Playfair Winners' Football, Rugby and *Cricket annuals*

Rothman's Football Yearbook

Sky Sports Football Yearbook

Football Association Year Book

Wisden's Cricketer's Annual

Words

Oxford English Dictionary and *Collins English Dictionary* (includes many proper names of people, places and events)

Roget's Thesaurus

Oxford Dictionary for Writers and Editors

Dictionary of Quotations

Brewer's Dictionary of Phrase and Fable

Other

The Bible and a concordance for looking up people, quotations and references

Black's Medical Dictionary and *Black's Veterinary Dictionary*

Education Committees Year Book and *Public and Preparatory Schools Year Book* for education

Jane's All the World's Aircraft, Fighting Ships and similar volumes

Lloyd's Registry of Shipping

Local Government in the UK, Politics UK and *Dictionary of British Politics* for central and local government

And, of course, the latest *McNae's Essential Law for Journalists* or *Scots Law for Journalists*

WEBSITES

Business & Industry

Bankruptcies
insolvency.co.uk

Business information
business-knowledge.com

Companies House
companies-house.gov.uk

Confederation of British
Industry *cbi.org.uk*

Patents Office
patent.co.uk

Trade Union Congress
tuc.org.uk

Education

Office for Standards in Education
ofsted.gov.uk

Europe

European Commission
cec.org.uk

European Parliament
europarl.eu.int

Government

All departments
direct.gov.uk

Central Office of Information
coi.gov.uk

Charity Commission
charity-commission.gov.uk

Consitutional Affairs
lcd.gov.uk

Culture, Media & Sport
culture.gov.uk

Defence *mod.uk*

Education & Skills
dfes.gov.uk

Environment, Food &
Rural Affairs
defra.gov.uk

Foreign & Commonwealth
fco.gov.uk

Government news network
gnn.gov.uk

Health
doh.gov.uk

Health and Safety Executive
hse.gov.uk

Home Office
homeoffice.gov.uk

International Development
dfid.gov.uk

National Heritage
heritage.gov.uk

National Assembly for Wales
wales.gov.uk

National Health Service *nhs.uk*

Northern Ireland
nio.gov.uk

Northern Ireland assembly
ni-assembly.gov.uk

Parliament (includes Hansard)
parliament.uk

Prime minister's official site
cabinet-office.gov.uk

Prime minister's public site
number10.gov.uk

Public Record Office
pro.gov.uk

Quangos
open.gov.uk

Scotland
scottishsecretary.gov.uk

Scottish Executive
scotland.gov.uk

Scottish Parliament
scottish.parliament.uk

Standards Board for England
standardsboard.co.uk

Trade & Industry
dti.gov.uk

Wales
ossw.gov.uk

Two things I always say to trainees are:

1. Self-indulgence is the enemy of good reporting; the news editor and the reader are the only two people you need to indulge – and not necessarily in that order.

2. The tried and tested marketing maxim 'Make it easy and they'll come' translates into good journalism as 'Write it simply and they'll get it.'

JANE REED
Director
Times Newspapers

Eight works of fiction about life as a reporter that you should read:

Alphabetical Order (Michael Frayn)

Arizona Kiss (Ray Ring)

Don't Print My Name Upside Down (Michael Green)

Hacks (Christopher Wren)

My Turn To Make The Tea (Monica Dickens)

Pratt Of The Argus (David Nobbs)

Scoop (Evelyn Waugh)

The Truth (Terry Pratchett)

Ten magazines you should read as often as possible: British Journalism Review; The Economist; Newsweek; New Statesman; Press Gazette; Private Eye; The Spectator; New Statesman; The Week; Time

Welsh Assembly
Wales.gov

Law

Court lists
courtservice.gov.uk

Crown Prosecution Service
cps.gov.uk

Police
police.uk

Press Association media law site
medialawyer.press.net

Local government

Association of Directors of Social Services
adss.org.uk

Audit Commission
audit-commission.gov.uk

Local Authorities Coordinators of Regulatory Services
lacors.gov.uk

Local Government Association
lga.gov.uk

Local government information
local-government.net

Local Government Ombudsman
lgo.org.uk

Welsh Local Government Association
wlga.gov.uk

Convention of Scottish Local Authorities *cosla.gov.uk*

Media

BBC
bbc.co.uk

Campaign for Freedom of Information *cfoi.org.uk*

Campaign for Press and Broadcasting Freedom
cpbf.org.uk

Chartered Institute of Journalists
cioj.co.uk

Commercial Radio Companies Association
crca.co.uk

HoldtheFront Page
holdthefrontpage.co.uk

International Federation of Journalists
ifj.org

Journalism links
journalism.co.uk,
journalismuk.co.uk,
journalismnet.com

Media ethics charity
presswise.org.uk

National Union of Journalists
nuj.org.uk

News links
newsnow.co.uk

Newspaper Society
newspapersoc.org.uk

Office of Communications (broadcasting regulator)
ofcom.org.uk

Online newspapers (global)
onlinenewspapers.com

Periodical Publishers Association
ppa.co.uk

Press Complaints Commission
pcc.org.uk

Press Gazette
pressgazette.co.uk

Press Association
pa.co.uk

Society of Editors
societyofeditors.co.uk

People

Electoral rolls
192.com

Friends Reunited
friendsreunited.co.uk

Phone directories
bt.com, 192.com

Tribute sites:
missyou.org.uk memory-of.com

Places

Street maps
multimap.com
upmystreet.com

Police

Association of Police
Authorities
apa.police.uk

Police forces
police.uk

Politics

Conservative Party
conservative-party.org uk

Electoral Commission
electoralcommission.gov.uk

Labour Party
labour.org.uk

Liberal Democrats
libdems.org.uk

Parties, elections:
ukpol.co.uk
party-register.gov.uk

Plair Cymru
plaidcymru.org

Scottish Nationalist Party
snp.org.uk

Research

Search engines
ask.com
dogpile.com
google.com

Source tracking:
facsnet.org

UK national statistics
statistics.gov.uk

Training

National Council for the
Training of Journalists
nctj.com

Broadcast Journalism
Training Council
bjtc.org.uk

Words

Plain English Campaign
plainenglish.co.uk

> *Look after your contacts as if they are family. And if a reader dares to bother you with something mundane, beware before you bite off their head ... tomorrow they might have the splash.*

ANDY PLAICE
Former editor
Melton Times

APPENDIX 2
GLOSSARY

ABC: The Audit Bureau of Circulations, a body which monitors newspaper circulation figures

Add: Additional copy for story

Ads: Advertisements

Advance: (1) Copy of speech or statement issued to media before delivery; (2) Story written about future event

Advertorial: Advertising material designed to look like editorial

Anchor: Horizontally-displayed story at foot of page

Angle: Approach to story

Art desk: Place where pages are laid out and illustrations edited

Artwork: Illustrative material

Attribution: Identification of source of quotes or information

Back bench: Senior production journalists

Backgrounder: Feature backing-up news story

Back issue: Previous issue of newspaper

Banner: Large headline across front page

Bastard measure: Type set in non-standard column width

Beat: Area or subject regularly covered by reporter

BDMs: Birth, marriage and death announcements

Bill: Poster advertising newspaper's content

Black: Duplicate copy of story

Blob/bullet: Circular black symbol at start of sentence or item in list

Blurb: Text promoting material inside newspaper or to be used in future edition

Body: Main text of a story

Bonnet: Rules tying text to material below

Bot: Black type on tinted background

Box: Copy enclosed in ruled border

Breaker: Typographical device to break text into sections

Breaking story: News happening now

Brief: (1) Short story; (2) Information and instructions about story given to reporter or photographer

Bucket: Story below illustration, tied to it by rules

Bump out: Expand by adding words or increasing type size

Bump up: Make story appear more important

Bust: To exceed the width available (as in a headline)

Byline: Writer's name on story

Calls: Regular inquiries made to emergency services and other information providers

Caps: Capital letters

Caption: Copy describing content of picture

Cast off: Gauge length of piece of copy

'When I use a word,' Humpty Dumpty said in a rather scornful tone, 'it means just what I choose it to mean – neither more nor less.'

LEWIS CARROLL
Alice Through The Looking-glass (1872)

👍 **Eight films about journalism that you should see:**

Absence of Malice (Paul Newman, 1981)

All The President's Men (Dustin Hoffman, 1976)

Citizen Kane (Orson Welles, 1942)

Live From Baghdad (Michael Keaton, Helena Bonham Carter, 2002)

The Day The Earth Caught Fire (Arthur Christiansen, Daily Express editor, as himself, 1961)

The Front Page (Walter Matthau, Jack Lemmon, 1974)

The Insider (Al Pacino, Russell Crowe, Christopher Plummer, 1999)

The Paper (Robert Duvall, Michael Keaton, 1994)

👍 **Contact suggestion: postmen. They know the name of everyone on their round, and where they live. Invaluable for tracking people down.**

Catchline: File name for story

Centre spread: Story/stories occupying centre pages

Change page: One that can be altered between editions

Chief sub: Chief sub-editor

Circulation: Number of copies sold

Classifieds: Small advertisements grouped in sections

Clippings: Cuttings

Close quotes: Quotation marks at end of quotation

Col: Column

Colour piece: Personalised, descriptive soft news story

Column: (1) Vertical division of page; (2) Regular item written by one person or several under same byline

Conference: Meeting of senior journalists to discuss newspaper content and news agenda

Contacts book: List of contacts with phone numbers, email addresses, etc

Copy: Material written for publication

Copytaker: Typist who takes down telephoned copy

Copytaster: Journalist who selects copy for possible publication

Corr: Correspondent

Credit: Originator's name printed beside illustration

Crit: Review of performance, book or other work of art

Crop: Cut picture or other illustration

Cross-head: Word(s) centred between paragraphs to break up text

Cross-ref: Text referring to material elsewhere

Cut-out: Picture with background removed

Cuttings: Published stories cut out of newspaper

Cuttings job: Story put together solely from cuttings

Dateline: Place from which reporter sent copy

Death knock: Interview with relative of someone who has died

Death notice: Small advertisement announcing death

Deck: One line or section of a headline

Delayed drop/drop intro: Story structure delaying main point

Desk: Editorial department

Diary: List of jobs to be carried out by reporters

Display ads: Advertisements with large type and/or illustration

District reporter: One working away from main office

Dog's cock: Exclamation mark

Doorstepping: Waiting outside home or other premises for potential interviewees

Double/double-up: Story unintentionally printed twice

Downtable: Less senior

Drop cap: Large initial letter of first word in a story

Drop intro: Story structure delaying main point

Dummy: (1) Scaled-down copy of newspaper showing space allocation; (2) Mock-up of pages showing design changes

Ear-pieces: Advertisements or other material placed each side of masthead

Edition: One of a number of printings for a specific time or place

Editorial: (1) Non-advertising material (2) Article giving newspaper's opinion

Editorialise: To write in an opinionated way

Embargo: Prohibition on publication until a specified time

Exes: Claims for reimbursement of expenses incurred (in theory, at least) while working

Facility trip: Expenses-paid visit offered by external publicity-seeker

Features: Non-news editorial material

File: To send copy

Files: Archived material

Filler: Brief news item

Flashback: Story or illustration reproduced from previous issue

Flush left/right: Align type to left/right margin

Fold: Position on page where newspaper is folded

Folio: Page

Follow-up: Story developing one previously published

Free: Newspaper distributed without charge

Freebie: Trip or other gift given to journalist in hope of favourable publicity

Freelance: Self-employed journalist

Free sheet: Free newspaper, raising all revenue from advertising

Full out: Type filling whole width of column

Gash copy: Unwanted material

Ghost: To write copy under name of someone else

Graphics: Hand-drawn or computer-generated illustrations

Gutter: White space between centre pages

Hamper: Horizontally-displayed story at top of page

Handout: Printed or emailed information sent to media

Hanging indent: Copy set with all but first line indented (as here)

Hard copy: Printed version of story

Hard news: Fact-based news of current events

Heading: Headline

Head shot: Picture showing head only

Hold: Keep for later use

Hood: Headline above picture, tied to it by rules

House ad: Advertisement for newspaper itself or its promotions

House style: Rules about presentation, word use, abbreviations, etc

Human interest: Stories focusing on people

Imprint: Details of publisher and printer

Indent: Space between side of column and text

Insert: Additional copy added to story

Intro: First paragraph of story

Issue: All copies of one edition

Justified: Type aligned to both left and right margins

Kicker: Story designed to stand out on page

Kill: To erase

Label: Headline without a verb

Layout: Arrangement of items on page

Lead (pronounced *leed*): Main story on page

Leader: Main article giving newspaper's opinion

Lead-in: First few words of intro

Leading: (pronounced *ledding*) Space between lines of type

The quirky stories are the best. A leaked confidential document revealed that shire horses which pulled wagons around Bradford city centre on litter-picking duties were threatened with redundancy because they were too slow – mainly because too many people stopped to pat them.

We launched a Save the Shires campaign. It was a record-breaker. Letters from readers even outnumbered those about a major shake-up of schools in the city.

Within a week the shires were saved. They still plod around the city – now with the newspaper logo emblazoned on the wagons, a great advert for the paper.

OLWEN VASEY
Former municipal reporter
Telegraph & Argus
Bradford

👍 **Ten reference books worth getting your own copy of:**

Brewer's Dictionary of Phrase and Fable

Chambers Book of Facts

Eric Partridge's Usage and Abusage

Guardian Media Directory

Harold Evans' Essential English

McNae's Essential Law for Journalists

Oxford Concise English Dictionary

Oxford Dictionary for Writers and Editors

Penguin Dictionary of Quotations

Roget's Thesaurus

Leak: Unauthorised disclosure of information

Leg: Section of text occupying one of two or more columns

Lift: (1) To use material from elsewhere; (2) Subs' storage area

Linage: Payment for copy based on number of printed lines it occupies

Listings: Lists of forthcoming events

Literal: Typographical error

Logo: Illustration or symbol identifying section of newspaper or other item

Lower case: Non-capital letters

Masthead: Newspaper's title on front page

Mf: More follows

Mfl: More follows later

Morgue: Newspaper cuttings library

Mug shot: Picture showing head only

Must: Story that must be published

News blackout: Ban or delay on publication of material, agreed between police and media

News list: List of stories to be covered

Nib: Short piece of copy (News In Brief)

Non-attributable: Information that can be used so long as source is not revealed

Nose: Intro

Obit: Obituary

On-diary: Listed in diary

Off-diary: Not originating from diary

Off the record: Information that must not be reported

On the record: Information that can be reported and attributed

Op-ed: Page opposite the one carrying editorial

Open quotes: Opening quotation marks

Overline: Line of type above main headline

Over-matter: Copy left over and unpublished

Over-night: Story or page produced for next day's use

Page lead: Main story on page

Pagination: Number of pages in an edition

Panel: Copy enclosed in ruled border

Par(a): Paragraph

Patch: Geographical area or specialised subject covered by reporter

Peg: Event or other reason for story being written

Pic: Picture

Pick-up: Item for collection

Piece: Article

Pix: Pictures

Press conference: Meeting to which media are invited

Press pack: Documents given to media, containing background information

Press release: Information posted or emailed to media

Press trip: Visit arranged for media

Print run: Number of copies printed of one issue

Promotion: Publicity exercise

Proof: Print-out of story or page, for checking before publication

Puff: Promotional copy, as advertising

Pull-out: Supplement separate from main newspaper

Pull-out quote: Brief extract from article repeated as design device

Quote: Quotation

Quotes: Quotation marks

Ragged left/right: Type aligned to right/left margin only

Rag-out: Picture with ragged edges, reproduced from previous issue

Range left/right: Align type to left/right margin

Readership: Total number of readers

Re-jig: Re-organise story on page

Re-nose/re-top: Change intro

Reverse: White type on black background

Reverse indent: Hanging indent

Ring-around: Telephone interviews to obtain information

ROP: Run of press: not pre-printed

Rough: Sketch of page layout

Round-up: Story gathering several different elements together

Running story: Developing story requiring regular updating

Sans: Non-seriffed type

Sched, sked, schedule: List of stories planned for future issue

Scoop: Exclusive story

Screamer: Exclamation mark

Seal: Logo accompanying newspaper's masthead

Serif: Tiny projection finishing off strokes on letters in some typefaces

Set and hold: Put into type for future use

Set flush left/right: Align to left/right margin

Shorts: Short stories

Shy: Short of required length

Sidebar: Second story accompanying main copy

Sidehead: Cross-head set left

Size: Make picture fit allocated space

Sketch: Light-hearted article

Slip page/edition: Page/edition produced for specific place

Slow burner: Story in which main point appears well after intro

Small ads: Classified advertisements

Snapper: Photographer

Snatch pic: Picture taken in a hurry, often without subject's agreement

Soft news: Lighter stories, often timeless, entertaining as well as informing

Source: Origin of information

Spiked: Rejected

Splash: Main front-page story

Spoiler: Story written to diminish effect of rival newspaper's exclusive

Spot colour: Single colour used to highlight item on page

Spread: Main story across more than one page

Stake-out: Wait outside building for occupant to emerge and face the media

Standfirst: Introductory copy, printed separately from main story

Stet: Ignore alteration marks

Strap: Additional headline set above main one

Streamer: Headline across top of page

Stringer: Freelance journalist on contract

Sub: (1) Sub-editor (2) To convert copy into form suitable for publication

Sub-head: Secondary headline

Tagline: Line of text explaining or attributing headline above it

Take: One page or section of longer story

The reporter's calendar: New Year babies – New Year's Honours List – Summer Holiday features – Chinese New Year – Burns Night – Valentine's Day – St David's Day – Spring Clean DIY features – St Patrick's Day – Pancake Day – Budget Day – Spring Brides features – Easter Days Out features – St George's Day – Football season climax – Local elections – Whitsun Days Out features – Birthday Honours List – Village shows – Silly Season starts – Heatwaves – Droughts – Hosepipe bans – Storms – Glorious Twelfth – Football season starts – GCSE results – A-Levels – Back to School features – Cricket season climax – Halloween – St Andrews Day – Bonfire Night – Christmas Shopping features – Panto season starts – Where's the snow? features – Christmas babies – New Year Sales – New Year babies again...

Taster: Text promoting material to be found elsewhere in newspaper

Tear-out: Picture with ragged edges, reproduced from previous issue

Teaser: Taster omitting detail to entice reader to seek main story

Think piece: Feature provoking debate

Tie-in: Story linked to another

Tip-off: Information from contact, freelance or member of public

Title-piece: Newspaper's name as it appears on front page

Top: Story at top of page

Trim: Reduce story length

Turn: Section of story continued from previous page

Turn head: Headline above turned copy

Turn line: Text indicating where copy turns to

Typo: Typographical error

Umbrella story: Round-up

Unjustified: Text unaligned to margin

Upper case: Capital letters

Vox pop: Interviews to obtain public opinion

Write-off: Summary of story to go on front page

Wob: White type on black background

Wot: White type on tinted background

Xref: Cross-reference

APPENDIX 3
FURTHER READING

YOU will find plenty of excellent books on journalism, many exploring in greater depth the areas introduced in *Essential Reporting*. Here are a few suggestions of books to look out for. Dates are the year of first publication unless otherwise indicated: you will find later editions of many.

A Guide to Commercial Radio Journalism. Linda Gage. *Focal Press, 1990.*

A Journalist's Guide to Sources. David Spark. *Focal Press, 1996.*

An Introduction to Journalism. Carole Fleming, Emma Hemming-way, Gillian Moore & Dave Welford. *Sage, 2006.*

An Introduction to Journalism. Richard Rudin & Trevor Ibbotson. *Focal Press, 2002.*

Broadcast Journalism. Andrew Boyd. *Focal Press, 1988.*

Dictionary of British Politics. Bill Jones. *Manchester University Press, 2005.*

Doing it in Style. Leslie Sellers. *Pergamon Press, 1968.*

Essential English for Journalists, Editors and Writers. Harold Evans & Crawford Gillan. *Pimlico, 2000* (originally **Newsman's English,** *Heinemann, 1972*).

English for Journalists. Wynford Hicks. *Routledge, 1993.*

Inside Journalism. Sarah Niblock. *Blueprint, 1996.*

Interviewing for Journalists. Sally Adams & Wynford Hicks. *Routledge, 2001*

Interviewing for Journalists. Joan Clayton. *Piatkus 1994.*

Journalism in the Digital Age. John Herbert. *Focal Press, 2000.*

Journalism: Principles and Practice. Tony Harcup. *Sage, 2004.*

Law for Journalists. Francis Quinn. *Pearson Longman, 2007.*

Local Government in the United Kingdom. Wilson & Game. *Palgrave Macmillan, 2002.*

Local Radio Journalism. Paul Chantler & Sim Harris. *Focal Press, 1992*

McNae's Essential Law for Journalists. Tom Welsh, Walter Greenwood & David Banks (eds). *Oxford University Press, 19th Edtn 2007.*

Newspaper Journalism. Susan Pape & Sue Featherstone. *Sage, 2005.*

Newspaper Language. Nicholas Bagnall. *Focal Press, 1993.*

News Writing. Anna McKane. *Sage, 2006.*

Politics UK. Bill Jones et al. *Pearson Longman, 6th Edtn 2005.*

Practical Journalism: How to write news. Helen Sissons. *Sage, 2006.*

Practical Newspaper Reporting. Geoffrey Harris & David Spark. *Focal Press, 1966.*

Reporting for Journalists. Chris Frost. *Routledge, 2002.*

● Books to look out for

'Tis pleasant, sure, to see one's name in print;

A book's a book, although there's nothing in't.

LORD BYRON
English Bards and Scottish Reviewers, 1809

FURTHER READING

Final contacts suggestion: everybody else. And when you've done them all, start again at the beginning.

Sports Journalism: A practical introduction. Phil Andrews. *Sage, 2005*

The Broadcast Journalism Handbook. Gary Hudson & Sarah Rowlands. *Pearson Lognean, 2007.*

The Journalist's Handbook. Kim Fletcher. *Macmillan, 2005.*

The Newspapers Handbook. Richard Keeble. *Routledge, 1994.*

The NCTJ Essential Guide to Careers in Journalism. Andy Bull. *Sage, 2007.*

The Simple Subs Book. Leslie Sellers. *Pergamon Press, 1985.*

The Universal Journalist. David Randall. *Pluto Press, 1996.*

Understanding Journalism. John Wilson. *Routledge, 1996.*

Waterhouse on Newspaper Style. Keith Waterhouse. *Viking, 1989.*

Writing Feature Articles. Brendan Hennessey. *Heinemann 1989.*

CONTRIBUTORS

Peter Aegenheister 85
Mike Amos 25, 161, 177
David Armstrong 19
Lynn Ashwell 29, 121, 161
Kate Barney 173
Peter Barron 5, 41, 89, 103, 131, 257
Neil Benson 39, 131
Clare Bourke 189
Adrian Braddy 35
Danny Brierley 11
Bill Browne 27, 163
Naomi Bunting 143
Nigel Burton 147
Neil Butterworth 53, 125, 167, 227
Dorothy Byrne 5, 159
Alex Cameron 81
Chris Chandler 123
John Chipperfield 95, 117, 165
Tom Clarke 207
Andy Cooper 7
Glen Cooper 145, 159
Sarah Cosgrove 157
Bev Creagh 229
Richard Davies 97
Mark Dickinson 133, 187
Andrew Douglas 41, 139
Andy Downie 33, 93, 243
Bob Drayton 41
Alan Ducat 107
David Duffy 113
Sean Duggan 49
Kieran Fagan 135
Simon Fearnley 81
Phil Fleming 39
Martin Forster 219
John Francis 9, 95, 165, 237
Nicole Garnon 25, 149
Jeremy Gaunt 157

Stuart Gilbert 225
Mike Glover 61
Tim Gopsill 77, 153, 233
Susan Greenberg 83
Liz Griffin 27
Sharon Griffiths 11, 51, 63, 69, 129, 183, 233, 257
Anne Hayes 197
Fiona Heavey 85
Kate Helyer 107, 129, 203
David Hetterley 139
Olwyn Hocking 151, 217, 231
David Horne 43
Paul Horrocks 9
Barry Hunt 9
Graeme Huston 15, 99, 185
Andrea Hyam 37, 175
David Jackman 17, 65, 103
Matt Jackson 185
Tony Jaffa 141
Rob Jerram 195
Mark Jones 5, 135, 187
David Kelly 109
Alan Kirby 21, 83, 217, 243
Gavin Ledwith 69, 119
Chris Lloyd 163, 213
Anthony Longden 87, 191
Brian Macarthur 97
Tom Malloy 113
Jean May 17
John McLellan 59, 121
Colin Mooney 39, 127
John Murphy 67, 179
Ian Murray 67, 99, 245
Jenny Needham 127
Nick Nunn 51, 201
Simon O'Neill 47, 125, 183, 223
Barry Peters 149
Fiona Phillips 63, 131
Andy Plaice 251

Arthur Pickering 167
Malcolm Powell 79
Graeme Pratt 79, 187, 211
Jane Reed 249
Simon Reynolds 5, 221
Paul Robertson 151, 245
Michaela Robinson-Tate 67, 221
Helen Rossiter 111
Bob Satchwell 27
Joe Scicluna 55, 215
David Seymour 235
Deanne Shallcross 109
Jack Shennan 57
John Simkins 257
Steve Singleton 105
Dennis Sissons 23
Les Snowdon 121
Keith Stafford 71
Helen Stanley 51, 201
Pat Stannard 7, 115, 181
Sally Stevens 241
David Summers 91
Anita Syvret 25
Richard Thomas 175
Brian Tilley 111, 181, 209
Nick Tite 45
Mark Turnbull 11
Steven Tyler 137
Olwen Vasey 193, 255
Jeremy Vine 171
Skip Walker 179, 197
Malcolm Warne 223
Mark Wood 37, 211, 239
Jeff Wright 169
Malcolm Wright 155
Robin Young 135
Requested anonymity 53, 73, 75, 123, 199, 205

INDEX

Page names in Roman type indicate items in the main text; those in italics are items on the lefthand tips panels. Contacts have far and away the most references: trainee reporters please note.